Models of Jesus Revisited

John F. O'Grady

PAULIST PRESS
New York/Mahwah, N.J.

Library of Congress Cataloging-in-Publication Data

O'Grady, John F.
    Models of Jesus revisited / John F. O'Grady.
        p.   cm.
    Includes bibliographical references and index.
    ISBN 0-8091-3474-8   (pbk.)
    1. Jesus Christ—Person and offices. 2. Jesus Christ—Person and offices—History of doctrines. I. Title.
BT202.0343   1994
232—dc20   94-11962
                                                                            CIP

Published by Paulist Press
997 Macarthur Boulevard
Mahwah, New Jersey 07430

Printed and bound in the
United States of America

CONTENTS

I thank my God in all my remembrance of you, always in every prayer of mine for you all, making my prayer with joy, thankful for your partnership in the gospel from the first day until now.

—Philippians 1:3-5

For the Barry University community:
Students, Faculty, Administrators and Staff;

The Adrian Dominican Sisters who have given and give without counting the cost;

The Presidents of Barry:
Mother Gerald Barry, O.P. 1940-1962
Mother Mary Genevieve Weber, O.P., 1962-1963
Sister Dorothy Brown, O.P., 1963-1974
Sister Trinita Flood, O.P., 1974-1981
Sister Jeanne O'Laughlin, O.P. 1981-

And especially,
Dorothy Inez Andreas, Chair of the Board of Trustees, 1977-

PREFACE

Thirteen years after I wrote the original *Models of Jesus*,[1] I have returned to write *Models of Jesus Revisited*. In the preface of that first edition I made reference to a personal spiritual odyssey. I have struggled for many years in my efforts to understand the meaning of Jesus of Nazareth both personally and within the church. The odyssey continues. Jesus still intrigues and surely challenges the church. All believers experience different stages in their acceptance of the Lord and with those stages come new insights and new understanding. The same has been true for me over the past decade. The church also has grown in its understanding of Jesus in the same period.

My model of Jesus changed long before I adverted to what was happening. To someone who has grown up accepting Jesus as the second person of the Blessed Trinity, and really just "God," it might seem difficult to change models. For me, it happened long before the model change was formulated or even adverted to and long before I had done any studying of models in theology. Growth in faith always suggests subtle changes which often take place without much awareness. Then, suddenly, people find themselves far removed from the starting point. Theology, faith seeking understanding, never stands still. Thank God for change and continual becoming!

This revised book hopes to give further direction, greater clarification and to provoke continued new movements in thought, and then, perhaps, in faith. I hope to continue to open up some of the various approaches to Jesus that are not only possible, but actual, in the church today, learning from what has been written and lived in the past unusual decade.

Originally I thought that I would eliminate the model "man for

1

others," but on further thought I concluded that this model not only represents the thought of Bonhoeffer but also expresses how many Christians understand Jesus even if they have never heard of Bonhoeffer. The model also exists in the minds of others who are not Christians but who have either accepted some Christian principles or who may even have personally accepted Jesus, but just as a good human being. For some, or perhaps for many, the divinity of Jesus is not nearly as important as his life of service. Jesus makes sense precisely because of what he offered to others. Those who follow him need only follow his example and not bother with the subtleties of theological discussion. The model stays!

Also over these years I have rethought other models or approaches to Jesus. Willingly I would have added others, but upon more careful examination I have decided to once again advance only six.[2] Any reader acquainted with the first edition of *Models of Jesus* will notice the subtle changes that have taken place. With age comes wisdom, or at least a lessening in surety and a more careful awareness of history. My original critique of the model of Jesus as the second person of the Blessed Trinity has also been modified. While it may not be the paradigm for preaching and for religious education, for theology and especially for the maintaining of the tradition, this model probably should remain paradigmatic.

Over the past ten years many people have often discussed with me *Models of Jesus*. Colleagues have offered valuable critiques and many students have used it as a textbook. I have continued to learn from them all. In this revised work, I have added significantly on the various models in the New Testament. This section may be studied first or postponed until after the six models have been examined.

In the preparation of this revised work, I am indebted to the Rev. Joseph P. McClain, C.M. for his assistance in reading and offering improvements on the chapter on the second person of the Blessed Trinity. Dr. Edward Sunshine, and Dr. Ralph del Colle, both of Barry University, also offered their comments, respectively, on Jesus as liberator and Jesus as Lord and Savior. Dr. Mary Ann Jungbauer, also of Barry University, read this manuscript as she has done in the past for other manuscripts for me, offering her assistance editorially. To each I offer my gratitude. Finally, I hope that this new book will further contribute to the work of evangelization, the heart of the mission of Jesus of Nazareth.

Treasure Coast, Florida   Spring 1993

1. Since the publication of *Models of Jesus* several people have suggested that in fact I mean models of christology rather than models of Jesus. They are correct. I have chosen to use "models of Jesus" because I want to emphasize that people have personal approaches to Jesus apart from any formulated christology. The theologian more properly has models of christology.

2. Daniel Helmeniak in *The Same Jesus* (Chicago: Loyola University Press, 1986) attempts to combine some of my approaches and proposes a rather involved seventh model: "What is needed is a seventh 'model' of Jesus....The complete name of this model would necessarily be cumbersome: 'Jesus as the Eternal Son of God Become Human and in His Humanity Divinized so that All Humans Might Likewise Be Divinized" (pp. 157-158). While accepting the critique offered by Helmeniak, I will keep the six original models.

PART I

The Present State of Christology

Biblical Studies

Discussions about the Old Testament and its meaning cause little reaction among Christians. Anyone can question any aspect of history or archeology or linguistics or theology and make applications and draw conclusions with immunity. Most Christians view what happened to the Jews and the record of their relationship with God as not as important as what happened to Jesus. If there are mistakes or errors or misunderstandings in the Old Testament brought to light by contemporary studies, such findings have little effect on Christianity. This attitude, especially in Roman Catholic circles, has created a situation that encouraged for many years the scientific study of the Old Testament but remained wary of a similar approach to the New Testament.

In 1943 Pius XII published his encyclical *Divino Afflante Spiritu*[1] and for the first time Roman Catholic scholars were encouraged to use a scientific method in the study of the Bible. The green light was given, however, mainly for the Old Testament, not for the New. It was not until the "Declaration on the Truth of the Gospels" in 1964[2] that Roman Catholic scholars could feel free to use the methods of contemporary scholarship in regard to the New Testament. Since that time the interest in biblical studies has profoundly altered the understanding of Christianity and has implications for the church of the next century. In the past thirty years biblical scholarship has flourished in the United States among Roman Catholics. Even weekly news magazines find it interesting enough to make comment. The results of this scholarship have clearly affected the understanding of Jesus. As a result of the new atmosphere in the church after the Second Vatican Council, believers are continually faced with new understandings of Jesus and the Jesus tradition as recorded in the New Testament.

In the past ten years, however, some caution seems to have arisen again in the Roman Catholic Church with regard to the study of the New Testament and to the meaning of Jesus. As much as some might wish to return to a different period in church history, most Christians are aware of what some theologians are saying about Jesus even if sometimes they are confused by the publicity involved. Different approaches exist among the various Christian denominations and even within the Roman Catholic tradition. The present state of christology contains various hues and no one approach or understanding captures the fullness of the reality just as no one color can capture the fullness of color. Various approaches have characterized theology over the centuries. Each one has made a contribution. Christians can always gain by studying what has preceded as well as by examining certain of the ideas that are prevalent today.

Images of the Church

Theologians have also studied the church, seeking to understand how personal images of the church might influence attitudes and behavior.[3] Today people seem to have become accustomed to the different ways in which many respond to the church. The image of an institutional and hierarchical church with detailed ritual and organization and lines of authority suits well some members of the church but not all. Even the increase of the use of the Tridentine liturgy can be helpful for some people's piety provided this is not used as a means to deny the reality of the Second Vatican Council. Latin liturgies can prove helpful to faith. Moreover, a folksy home liturgy with people sitting on the floor and singing folk music can do much to create the image of the church as a community of people on pilgrimage. Such an approach is helpful to others in the faith community. The result has been a healthier attitude toward the divergent opinions that can exist within the church without doing harm to its basic meaning. The same should be true with regard to Jesus.

> **Institution and Hierarchical**
> **Mystical Communion**
> **Sacrament**
> **Herald and Prophet**
> **Servant**
> **Community of Disciples**
> **People of God**

Church Concerns

At the outset, however, a certain resistance might be expected. When a scientific methodology is applied to the New Testament, and to Jesus, more traditional-minded individuals are apt to react negatively or at least cautiously. The same might be true if some begin to entertain the thought that divergent views on christology can well be admitted within the church. But not everyone has to have the same approach to Jesus. Nor can any one approach fully manifest the truth of Jesus as the revelation of the Word of God and the veritable Son of God.

In 1972 the Congregation for the Doctrine of the Faith published a declaration entitled "Safeguarding Basic Christian Beliefs."[4] In this document the Congregation saw the need to reiterate certain traditional Roman Catholic teachings with regard to Jesus and the Trinity. Concern existed in Rome. Some of the teachings of the Christian faith were being undermined by certain contemporary theologians, and thus the church would have to react to affirm the traditional approach to christology and to the Trinity.

Much of the concern seems to have arisen because of the new terminology in christology as well as the efforts to encounter again what has been the Christian heritage on Jesus through the study of the New Testament. Any effort to re-examine such teachings as the meaning of pre-existence, how in Jesus there exists the one divine person, and the presence of the human person in Jesus is presented in the declaration as contrary to true belief in Christ.[5]

After the declaration was published, Pope Paul VI called attention to the statement in his usual Sunday audience and explained why such a statement was necessary. He said that recently the teachings on Jesus had not been properly interpreted.[6] The pope continued that such statements had spread even among "us believers." Therefore, the Congregation responded. The conclusion of the declaration, however, should not be overlooked. In spite of their anxiety, the authors of the statement admit the need for updating traditional dogmatic formulations.[7] More recently, the decision by the Congregation for the Doctrine of the Faith to investigate and censure certain European and Latin American theologians may be read as continual signs of anxiety with regard to the contemporary research on the meaning of Jesus.

In June of this past year Pope John Paul II reaffirmed the belief that Mary was physically a virgin before, during and after giving birth to Jesus. "The church feels the need to recall the reality of the virginal conception of Christ."[8] The gospel accounts of Luke and Matthew "cannot be reduced to simple stories to give a solid reason for the faithful to believe in the divinity of Christ. Rather, they go beyond the literary style adopted by Matthew and Luke and express a biblical tradition of apostolic origin."[9] The pope seems to imply that certain questions from the New Testament and others concerning Jesus are out of bounds for further research.

Raymond Brown, a well-known American New Testament theologian, has stated: "The scientifically controllable biblical evidence leaves the question of the virginal conception unresolved."[10] He also acknowledges that for Roman Catholics the long-standing church tradition supplies a different answer from what can be gained in the study of the New Testament.

During the same year that the pope made his statement on the virginal conception of Jesus, John Meier, another American Roman Catholic biblical scholar, wrote in *The Catholic Biblical Quarterly*: "A historian prescinding from what is held by faith and later Church teaching and working solely with the historical and philological data available would most likely come to the conclusion that the brothers and sisters of Jesus were his true physical brothers and sisters."[11] Meier goes on to say that the whole question of the perpetual virginity of Mary "is so obscure and ambiguous that it enjoys at best a remote and unclear relation to the foundation of Christian faith and the foundational truths that flow from it."[12]

Scholarly Activity

The research continues. The recent publication of *The Marginal Jew* by J. Meier[13] and *The Historical Jesus* by D. Crossan[14] amply exemplifies that Roman Catholic New Testament scholars have not ceased in their study of Jesus. Nor have they written books that merely support the general tendencies of official church documents. The publication of *God's Beloved* by B. Cooke[15] and *Christ is Community* by J. Neyrey[16] and *Jesus Before Christianity* by A. Nolan[17] and *A Christological Catechism* by J. Fitzmyer[18] also demonstrates that contemporary Roman Catholic scholars continue to examine every aspect of the Jesus tradition in Christianity. No one seems to have abated in efforts to further understand the meaning of Jesus.

If theology is faith seeking understanding, growth in an appreciation of Jesus and his gospel will continue. No one generation can claim to speak the last word or disclose the final expression. Each generation must examine the insights of the past in order to offer new generations of believers an understanding of Jesus that will be intelligible to the contemporary spirit. Often enough, in the contemporary research on Jesus, scholars are not concerned with faith as much as past interpretations of faith. For a theologian to re-examine some of the fundamental tenets of Christian belief does not imply a doubt of those beliefs. With the passage of time, words change in meaning, or at least in nuance. To be faithful to its task, theology will always demand a study of what words have meant in the past and what they might mean today. The theologian is conscious of the common Christian heritage, but also of the responsibility to reinterpret that heritage.

If Christian theology in general continually needs updating, this is certainly true of the heart of Christian theology, the study of Jesus. When the church encouraged the scientific investigation of the New Testament, it was also commending the careful methodological approach to Jesus as advocated by most contemporary theologians. Further insights into the origin and development and theology of the various books of the New Testament must of necessity bring about changes in the understanding of Jesus.

In a speech prior to the Second Vatican Council, Pope John XXIII was most careful to distinguish the content of faith from its expression:

> The deposit of faith is one thing; the way that it is presented is another. For the truths preserved in our sacred doctrine can retain the same substance under different forms of expression.[19]

Problems seem to arise when theologians actually try to fulfill their function in the church and begin to use new terminology which is either not understood by the church hierarchy or does not meet with approval among the majority of believers. The problem is compounded when popular news magazines take learned articles and digest them into one-page religion sections with startling headlines announcing that theologians question the divinity of Jesus or hold that Jesus was not born of a virgin or do not believe in the physical resurrection of the Lord. When other theologians write of Jesus the liberator, emphasizing his humanity, and de-emphasizing the divinity, oppressed people might find such an image helpful but others find in liberation christology the loss of the true Jesus Christ.

Scholastic philosophers often remarked that whatever is perceived is perceived according to the mode of the perceiver. In contemporary language: "People hear what they want to hear." Surely that is true with regard to the present state of christology, whether the listeners are pope or cardinals or bishops or clergy or religious or laity or even theologians, liberal, centrist or conservative.

Many Images of Christ

For those who have been nurtured on a "docetic" or a totally spiritual or divine Christ, anything that seems to emphasize the humanity of Jesus will be suspect. For someone who has viewed Christ as the suffering servant going to his death meek and humble, any effort to make him a social reformer is simply out of order and contradicts the gospel. For a Roman Catholic who has grown up with a formal liturgy, any effort to make Jesus the source of enthusiastic singing of "Jesus my Savior" must be not only suspect but even a bit "mad."

Many regard Jesus as the all-knowing God in human form. Then how can some of the attitudes of Jesus in the gospels be explained?[20] How could he ask questions when he knew everything? If Jesus is the all-knowing God, then the only explanation based on the previous premise would be that Jesus, like Socrates, questions as a pedagogical technique. But such a response does not satisfy many careful readers of the New Testament.

Someone who sees Jesus as a good man, an individual who could identify with the human condition and could rise above that condition, would consider any attempt to deny that he lived a human life (by making him out to be God) as tantamount to the destruction of the meaning of Jesus.[21] Anyone who sees the need to reform the social order on the basis of the gospel will not be content to adhere in belief to a God-man who is content to live under any social system, even an unjust one.[22]

In reality history has many images of Jesus. "Who do you say that I am?" (Mk 8:27). Not everyone has given the same answer. History offers as many answers as people who choose to respond. Even those who refuse to respond often have their unspoken answer. People still hear what they want to hear. If a person adheres in faith to a Jesus who is the second person of the Blessed Trinity, then everything about Jesus is judged in that light. If someone else sees only the good man who suffered and died unjustly, no amount of rhetoric will persuade that person to see Jesus as the all-knowing, pre-existent Son of God.

Models of the Church

The Roman Catholic tradition has accepted for some time many models of the church. Some see the church as a visible institution, others as a mystical communion, as a sacrament, as a herald or as a servant, or as a gathering of disciples. Each model offers some insight into the meaning of the church; each offers some understanding. But if viewed exclusively, each model breaks down and fails in its ability to represent the true reality in any complete or final fashion. The church lives as more than any one approach or one person's or one group's understanding.

People who read A. Dulles' book *Models of the Church* usually can quickly identify with one or the other of the models. This colors not only their reaction to opinions about the church, but also their lived actions as members of the church. The scholastics also had an axiom: Action follows being. What a person is will determine the activity; actions follow being. If a person accepts the institutional model as the only model or as the primary model, then a person's activity will follow suit. Whatever will lessen the institutional aspect of the church in any way must be countered. If a person's primary model is the church as sacrament or as servant, then often what we would call the visible structure of the church presents little interest with little regard for such things as hierarchy and official teaching.

Gradually the notion that the use of models provides a good approach seems to have penetrated within the body of the church, affecting hierarchy and laity alike. Individuals can now acknowledge their opinions of the church and not feel afraid of professing one model, since they know that it is only one of several and should not be accepted as the exclusive model without some consideration of other opinions. Even when people choose a primary model, they know that complementary or even opposing opinions have a right to be heard. In parishes this seems to have become commonplace as even liturgy is expressed differently to respond to the particular approach or needs of the members and various groups within the congregations.

Jesus and Models

At this point in the history of Christianity people find it accept-able to maintain different models of the church without detriment to the unity of belief. Believers should also be able to accept a similar position with regard to Jesus. In the past some felt that such a propos-al may well lead to the sacrificing of the clarity that has been part of the Christian tradition for centuries. Many felt that there should not be many models of Jesus, but only one model. The one approach has been expressed in the official teaching of the church in the course of its development, in particular through the ecumenical councils.

No doubt, the church did have clarity in the past with regard to christology. The Council of Chalcedon made its declaration and pur-ported to have settled the question for all times:

> . . . one the same Christ, the Son, the Lord, only begotten, in two natures unconfused, unchangeable, undivided, insep-arable. The difference of natures will never be abolished by their being united but rather the properties of each remain unimpaired, both coming together in one person and sub-stance, not parted or divided among two persons but in one and the same only begotten Son, the divine Word, the Lord Jesus.[23]

But how much of these statements is understood today? Do the words have the same meaning? Does this declaration respond to the needs of the church in the twenty-first century? Was there ever agree-ment, or unanimity, in the understanding of Jesus in the early church or even in the conciliar period?

On the fifteen-hundredth anniversary of the Council of Chalcedon, a group of German scholars published a series of articles. Karl Rahner's contribution was entitled "Chalcedon, Beginning or End?"[24] For this renowned theologian, the Council of Chalcedon did not represent the end of theological speculation, nor the end of the debate within the Christian community as to the meaning of Jesus, but a beginning. The council was a starting point that would allow further development and refinement, and continual updating. The clarity of the conciliar definition has often been paid for with the loss of continual rethinking. Continuing to examine the meaning of Jesus is essential. Only then may Christianity make sense of the central mystery of the faith to all generations.

Fortunately, while the councils have made efforts to clarify and control, they have also consistently pointed out that in the end we are dealing with mystery.[25] Such an impetus, far from discouraging continued thought, discussion and debate, actually promotes it.

Mystery

The term "mystery" has been used in many ways in the Bible as well as in the history of theology. History provides a starting point for the continual quest that challenges the theologian. In scripture the word "mystery" does not mean something that no one can ever know, but rather the plan of God that brings salvation to all through the coming of Jesus of Nazareth. In Jesus "the manifold wisdom of God is made known" (Eph 3:8); "in him dwells the fullness of divinity" (Col 3:9). In him the mystery that God has preserved for all times has been revealed: "To unite all things in him, things in heaven and things on earth" (Eph 1:10).

> **Mystery:** Is a primordial aspect, essential and permanent, of total reality, in that reality as a whole (that is as infinite) is present for the finite, created, spirit in the latter's intrinsic openness to the infinite. Spirit, as this openness to the infinite, is the capacity to accept the incomprehensible as such, i.e. as permanent mystery.[26]

This great mystery concerns not so much God as God, nor even Jesus in himself, but rather the relationship between God and creation. The mystery involves a plan to unite all things in heaven and on earth, a destiny for all creatures to share in the unity of God and realize the perfection inherent in creation. Paul writes in Romans:

> We know that the whole of creation has been groaning in travail, together until now, and not only the creation but we ourselves who have the first fruits of the Spirit groan

inwardly as we await for adoption as sons, the redemption
of our bodies (Rom 8:22-23).

God the Father has involved himself in creation through Jesus, and his
plan is to accomplish the unity of all reality through Christ.

In the course of centuries people of faith have always sought to
understand this mystery. As a result people found themselves brought
into a greater awareness of the meaning of God and the plan of salvation. No one person could ever reach the point of a full understanding
or complete appreciation of this mystery. Even the collective experience of the church has not exhausted the reality that was the meaning
of Jesus and his salvation. At the outset of this study all face mystery,
inexhaustible intelligibility as they try to encounter, in a personal way,
the meaning of Jesus the Christ.[27] This richness cannot be captured in
any one model nor in any one period of time nor by any one individual.

Jesus can be known and experienced more fully and immediately
than he can be explained and expressed. A connaturality exists
between believer and the believed. In the presence of such an intimate
relationship all attempts at analysis, at moving from the non-conceptu-
al to the conceptual, and then to the verbal in oral or written form, are
doomed to frustration. People who live and are involved with the mystery of Jesus never can objectify its meaning. A certain intersubjectivi-
ty, the very basis of faith in the first place, precludes a complete cate-
gorical expression. People of faith live that faith and depend on that
faith prescinding from any efforts at formulation found in official documents or in theology textbooks.

The church fathers of the Second Vatican Council were well
aware of the continual need to grow in understanding of this mystery.
They related the mystery of Jesus to that of the church and saw all as
part of the divine plan to unite all things in Jesus.[28] The concept of
mystery not only places certain limitations on the content of this study,
it also affects methodology. Theologians cannot easily extrapolate
from clear, unequivocal concepts or definitions to others. They cannot
simply take the pronouncement of a council and maintain that these
concepts and words express the final and irrevocable approach to the
understanding of Jesus. Neither can theologians simply apply the concepts abstracted from personal experience to the mystery of God nor
to the mystery of Jesus. Everyone may know something of the meaning
of personhood, since all have the experience of being persons, but to
presume to extend this interpretation to the mystery of God should
cause hesitation. People also have some concepts of the meaning of

being human, not just through personal experience, but also by means of the human history. But to delineate what it means to be divine should stop all people in their tracks. Learned concepts do not directly apply to the mystery of God uniting all things. They tell something but far from everything.

As a result, some people just give up the quest. Believers can become quietists if they so choose and ignore the theological endeavor. Since no one will ever have all the answers and since even what approximates an answer is provisional, why should the Christian engage in any theological speculation? Prayer and the efforts to live a good life suffice.

Evidently, however, God has chosen to communicate through Jesus. Some value must exist in struggling with the interaction of the divine and human, even if the final outcome remains in shadow. Furthermore to retreat and remain silent about the meaning of God in Jesus denies the gift of the human spirit to always seek truth and to live for the inquiring. Besides, people have engaged in theological discourse for centuries and the proliferation of books shows no sign of abating.

Images of Jesus in Art

The history of Christianity contains various images of Jesus. Nowhere is this more evident than in various portrayals of Jesus in Christian art. A comparative study through the ages would find a clear relationship between popular piety (another form of images) and the artistic depictions of the Lord. The statue of Jesus at the portal of the Cathedral of Chartres commands with power. He holds a book. The statue is entitled "The Teaching Lord." The artist had a clear image of Jesus as one who commands respect and teaches with authority. At the same time, the facial expression is kind and gentle. Jesus' eyes are soft and warm, his lips curved slightly in a smile.

Compare this image from the twelfth century with the figure on many of the holy cards of the twentieth century associated with devotion to the Sacred Heart. The features are usually weak and ethereal with little power, often with a sadness that does not tend to inspire.

The history of theology also has its images, models, symbols, or paradigms. These approaches or images or models have a long history in the learned traditions of Christianity as well as in the ordinary heritage of believers. The basis for such diverse images can be found in the New Testament itself.

Jesus in the New Testament

In the gospels and the other writings of the early church we find myriad images of Jesus which formed various foundations for speculation about his meaning. Jesus is the Lamb of God, the Word, the prophet, the messiah, the almighty Lord of heaven and earth; he is the servant who assumes humble tasks and who suffers unjustly. Jesus is the teacher who teaches with power; he is the miracle worker who performs prodigies as the healer. Jesus is also the vine, the shepherd, the door, the gate, the light. Each of these images of Jesus captures some aspect of his person. No one image can claim the exclusive portrayal of the meaning of the Lord. Each one contributes to an overall picture. The New Testament teems over with images. As the record of the experience of the early church, the writers of the New Testament present in their collective consciousness and individual writings the many faces of Jesus.

TITLES
Lamb of God
Word
Prophet
Messiah/Christ
Lord of All
Son of Man
Servant
Teacher
Miracle Worker and Healer
Shepherd
Suffering Servant
Perfect Greek Gentleman
All-knowing Son of God

The study of the history of christology also shows the use of many images and approaches or models. For some early believers he was a divine man (*theios aner*). Some heretics saw him as a gnostic redeemer come to gather together the various sparks of light that had been scattered in the human race. Later theology would see him as the second person of the Blessed Trinity. Certain contemporary theologians see him as the man for others; still others regard Jesus as the great liberator.

Signs and Symbols

All of the above images, whether from the New Testament, or from the history of theology, from Christian art or common piety, reveal psychological and existential aspects of people who believe in Jesus. They are signs and they are symbols.[29] They reach down into the very depth of the reality of Jesus and bring up some aspect of his person that appeals to the human psyche and to faith. How much of the reality is actually made present depends upon the particular choice of image or symbol. Some symbols communicate through evoking a response. The face of Jesus from Chartres, for example, evokes a sense of trust and confidence. The image of holy cards might also help some to accept a tender and compassionate Jesus. Other images appeal more to the conceptual side of human nature. Symbols of Jesus can transform a person's attitude toward life; they can integrate perceptions, change value systems, reorient loyalties and create a sense of commitment and attachment far stronger than abstract concepts. Good symbols have more than just an intellectual appeal and more than just an aesthetic appeal. They are involved with the whole person—with all of the facets that create a human being in concrete human existence. When symbols make the reality known, more than an academic exercise results. The symbol actually contains the reality it expresses and thus can engage the person and focus the human experience in a definite way.

Any group of people that hopes to remain bound together in some sense of unity will depend on symbols to help them accomplish that task. All are familiar from the history of Christianity with the symbol of the fish used by early believers to remind them of Jesus. The five Greek letters for fish were an acronym for: Jesus Christ, Son of God, Savior. Recent secular history used the swastika which helped unite people in a fanatic commitment to a dictator and still causes anxiety whenever seen. People in the 1960s and 1970s used a peace symbol. The clenched fist still is used to symbolize power, especially for those who have no power. The Olympic torch and five rings finds recognition throughout the world. Good symbols arouse courage, peace, authority, love and even hatred.

When examining the many images of Jesus they suggest attitudes, feelings, courses of action and devotion. They help to unite people in a common bond of affection and commitment. But always, as images, they are incomplete and should not be seen as perfect in themselves. The images express the reality toward which they lead but for which they cannot substitute.[30]

For an image to gain acceptance it must conform to the experience of people of faith. At the same time the images help to shape that faith. The community must learn from the experience of its individual members with regard to images and at the same time must help inspire images for edification. To be effective the image or symbol must be deeply rooted in the experience of the community of believers. One person's approach never suffices. The church depends not upon an image that is short-lived or based upon the experience of a limited few nor of a particular period in the history of faith. True symbols will eventually rise to the surface, even in the midst of a period of confusion and a multiplicity of inadequate and unworthy images. But even the best of images have limited value precisely because the believer always faces mystery, inexhaustible intelligibility. They help, but should never perdure as absolutes.

Crisis of Images

The present period of church history seems to be experiencing a crisis of images. The crisis persists and is not limited to the religious sphere, for the previous relatively stable culture suddenly seems no longer firmly established. The rapid change in the western arena has caused a breakdown in some of the most common symbols and images of human life. Kings rise and fall; presidents who are supposed to epitomize the best of American traditions misuse power and become symbols of the worst. The stability of great universities as symbols of longevity and learning and integrity is compromised by involvement with government or business control and a lack of ethics. Schools are torn in many directions, with student and faculty crises. Banks, considered to be the foundation of economic stability, actually close their doors. Even the Soviet Union no longer exists. For more than forty years that particular political system symbolized for many westerners the power of evil. The Berlin wall fell and with it the mighty dominant communist system shook and disintegrated. People may have been united by opposition to a particular regime, but now the symbol of that regime lies broken. If the symbols that help to unite disparate elements of society, even if they unite in opposition, begin to crumble, no wonder that people are afraid and confused.

With regard to the church, perhaps rather than a crisis of faith, believers face a crisis of images. The Roman Catholic Church used to convey stability; the rock of Peter was truly a rock. Religious men and women portrayed a sense of commitment and symbolized this commitment in action and even in dress. Now the images have been altered and people feel insecure. Church leaders resign in disgrace, acknowledging their sins. Laity and members of the hierarchy openly profess differing views where once all walked to the same rhythm. Dissent has become commonplace.

The crisis concerns of course, more than just the understanding of the church. The entire Christian message is based upon images. These images, however, are often taken from pastoral scenes in first century Palestine and never from the twentieth century technological society. Most people have little contact with lambs and shepherds, or even with vines and grapes. Servants, where they exist, are not in the same social category as in the time of Jesus. Even the developments in the later writings of the New Testament involve some urban society but still fall short of the global village society of today.

People need to examine the images of the past and to supplement these images with others, more in conformity with the faith community that has been reforming itself for the past four hundred years. The development of the new images will continue wherever the faith lives a vibrant and exciting vision. The church has already decided to make many changes in its outward appearance, in consonance with changes that have taken place in the secular culture. The images of Jesus also need to relate to the experience of the larger community. Religious language has become impoverished with regard to imagery because there seems to be so little in experience that bears the stamp of the numinous. Mundane and this-world-centered-life needs to experience an awareness of the transcendent present in life. "'Tis ye, 'tis your estranged faces that miss the many splendour'd thing."[31]

New Images of Jesus

Examples of creative theological thinking do exist. J.A.T. Robinson derived his image of Jesus as the human face of God[32] from the theology of the later Karl Barth;[33] Dietrich Bonhoeffer was the first to speak of Jesus as the man for others.[34] Edward Schillebeeckx coined the phrase "Jesus as the sacrament of encounter" to explain his sacramental theology.[35] Karl Rahner sees Jesus in relationship to the evolution of humanity and thus the image is that of a perfected human person.[36] Bernard Cooke views Jesus as the compassion of God.[37] Each of these images must encounter a *kairos*, the right time. The religious community must be psychologically set for the image. Paul Tillich made all aware that images are not created or destroyed by human effort; they are born or they die. They often acquire a mysterious power that seems beyond human control or even beyond human comprehension.[38]

All know the importance of images in human life and how essential they are for the life of the believer. People live and die with images and by images. In the efforts to communicate faith, believers must constantly try to find new images that can convey something of that faith. When St. Patrick stumbled upon the shamrock as the image of the Trinity, he was being faithful to the human need to express concretely an abstract notion. The archdiocese of Miami chose to use a logo of people gathered together with uplifted hands to symbolize the archdiocese as a community of people praising God together. This logo appears on all the official stationery of the archdiocese and helps to raise people's awareness of the meaning of church.

Images and Analysis

Theology also depends upon images and symbols. For a true theology, however, along with the symbol comes analysis. The church cannot settle for the shamrock for the symbol of the Trinity without analysis. What meets the needs on the level of catechetics does not always reach the level of theology. Nor must the theologian limit interest to those images that are current. Studying the symbols of the past proves worthwhile, even if they have lost some of their power. They once vitalized the church and maybe today believers can uncover some of that vitality that can be used again. People should also examine some of the current symbols and see what value they are actually conveying. The theologian is not always the preacher, and so the person who proclaims Jesus to the ordinary believer must be careful to choose images that convey some sense of understanding, just as the theologian must be aware of what is actually being preached. The theologian always studies and analyzes symbols. In a *kairos*, the person devoted to the study of Jesus may actually help to form a symbol that is acceptable to the collective spirit of the faith community.

When a theologian uses a particular image in theology, the primary interest lies in gaining some insight into the understanding of faith. The theologian knows the usefulness of the images, but also the limitations. No symbol contains the fullness of the reality, and thus no one particular image can be erected into an absolute, nor can it ever be construed as a substitute for the reality itself. The good theologian will use images reflectively and with sobriety. As someone dedicated to the careful study of the faith, the theologian carefully and critically evaluates the images of the past as well as the images of the present. The result distinguishes the valid expression of some aspect of the mystery of faith from that which is inadequate, invalid or even prejudicial to faith.

An image used theologically, reflectively and ontically deepens the theoretical understanding of a reality, and becomes a model. Some models are also images; that is, they can be imagined easily. Other models are more abstract. With regard to Jesus, the New Testament models him as a shepherd, or as a preacher or a prophet. To model him as the second person of the Blessed Trinity or the Word of God, however, does not connote the idea of an image, since the ideas are more abstract.

Models in Science and Theology

The physical sciences and the social sciences have used models extensively in the past. Only recently have models been used in theology. Avery Dulles titled his book on the church *Models of the Church*. I.T. Ramsey also demonstrates how the use of models can be helpful in theology.[39] There are obvious similarities and differences between the way the various sciences use models and the way theology uses them. In science the use of models is effective if the model allows for deductions as well as verification: "In any scientific understanding a model is better, the more prolific it is in generating deductions which are then open to experimental verification and falsification."[40] A model that fails to respond to some of the questions to be answered is by that fact limited in its usefulness. A model that does not allow for experimentation is also of limited value, since the researcher cannot verify the truth purported to be represented.

With certain restrictions, theologians have applied these notions to theology, even though developed primarily in other fields. E. Cousins explains clearly the use of models in theology:

> Theology is concerned with the ultimate level of religious mystery which is even less accessible than the mystery of the physical universe. Hence our religious language and symbols should be looked upon as models because even more than the concepts of science, they only approximate the object they are reflecting.[41]

The symbol, however, can never become an absolute. Cousins is convinced that the use of a model prevents this possibility:

. . . to use the concept of model in theology, then, breaks
the illusion that we are actually encompassing the infinite
within our finite structures and language. It prevents concepts and symbols from becoming idols and opens theology
to variety and development just as the model method has
done for science. Yet there is a danger that it will not go far
enough for it may not take sufficiently into account the
level of religious experience.[42]

The last comment of Cousins merits study. Certain disadvantages
arise from using a methodology from the physical sciences. Religious
experience involves more than the intellectual; it encompasses the
entire person. No one can compare religious faith with the analysis of
the universe in any complete fashion. Analysis can be used, but in all
analogies the differences predominate. Faith concerns more than can
be contained in any model. Recognizing this deficiency, however,
models can help the theologian not only in efforts to explain faith, but
in exploring faith.

On the level of explanation, models tend to synthesize what people have already experienced or have come to believe in a faith experience. Just as a good scientific model will synthesize and respond to
many facets and problems and questions, so the theological model will
synthesize the biblical experience as well as the experience of centuries
of lived faith in the history of Christianity.

The gospel models of Jesus as a shepherd, or the Lamb of God,
or one of the prophets convey certain aspects of the meaning of Jesus,
and the church has accepted them. He is the one who provides for and
protects; he is the one who offers himself without hesitation to God
his Father; he is the one who fulfills the aspirations of the Old
Testament and points out the religious dimension present or absent in
human life. Each model points out one specific aspect of Jesus and his
ministry, but each has its obvious limits. No model above takes into
account the specific relationship between Jesus and God his Father.
Nor do they deal with an appreciation of Jesus as one like his brethren
"in all things but sin" (Heb 4:15). Thus, other models must be used to
supplement these models taken from scripture. In the history of theology, Jesus has been explained as the second person of the Blessed
Trinity. More recently, Jesus is the man for others, the sacrament of
God, the human face of God, the great liberator, and the ground of
being.

Using Models

In the use of models, the more applications the models have, the better they suggest a true relationship between the reality of Jesus and the image that is used to convey the reality. No complete harmony is possible, since the symbol is forever limited in expressing the reality it contains. The exploratory use of models involves the specific theological task of breaking new ground and offering a means for the theologian to fulfill the task as one who is seeking understanding. Such a responsibility demands much and involves many pitfalls. Somehow the theologian must steer a course between the Scylla of exploration for its own sake and the Charybdis of theological stagnation in long-outdated ideas. Christian theology has a norm in the gospel of Jesus as experienced and expressed in the early church. Thus in some sense every exploration further enunciates the reality of Jesus always present in the church. The ongoing sense of revelation as the unfolding of the offer of a relationship with God demands Jesus living among his people now, continuing to offer himself in ways that are meaningful to people of every age. Exploring the present experience of Jesus by the faithful also forms part of the theological enterprise. A true development in theology and not just the unfolding of what was always known does exist. The present experience of the church is in a certain sense unique, and that experience itself will bring new insights into the meaning of faith.

The present pope, John Paul II, has learned from personal experience the role of the church in a Marxist regime. That has given him an understanding of Jesus that would not be possible at any other moment in history. The experience of faith in Latin America or in the emerging nations of Africa and Asia has developed new insights into the meaning of Jesus. In the Second Vatican Council the specifically American experience of faith gave birth to the decree on religious liberty. In each period of history, theological reflection has nourished insights that grew out of the interchange of human experience and Christian faith. The result has raised the consciousness of the entire church to appreciate another aspect of the inexhaustible meaning of Jesus of Nazareth.

Verification

A further problem in the exploratory use of models in christology involves verification. Dealing with the mystery of God and humankind precludes any easily deduced conclusions. Nor can any empirical tests be used to see if the model is actually helpful or harmful to Christian faith.

The model of Jesus as the great liberator causes some to suspect that this must imply the approval of violence and thus cannot be valid. This may not be the case. The model need not automatically entail the sanctioning of violence, thus contradicting the fundamentally non-violent stance of Christianity. Clearly, empirical tests cannot be used for verification of this model, since statistics in themselves cannot tell what is right or wrong in the struggle for justice. The number of people espousing liberation theology in Latin America and in other parts of the world is not a criterion for rightness, nor is the number of people opposed to liberation theology a sign that the model is wrong. Even the presence of some people in the movement who advocate violence does not, of itself, vitiate the value of the model.

Discernment

Just as the discernment of spirits is necessary in the spiritual life, so too a process of discernment is crucial in the realm of theology. Ignatius Loyola saw the need to seek guidance to discover the significant values in the life of faith. This concept can be applied here as well. K. Rahner faces the question of authority in the church and speaks of a certain "feel" for the rightness of a position. He speaks of a sense of peace that will be the sign that the person is on the right track:

> That serene, joyous, harmonious lucidity in which there can
> alone be any hope of finding the correct solution in individ-
> ually important affairs may also be the fruit of the spirit.[43]

A corporate discernment of spirits can be most helpful in coming to some judgment with regard to the use of models for Jesus:

As this life of Christ is deepened in us by the Holy Spirit there is created in the Christian a "sense of Christ," a taste and instinctual judgment for the things of God, a deeper perception of God's truth, an increased understanding of God's dispositions and love toward us. This is what Christians must strive to attain individually and corporately; theologians call it Christian connaturality. It is like a natural instinct or intuition but it is not natural, since it results from the supernatural reality of the divine indwelling and the impulses of grace.[44]

This feel for what is right or wrong, valid or invalid, is important in the evaluation of any model. Jesus had the same idea when he remarked, "By their fruits you shall know them" (Mt 7:20). The Christian community will recognize a model truly helpful for faith, even though this may take time and involve opposition. Where the model results in anger or discord or the destruction of individuals in any way, then the Spirit is not at work. The models may be evaluated by the effect they have on the church, the worldwide community of believers who profess the gospel on which every model must ultimately be based.

Faith is not just a theoretical engagement of the mind. Faith is lived. Theory and practice are not separate realities. Faith in Jesus exists in people and in history, neither divorced from them nor isolated from their historical experiences. The continual interplay between the individual believer working out of personal history in conjunction with other believers brings faith to birth. When these realities are in balance, one can confidently judge the validity of a model of Jesus.

Jesus as Ruler

An example from the history of theology should help to clarify this method of discernment. In medieval times the model of Jesus as the ultimate ruler of all gave birth to a sense of judgment and control that produced an authoritarian church in the late middle ages. If Jesus controlled all people and if the church shared in this power, then the church had an obligation to rule over everyone in an absolute manner. Consequently the church could forbid anyone to think differently from the official teaching.

Church leaders also saw themselves empowered to dethrone kings and force infidels to submit to baptism. The model was taken not from the role of Jesus in the gospels, but from the experience of secular, civil authority. Turning Jesus into a secular potentate and then using that model to control the society from which it arose demonstrates how questionable that particular model was from the outset.

All models used in theology are incomplete. They illuminate certain aspects of Jesus and obscure others. Certainly the model of Jesus as ruler has some foundation in the New Testament. The Father has given to *him* power and judgment (Jn 5:22; Mt 28:18) but this should not be interpreted by the understanding of rulers in secular society.

Paradigm

The study of Jesus discloses many models. Some will have outlived their usefulness based upon the continual growth and perception of the reality of Jesus as still present in his community. Images and models have always proliferated in the history of Christianity. With such a multiplicity, often enough the human mind will want to limit the plurality and search for one model that will be the summation or epitome of all. Can one model unify the data of scripture and that of the two thousand years of Christian experience? At various times in the history of theology, people have tried to offer such a model. In the terminology used in this book, that model would then become a paradigm. When a model successfully solves a great many questions and problems and allows for the greatest number of deductions and further invites a variety of personal understandings, then such is a paradigm as expressed. Paradigms are "concrete puzzle solutions which, employed as models or examples, can replace explicit rules as a basis for the solution of the remaining puzzles of normal science."[45]

In the past, the chief paradigm for Jesus was the second person of the Blessed Trinity. This formed the basis for scholastic christology and has been part of the official teaching of the church for the past fifteen hundred years. In recent years the church has chosen to use other models, at least in unofficial documents, but the paradigm has remained the same. The eternal only-begotten-Son-second-person-of-the-Blessed-Trinity is the model that responds to the most questions and problems and allows for the greatest expression of the reality.

Is this the paradigm that the church wants to use in the twentieth or twenty-first century? Are followers of Jesus and members of the church expected to maintain and hold to this model as a paradigm, or can they use it as one model and turn to some other paradigm? Must this model be a paradigm for preaching and religious education, or may it give way to other paradigms while maintaining its position in speculative theology?

Whatever one's personal position, the transition from one paradigm to another creates problems. Each model brings its strengths and weaknesses. When one model becomes a paradigm, the weaknesses are often forgotten and the strengths are emphasized. When paradigms shift, people who have grown accustomed to the strengths of one and have never been aware of its weaknesses will react sharply against the introduction of a new paradigm. Not only are theologians threatened who have worked out their own positions in terms of the previously reigning paradigm, but ordinary people are affected at the level of their beliefs and practices. Piety suffers.

No one should be surprised, then, to find polarization with regard to Jesus and his image in the contemporary church. Theologians often seem unable to communicate and the church officials fall back on a reaffirmation of more traditional models. In times of controversy the usual tendency is to solidify and reaffirm a previously held tradition. Such is the situation of the church at the end of the twentieth century; theologians and others must learn not only to live with that fact, but also to gain insights from it. If no one paradigm provides the final answer, then it seems that an acceptance of many models within a dominant paradigm is the rational and responsible approach. Only further confusion will result from an effort to convert a single model into a final and eschatological one.

Instead of seeking one absolute paradigm, since each one captures only part of the reality, the Christian community might choose to recognize the plurality and celebrate the complementarity of the models. A model may also be erected into a paradigm, but only for a time, and only with the realization that it must accommodate other models.

In the following pages some of the models that have been used with regard to Jesus in the history of christology will be presented, as well as those models that are currently most popular. The beginning is always the New Testament. From there, the church has developed its various approaches to Jesus. To be all-inclusive is impossible. Certain models will always deserve their place. The study delineates the various approaches to christology of the past as well as shows the avenues of development in the present and future. Theologians usually adopt a model or a combination of models. They commit themselves to a particular stance in systematic and practical theology. Believers do the same thing. Action follows being.

STUDY TOPICS AND QUESTIONS

1. Why do people bother to study the Bible?

2. Critically analyzing the New Testament can cause problems. Why do theologians insist on doing it?

3. The church must have concerns when people start rethinking fundamental doctrines.

4. Why are contemporary scholars so interested in the historical Jesus?

5. All approaches to Jesus are equally good.

6. The idea of "mystery" as inexhaustible intelligibility makes sense.

7. Is there a crisis of faith today? Is there a crisis of images?

8. What new images of Jesus appeal to you? What is your own image of Jesus?

9. Do models and paradigms help or hinder in understanding Jesus and the church?

10. Make a list of as many images of Jesus as you can recall. Put them in order of personal preference.

PART II

Models of Jesus in the New Testament

Chapter 1.

THE HISTORICAL JESUS
AND EARLY FORMULAE

Over the past two centuries New Testament exegetes have struggled with the search for the historical Jesus. Every student of Christianity knows that Christians have experienced for the past two thousand years not the Jesus of Nazareth but the Christ of Christian faith.[46] The New Testament can never be accepted as an historical biographical document, but rather the New Testament persists in its claim to offer assistance to a troubled world as a faith document.

The studies of the nineteenth century which sought first to discover an actual biography of Jesus and then a psychology of Jesus were doomed. The Jesus of history, the Jesus who was born, raised and preached in what is now contemporary Israel, can never be separated from the Christ of faith: the empowered Son of God, giver of the Spirit, and founder of the Christian church. The general conclusion that prevailed up to the past year or so was that the Christ of faith was not in fact separated from the Jesus of history. The Christ of faith found expression in the lived words and activities of the same Jesus of Nazareth.

The recent studies by J. Meier and D. Crossan have opened once again the quest for the historical Jesus. More information from the discovery of ancient documents, especially at Nag Hammadi, more studies on the social environment of the first century, and greater knowledge of linguistics and the various uses of language have all contributed to the rethinking of the historical Jesus.

Contemporary Christians may find it difficult to accept the limited knowledge on Jesus, the source of Christian faith. At the foundation level, historians can only state that Jesus lived in Palestine, was known as a good man and was crucified.[47] Much of what Christians associate with Jesus: his virginal conception, his bodily resurrection, his healing and raising from the dead, his preaching of himself as the messiah and the Son of God, his establishment of the church including the celebration of the last supper and institution of the eucharist—all are elements coming not from Jesus himself but from the followers that eventually gave to future generations the New Testament.

Such statements should not cause undue concern for the contemporary Christian. Christianity, like any religion, rises and falls on faith and not on the details of history. The survival of the Christian faith for two thousand years, the immense amount of good accomplished through the acceptance and living of the teaching of Jesus as attested to in the gospels, gives sufficient reason to maintain a faith rooted in a first century Jew of whom historians know very little.

Crossan offers his opinion of the very minimum of teachings of Jesus generally attested to as in truth going back to his actual ministry.

TEACHINGS FROM THE MINISTRY OF JESUS

The kingdom of God is now offering salvation for all
All sins will be forgiven
Parables: The sower, mustard seed, vineyard, weeds and wheat, the banquet, talents, settle account with servants, the prodigal son, workers in the vineyard, good samaritan, unjust steward, Lazarus, the lost coin
the equality of the sexes
the dispossessed, even the destitute, are all invited to share in the kingdom
true family ties are ties of faith in God
following him involves suffering
he is like a shepherd who cares for his sheep
forgive as you are forgiven
serving one another is the hallmark of the kingdom
seek reconciliation with all[48]

For any contemporary believer in Jesus no anxiety should exist in regard to the historical Jesus. Even the most limited approach, such as Crosssan's, will admit that the above teachings can in fact go back to Jesus of Nazareth. Surely such teachings form the basis of the

Christian gospel. One further element however needs to be affirmed before actually studying the documents of the New Testament: the self-understanding of the historical Jesus.

If the nineteenth century New Testament scholars gave up on composing an actual biography, they also gave up on constructing any sense of a psychological portrait of Jesus. Twentieth century scholars have returned once again into the fray with new appreciation of the self-understanding of Jesus.

God as "Abba"

Joachim Jeremias has devoted much of his life to the study of the religious experience of Jesus. For Jeremias Jesus used Abba regularly as his personal form of address for God.[49] E. Schillebeeckx speaks of the "Abba principle" as the foundation of the self-understanding of Jesus and his mission.[50] More recently B. Cooke writes of Jesus' Abba experience.[51] The conclusion generally accepted by both New Testament exegetes and systematic theologians recognizes that the self-understanding of Jesus rests upon an awareness of his special relationship to God. God loved him in a way unlike other people. Jesus was God's beloved one. Such an awareness does not in any way imply that Jesus saw himself as equal to God, but rather that God had entered into his life in a most unusual way. Neither the self-awareness of Jesus nor the New Testament teaches that Jesus was the second person of the Blessed Trinity. Rather, Jesus had a unique relationship to God characterized by his use of the word "Abba" when he addressed God. Later reflection on this distinctive way of relating to God assisted the New Testament writers in presenting Jesus as the Son of God, messiah, and Lord of all.

Apocalyptic and Eschatological

A fuller appreciation of Jesus in the New Testament and the various models of Jesus presented therein demands an understanding of apocalyptic and eschatological. For several decades many scholars viewed Jewish apocalyptic experience as the matrix of Jesus and his message as well as the writing of the New Testament.[52] Today sobriety has returned to this discussion. Most see Jesus and his message and the New Testament as primarily eschatological rather than primarily apocalyptic.[53] What the words mean deserve some careful discussion.

In general apocalyptic conveys "things will get worse before they get better" and it will all end in a cataclysmic experience of God. The world will come to an end including the traditional death, judgment, heaven or hell with the coming in power and glory of the Son of Man. All will recognize the powerful messiah, and the enemies, those who refused to believe, will meet destruction. The thirteenth chapter of the gospel of Mark with its imagery of the sun and stars falling paints a good apocalyptic picture. At the time of Jesus the Jews looked for an inbreaking of God in human history in which the hated Roman regime would be destroyed and God's people would be vindicated though power and might. The apocalyptic still lives on in the images of the end of the world through fire, especially when the world lived so closely under the threat of nuclear annihilation.

The eschatological also involves the future but as being made possible in the present. Living in peace and with justice and freedom for all, even those who live on the periphery of society, is eschatological. Not quite real yet but such a possibility exists and has already been achieved in a limited fashion. The eschatological good calls for a healing within, which then finds expression without. Jesus, in the opinion of many, was primarily eschatological, in line with the wisdom tradition of the Old Testament and within a limited prophetic tradition rather than the prophetic/apocalyptic tradition of Judaism. This shift from the apocalyptic to the eschatological may seem like so much useless discussion on the part of scholars. In reality, it marks a shift which will have repercussions for the actual living of the Christian life. Realized eschatology, salvation present for all now, gives more an impetus to live the gospel than looking for some future cataclysm in which the Son of Man will return in power and glory and believers will be vindicated. Within this context the New Testament and its various portrayals of Jesus should be studied.

The traditional image of Jesus as second person of the Blessed Trinity, virginally conceived, working miracles and prophesying the future, knowing all things and rising by his own power from the dead, exists in the minds of many believers. The same will be found in many catechisms,[54] but not all of these elements can be found in the New Testament. In fact many other additional images of this same Jesus appear in the documents upon which Christian faith rests.

Images of Jesus in the New Testament

Some have seen Jesus as a political revolutionary, dedicated to the overthrowal of the Roman authority in Israel.[55] Morton Smith examined the environment of early Christianity in Jewish and Greek culture and recognized Jesus as a magician, healing people by his own power.[56] Recent studies have attempted to recover the Jewishness of Jesus, seeing him as a Jewish charismatic, or as a monastic Essene, or as a rabbi or even as a proto-Pharisee or as a Jew in the tradition of Old Testament prophets. The New Testament gives evidence, more or less, for all of these approaches. To them can be added the more traditional images as the kind and passionate benefactor, or the suffering human being, the teacher, the benevolent shepherd, the friend of outcasts. The New Testament also has many titles used of Jesus: messiah, Christ, Lord, Son of God, Son of Man, Son. And so the list goes on. The New Testament comes from the pens of many authors over at least a seventy year time period. During this period development took place as the early followers of Jesus realized more and more the meaning that his life and message had for themselves and for future generations. The images or models of Jesus extend from the Jesus for Paul in 1 Thessalonians to the cosmic Christ of Colossians to the Jesus of the pastorals supporting organization and control.

Christology seeks to offer a systematic presentation of the meaning of Jesus of Nazareth. Concerned with the human effort to understand faith in Jesus, the writers of the New Testament gathered together many strands into a unified whole. In the past, many authors have attempted to construct a consistent and often harmonized christology founded on the New Testament. Such a claim, however, often demonstrates little knowledge of the various theological traditions associated with, and coming from, the early communities. The New Testament contains many christologies of many different authors coming from diverse communities—all making a just claim to offer some true insights into Jesus of Nazareth.

The Bible, and in particular the New Testament, is not primarily a listing of doctrine or a grouping of articles of faith. The Bible offers a record of a conscious religious life lived by the Jewish people, and in the New Testament by Jesus and his followers. The New Testament documents the faith of the members of the Christian community after they had the experience of the risen Lord, and believed in him as the messiah in power (Rom 1:4). When people read the Bible today they can become aware of the experience of Jesus and the faith of the early followers. But the reader experiences the record of that faith and not the faith itself. The New Testament shares in the mystery of God and the mystery of human life. This means that anyone who reads this document of faith can reach some understanding but can never reach complete clarity.[57] Not that believers know nothing, but that they will never know everything. If the individual can never reach a complete understanding of self, how can anyone expect to understand the mystery that is Jesus of Nazareth?

Christology and the New Testament

Although believers rely on the presence of God's Spirit in the church, the source for the life and the meaning of Jesus is the record left by writers some two thousand years ago. This makes the task all the more difficult. If no one can reach a complete understanding of Jesus today, the same thing holds for any believer or group of any period of history. Even those who were privileged to know Jesus and to live with him and learn from him were limited in their appreciation of him. Thus theologians cannot expect to develop a complete, accurate and systematic christology even from the earliest documents of Christianity. The New Testament authors display neither harmony in their sayings about Jesus nor a sense of a unified doctrinal approach to him. These documents come from a specific time and place; they are human, with all of the defects and limitations of any human accomplishment. The careful reader can certainly gain much from a study of the New Testament in a search for christology, but that includes an awareness of the historical ambit, the social and cultural and religious milieu of Jesus' time and place. The study may well end up knowing less than what was presumed at the outset.

God chose to act with people in a human way; thus the gospels would have to be limited and expressed within certain spiritual ideas common to all people. The Word was made flesh, but not flesh in general. Jesus was a man, a Jew born in a specific era in a particular country. What he did and what he taught have been expressed in human terms taken from that time and that region, and thus part of the heritage of Judaism.

The first preachers of Jesus also lived within the confines of a particular education and culture.[58] When Jesus spoke of God he did so in terms of his own understanding of God, and his listeners understood him in terms of their own perceptions. If he spoke of Father, the listeners formulated their image of father according to their own lights.[59] And so the christology of the New Testament is limited by the people and events that surrounded Jesus of Nazareth, as well as by the limitations of the earliest preachers.

Each author of the epistles and gospels understood Jesus within a certain harmony and unity of viewpoints. For some who knew Jesus, they compared their appreciation of Jesus as risen Lord to what they had known before. They integrated this new experience with their own understanding of human personality, and formulated it in their own way and with their own categories. All of this resulted in a great diversity in the New Testament images of Jesus. The only honest approach to biblical christology is to admit that no one biblical christology exists; there are as many christologies as there are authors and communities that tried to express in writing something of their experience of Jesus. Even individual writers can offer an early christology and a later christology. Paul, for example, presents a slightly different understanding of Jesus in his earlier epistles than in the later ones. The gospels give evidence of several christologies in the community along with a contest as to the superiority of one over the other.

A complete overview of New Testament christology lies beyond the limits of this study.[60] Some general guidelines and approaches, however, will help situate the historical foundation for the various contemporary approaches found both on the level of developed theology as well as on the level of popular piety.

Earliest Christological Formulae[61]

The New Testament evidences a certain natural evolution in the understanding of Jesus. Since the writings in the New Testament are collections of pericopes elaborated over a period of time, the reader cannot easily detect precisely what the early church preached. For example, Acts 3:12-26, 4:9-12 and 5:3:31 seem to be basic and to date from the time immediately after Pentecost. Today, however, scholars generally admit that even they have been theologically elaborated. They are more than just the immediate reaction to the meaning of Jesus as crucified and risen Lord.

> The God of our fathers raised Jesus whom you killed by hanging him on a tree. God exalted him at his right hand as leader and Savior, to give repentance to Israel and forgiveness of sins (Acts 5:3.31).

Authors will not even agree on the primitiveness of "Maranatha" ("Come, Lord Jesus," or "May the Lord Jesus come"). Some authors construct ancient formulas from Matthew 25:31-36, Mark 14:61 and Luke 12:8.

When the Son of Man comes in his glory, and all the angels with him, then he will sit on his glorious throne. Before him will be gathered all the nations, and he will separate them one from another as a shepherd separates the sheep from the goats, and he will place the sheep at his right hand, but the goats at the left. The king will say to those at his right hand, "O blessed of my Father, inherit the kingdom prepared for you from the foundation of of the world, for I was hungry and you gave me food, I was thirsty and you gave me drink, I was a stranger and you welcomed me, I was naked and you clothed me, I was sick and you visited me, I was in prison and you came to me (Mt 25:31-36).

Are you the Christ the Son of the Blessed? (Mk 14:61b).

And I tell you, everyone who acknowledges me before men, the Son of Man also will acknowledge before the angels of God (Lk 12:8).

The above seem to have come from a Palestinian milieu, which would suggest a more ancient origin, but the theory still has serious drawbacks. Each statement shows signs of development far beyond what might be considered the earliest understanding of Jesus as an itinerant preacher of the kingdom of God.

Exaltation

The chief stumbling block in Matthew and Luke is the question of the parousia. Was the parousia part of the earliest testimony of Jesus or not? Some maintain that the most ancient Judaic-Christian christology contained a theology of exaltation without a second coming. Jesus after his death was raised by God and was justified and as such now lives with God; another coming in glory was not expected; the eschatological time of salvation exists now, as proven by the outpouring of the Spirit.

A second opinion maintains that the Christian community expected a second and definitive coming of the Lord. Therefore they did not consider the exaltation as full nor the institution of Jesus in power as complete. Christ was taken for a time, and only in his second coming will he be instituted as messiah in the sense of the Son of Man in Daniel (Dan 7:13-14).

"And that he might send the Christ, appointed for you, Jesus, whom heaven must receive until the time for establishing all that God spoke by the mouth of his holy prophets . . ." (Acts 3:20-21)

Certainly the earliest christologies were formulas of exaltation. Jesus was exalted, raised up in power (Rom 1:4; Acts 2:36), and since the Spirit was actually given, perhaps there was no need for a further exaltation in a second coming. But since the Jews expected a glorious messiah, a role Jesus did not fulfill, in all probability the thought of a parousia was soon added to this earliest christological formula. Without a second coming in glory it would be difficult for Jews to accept a crucified messiah.

The advantage of an exaltation christology without a second coming is that it accentuates the salvation already present among the followers of Jesus. This gives the foundation for a realized eschatology which the New Testament will develop at a later stage.[62] The parousia adds the future element to salvation and gives the foundation for what has come to be known as traditional eschatology.

Evolution in the New Testament

The New Testament also allows us to chart a development in the church's understanding of the divinity of Jesus.[63] The earliest formulation in the kerygma emphasized that Jesus was made messiah in his resurrection (Acts 2:36). Thinking would have centered on Jesus becoming the Son of God in the experience of his resurrection. The Father raised Jesus up as a final testimony of his acceptance of the life and death of his faithful Son, and by this means Jesus was made Lord and messiah.

At this point there might have been a further development into the future with the advent of the parousia. For some, this would be the final manifestation of the favor of God on Jesus his Son. Jesus would become Lord and messiah in the fullest sense in his second coming. Later thinking on the ministry of Jesus encouraged seeing Jesus as already the messiah in his activity and in his preaching. In the gospel of Mark the baptism begins his ministry (Mk 1:11). Since he fulfilled the expectations of Israel in his ministry he was God's favored Son in his baptism. Later theologians would falsely interpret this scene in the light of an adoptionist christology: the Father adopted Jesus as beloved Son in his baptism.

Still further thought situated Jesus as God's unique Son, not only in his ministry but from his very conception. Matthew and Luke offer infancy stories which present the virginal conception as the sign of the unique Sonship of Jesus. Finally the Logos theology of John identifies Jesus with the pre-existent Word of God, the one who exists in the form of God (Jn 1:1). This highest christology of the later writings of the New Testament concludes the natural evolution in thought that began with an experience of Jesus. The New Testament does not attempt to relate all of these ideas; it shares no great concern to explain how Jesus was divine and human. Rather, it simply presents from a variety of viewpoints the attestation in faith of the uniqueness of Jesus as Son and one like us in all things but sin (Heb 4:15).

STUDY TOPICS AND QUESTIONS

1. Is the historical Jesus important?

2. Do you see any value in studying the primitive christologies?

3. How would the early christology of exaltation be related to the understanding of the resurrection?

4. What affect do the different christologies in the New Testament have on the study of Jesus today?

5. Does the parousia, the second coming, make any difference?

Chapter 2.

JESUS IN THE WRITINGS OF PAUL

Paul never knew the historical Jesus. The author of so much of the New Testament experienced the risen Lord on the road to Damascus. His life and the future of Christianity changed forever.[64] The Jesus of Paul was the Jesus, primarily, of his personal experience. A reading of his letters makes clear his reliance not on the testimony of apostles or other eye-witnesses, but on his personal revelation. Paul did however make efforts to assure that what he preached was in accord with the Jesus tradition of other preachers. He did not wish to preach another gospel and did not want to separate himself and his converts and communities from the larger Christian community.

Traditions

In 1 Corinthians Paul writes of that tradition; Jesus died, was buried, rose and appeared to certain members of the community (1 Cor 15:3-5). In these and other writings Paul demonstrates his awareness of the sufferings of Jesus (Phil 3:10) and his cross and crucifixion (1 Cor 1:17-18, Phil 2:8; Gal 2:20; 3:1; 1 Cor 1:23) and his death (1 Thes 5:10; 1 Cor 11:26; Rom 6:3) and his burial (1 Cor 15:4; Rom 6:4). Most of what Paul preaches, however, rests upon Paul's interpretation of Jesus in the light of Paul's own understanding of Judaism. Jesus saved all, Jew and Gentile, from the burden of the law, from the impossibility of living a righteous life based on works. For Paul the Jesus tradition meant that people could be justified in the sight of God not for anything they did or failed to do, but solely because of what God had done for them in Jesus. As Savior, Jesus truly saved all of

41

humankind from the great sin of trying to save themselves. Salvation, grace, justification and reconciliation belong to all of humanity now through the one gracious Savior, who lived and died and rose for justification because of the graciousness of God. On the road to Damascus Paul encountered a suffering messiah risen in power, who had become for Paul the compassionate and forgiving Savior. Paul met a supportive Lord who invited Paul to share in his suffering and death and so share in a glorious resurrection to come. Christ lived in Paul and Paul lived in Christ. The troubled Pharisee in Paul gave way to the peaceful follower of Jesus, his personal Savior. Jesus delivered him from the impossible task of fulfilling the law. Paul accepted Jesus as personal Lord and Savior and deliverer. Jesus alone could forgive all sins and promise the beginning of a life of justice and peace and an unfolding of that life into a future with God.

Development

Reading the various letters of Paul can demonstrate a development in Paul's christology. Above all, however, he sees Jesus as Savior; God has communicated and offered himself through Jesus and unites and reconciles people and the world through this same Savior. Paul recognized the speaker who introduced himself on the road to Damascus as "Jesus, whom you are persecuting," as the exalted Son of God. This Lord, however, was for Paul the same as the historical Jesus of Nazareth who had been crucified some three years previously. Since Paul did not know this historical Jesus, his perspective would of necessity differ from that of the twelve apostles or those other earliest followers of Jesus.

Nevertheless, Paul was the first to write about this historical Jesus of Nazareth since his letters are the first literary expressions of Christianity. Jesus was a descendant of Abraham (Gal 3:16) and David (Rom 1:3), lived under the law (Gal 4:4), endured crucifixion (Gal 3:1), and was experienced as risen by Paul himself (Gal 1:16).

Paul also knew Peter, James and John (Gal 1:19; 2:9), and although he does not quote actual words of Jesus, he seems to be well acquainted with the substance of his teachings. The reader need only to compare the ethical section of Romans (12–15) with the sermon on the mount to discover the close relationship between what Matthew presents as a way of living for believers and what Paul offers. What Paul says of the life and teaching of the historical Jesus fits well with the understanding of this same historical person as recorded in the gospels.

Some of the most familiar aspects of the historical Jesus in the gospels, however, find no place in Paul. In the gospels Jesus habitually teaches in parables, heals the sick, drives our demons. None of this appears in the letters of Paul. Nor would believers know of the controversies faced by Jesus and the events that led up to his death if they only had the testimony of Paul. The christology of Paul agrees with that of the evangelists and differs.

Paul's Christology

Some have tried to develop the christology of Paul from gnosticism, Hellenistic philosophy and a refined sense of Judaism. But Paul knew Jesus as risen Lord and understood the meaning of God's anointed not from a mixture of gnosticism and Hellenism and Judaism, but from personal contact. Often in the past scholars have tried to detect foreign influences in Paul and his theology. Surely he could not live in a pluralistic world without feeling some of its effects. His portrait of Jesus, however, comes from personal contact. His christology does not consist of some abstract doctrine but finds its foundation in the historical Jesus of Nazareth who died, whom he persecuted and who appeared to him on the road to Damascus. But now this same Jesus sits at the right hand of God and becomes the center of Paul's personal religion.

According to Paul, Jesus had been designated Son of God in power according to the spirit of holiness by the resurrection from the dead (Rom 1:4). The emphasis falls on God as the agent who made Jesus Son of God in power because he had already been endowed with the spirit of holiness. As a result, God raised Jesus from the dead. This same divine power works now among the followers of Jesus, conveyed to them through the indwelling Spirit. The christology of Paul also involves the continuing presence of the Spirit in believers which attests to the final consummation when all, Jew and Greek, will experience the fullness of salvation in the resurrection of the dead.

Jesus and Paul's Personality

While all of his christology results from personal experience, Paul's temperament also figured in his understanding of Jesus. Paul the Pharisee tried to fulfill all of the law but labored under an internal conflict, since he realized that he could never fulfill such law (Rom 7:7). In Jesus, Paul recognized a redeemer who brought the salvation of God, the saving presence of God and gave grace freely. The convert

Paul lived supremely conscious of the once fractured life that was made whole by the grace of God in Christ Jesus.

Glorified Christ

Paul's personal Christ was the glorified Jesus, living eternally in his definitive state as resurrected Lord and Christ. This same Jesus is also the mystical Christ united by reason of identity with his followers whom Paul had persecuted. People experience salvation by accepting the offer of the communication of the glorious life of Jesus (Gal 2:20), and Paul as an apostle proclaims this to Jew and Gentile alike.

Paul always related the Christ of the Spirit to the Jesus of the flesh in history (2 Cor 5:16), including in his personal understanding the pre-existing and transcendent Christ. All that Paul understood in his christology came from this personal experience, which was mystical and existential. In some ways this understanding of Jesus went beyond that of the twelve, for Paul started from the glorious Christ, affirmed his earthly existence and then, finally, preached some type of pre-existence which culminates his christology in the fullness of the life of the risen and glorious Christ with God his Father.

Paul Receives from Tradition

Paul based his christology on personal experience (Gal 1:12), but also clearly acknowledged his dependence upon the traditions of the early communities (1 Cor 15:3-5). He preached a risen Lord with a history received from tradition from the early church. He writes of the historical Jesus: "born of a woman, born under the law" (Gal 4:4); the seed of David (Rom 1:3); "crucified" (Gal 3:1). This same Jesus instituted the eucharist the night before he was betrayed (1 Cor 11:23); he suffered (Rom 15:3); was obedient unto death (2 Cor 1:5; Phil 3:10); and even records certain sayings of the historical Jesus (1 Cor 7:10; 9:14; Rom 14:4; 1 Thes 4:14). Paul continued the preaching of Jesus, especially the coming of the kingdom, the primacy of love, and the apostles as servants of all.

The combination of personal experience and the tradition of the early church flowed into each other to create a multifaceted portrait of Jesus that ebbed and rose, responding to the various needs of Paul and his listeners.

The Progression of Paul's Christology

Development characterizes human life. Surely a growth in awareness and understanding would characterize the church's understanding of Jesus. The same remains true for all believers, especially evidenced in Paul.

The early Paul (1 Thes and 1 Cor) emphasized the second coming of Jesus. This christology seems close to that of Acts but with further development. Jesus as Lord occupies the central place, equal to
the Father. The resurrection of Jesus constitutes the first moment and
prelude of the final act, which will be the second and glorious coming.
With the risen Lord, people can be sanctified. Salvation and the kingdom are no longer just future realities, but present *now*. At this period
of Paul's thought, the actual coming of Jesus into history has little
importance. The incarnate Word of God in Jesus of Nazareth gives
way to the glorious and risen Lord and Christ. Paul differs from the
gospels, for example, which often see the ministry of Jesus as one continuous epiphany of God in Jesus.

In 2 Corinthians, Galatians and Romans, Paul emphasizes Jesus
as the one who brings salvation. The law cannot justify people, but
only faith in Christ Jesus can bring the saving presence of God's grace.
This offer Paul proclaims to all. Law gives way to faith; Jew receives the
offer as does the Gentile; the church becomes the new people of God.
All of this Paul preaches in 2 Cor 5:18-19.

In Philippians and Ephesians (whether Paul wrote this or not
remains disputed), some of the controversies seem to have subsided.
Faith has overcome the law and Gentiles are freely welcomed into the
community. Now Paul concentrates on the mystery of Jesus the Christ,
prepared for in the wisdom of God before the foundations of the
world. His meaning had been announced in the scriptures and effected and completed in the Christ who lives now with full majesty and
glory at the right hand of God. The cosmic Christ, the transcendent
Savior, reigns eternally.

Philippians expressed the personal Christ who is Savior and Lord
of all (Phil 3:20), but this same Christ had emptied himself (Phil 2).
The pre-existent Christ becomes the center of all and the consummation of the universe. With an emphasis on dignity, the letter to the
Ephesians explained the Christ by attributes of wisdom and focused
on the saving power; God chose according to his good pleasure; by the
super liberality of God people share in the riches of the divine and all
live pre-destined in Christ (Eph 1:3-14).

The Hymn in Philippians 2:6-11

Perhaps no greater expression of Pauline christology can be found than that of the hymn in the second chapter of Philippians. In the past some have claimed that Paul actually composed the hymn; others, by far the majority, believe that Paul found the hymn already existing and incorporated it into his letter, adding some additional elements to suit his purpose.

Paul loved the Philippians more than any other community he founded. His personal attitude toward this group of believers becomes evident in the reading of the epistle. Everything written in this letter should be seen not as a missionary document, nor as an effort to correct problems, but rather that this favorite community might grow in the knowledge and love of their faith in Christ Jesus.

Paul viewed the Christians at Philippi differently from other communities. He wanted them to more fully understand and live the life of Jesus in their personal lives, and in this epistle he used hymns more so than in any other letter. For Paul this group of early believers had already reached a level of understanding that demanded him to encourage them to continue to imitate the living Christ. Paul loved this community and anxiously led them to ever greater understanding and love of their faith in the Lord Jesus. With this as background, the reader can better understand the hymn and what Paul hoped to accomplish in his writing.

> Have this mind among yourselves, which you have in Christ Jesus, who though he was in the form of God did not think this equality was something to be proudly paraded, but emptied himself, taking the form of a servant, being born in the likeness of men. And being found in human form he humbled himself and became obedient to death, even to death on the cross. Therefore God has exalted him and bestowed on him the name that is above every name, that at the name of Jesus every knee should bend in heaven and on earth and under the earth, and every tongue should confess that Jesus Christ is Lord, to the glory of God the Father (Phil 2:5-11).

Paul offered a full christological presentation with elements involving the person of Jesus, his ministry moving from pre-existence to the consummation of the world.

Pre-mundane (pre-existence), the historical phase and the escha-tological phase:

Pre-existence: **He was in the form of God but entered into human history as a servant.**

Earthly life: **Servanthood led him to death on a cross in obedience to God.**

Exaltation: **God glorifies Jesus in his resurrection and makes it possible for all to overcome death and share in the same glorification.**

The exalted Jesus is now Lord of the universe, and all, even adverse powers, must acknowledge him as such.

"The form of God" demands a comparison with "servant form." Paul presents Jesus as being equal to God, sharing in the glory of God but also distinct from God since God exalted Christ. This form is not to be proudly paraded. He never explains the equality. Surely he does not mean divine essence, for then "emptying" makes no sense. The form of God is not the essence of God, just as the form of a servant is not the essence of being human. He who did not have the form of a servant accepted it without losing the form of God. He (Paul does not name the "he") accepts not just human nature but the sinful humanity. As obedient servant, Jesus goes to the cross, and as a result God gives him a name above all names. In the biblical tradition, a name expressed the essence or meaning of a person. God enthrones Jesus as Lord and all must now acknowledge him as such.

The hymn does not form a complete theological treatise on christology. Rather, as a poem, the hymn expresses some understanding of Jesus by one who loved ardently and wrote poetically. Paul found the hymn and sent it on to the Philippians who could meditate on its meaning and acknowledge that their Savior Jesus was the exalted Lord of all. They could turn to him in worship and receive his comforting grace.

Crucified Messiah

Jesus was true messiah, but also crucified messiah. The crucified Jesus forms the foundation for Paul's preaching. Salvation by the law gives way to salvation by faith in the cross of Jesus. Thus Paul preaches the scandal of the cross (1 Cor 2:2; Gal 5:11; 6:12). Paul, however, will not remain on the level of the earthly death of Jesus. Faith in the cross of Jesus takes its strength from faith in the resurrected Lord (Rom 4:14). Cross and resurrection are constituted as one in the mind of Paul, which is expressed in his formula:

> Who was put to death for our trespasses and raised for our justification (Rom 4:25).

Both cross and resurrection need to be personally accepted by the Christian. In Romans, Paul sees this in baptism (Rom 6:3). The cross is the place of the expiatory death for all (Gal 3:13) and the resurrection is the giving of new life, made so by the Spirit (Rom 8:9-11). Only through Jesus as Christ can believers ever understand human existence. Cross and resurrection will constitute the life of the believer just as it constituted the life of Jesus.

Son

Paul used this title sixteen times and in diverse meanings and contexts: the pre-existent Son (Rom 8:3; Gal 4:4); crucified Son (Rom 5:10; 8:32). In Rom 1:3-4, Paul used an ancient formula: Son of David and Son of God in power. In Rom 8:3, what was impossible by law becomes possible in the coming of the Son in sinful flesh. Such a Son accepts a salvific office and is able to restore a sinful world. In Rom 8:32, God did not spare his own Son but gave him up for us. The love of God for the Son and vice versa and the love of God and Son for humankind form the reasons for the salvation of all. In Rom 8:8-11, the Son of God makes others share in this relationship. The same idea is present in Gal 4:1-7. Christ as God's Son sends his Spirit to make all adopted children of God. God himself had revealed his Son to Paul on the road to Damascus (Gal 1:16), and now Paul proclaims that all can relate to God as did Jesus.

Lord and Christ

The title Lord carries with it a sense of adoration. Paul accepted the title from the Christian community and gave it a proper character. In Rom 14:9, Paul relates the title to reigning. In the Old Testament it refers to God, and Paul used it forty-seven times either alone or in conjunction with Christ. The exalted Lord will come again and demand adoration. This same Lord accepted his death (Rom 14:8).

Jesus is the messiah, the anointed one, the Christ, the chosen one who will bring salvation to all. God had sent Jesus to live a human life in obedience unto death. Then, as chosen anointed one, Jesus the Christ became the Lord of all, offering salvation to all, Jew and Gentile.

Paul allowed his understanding of Jesus his Lord and Christ to unfold as his life unfolded. He never developed a complete christology since such would be possible for Paul only when he himself had completed his journey. He gives to every Christian community starting points for ultimately Paul believes that christology, the understanding of love of Jesus the Lord is personal. Such it was for him. So it shall be for all.

STUDY QUESTIONS AND TOPICS

Paul

1. Paul had a personal experience of Jesus. Is this true for everyone?

2. Is Jesus a Jew for Paul? Is he more than a Jew?

3. Paul preaches a crucified Jesus. Why is this model important?

4. Do the titles that Paul used for Jesus help in understanding Jesus?

5. How would you sum up Paul's model of Jesus?

Chapter 3.

JESUS IN THE GOSPELS

Mark

A study of the different gospels will demonstrate the further distinctions that existed in the early community. Each author's perspective flowed from the needs of the particular audience. Each presents a christology that is not meant to be exclusive or exhaustive. Only when the richness of this variety of approaches to Jesus is understood can anyone begin to appreciate the impact that Jesus had on people.

Christology and Anthropology

The gospel of Mark[65] has no infancy narrative and seems to locate Jesus' divine Sonship in his baptism. Such elements are of limited interest, for in this gospel Jesus is first and foremost the suffering Son of Man who must die. On three occasions Mark has Jesus give a prediction of his passion: Mk 8:31, 9:31 and 10:33-34. The general theology that pervades the gospel of Mark focuses on the fate of those who are faithful to God. They hear the word of God and preach it, they are rejected and are delivered up. John the Baptist preaches and he is delivered up (1:14); Jesus preaches and is delivered up (9:30; 13:33); the disciples preach and they too are delivered up (13:9). Death appears to be the fate of all.

The christology of Mark rests on his fundamental Christian anthropology. Whatever happens to Jesus will also happen to his followers. It is a sad gospel in many ways, filled with misunderstandings on the part of the disciples, and with pain inflicted on Jesus as he is abandoned by family and friends and eventually by the entire population. Mark wishes to speak about Jesus, but only in relationship to the sufferings that are part of the Christian experience. Jesus as the suffering Son of Man is the model for all who would be disciples.

However central the death of Jesus is to Mark's gospel, it is not his sole concern. The author is also concerned about how Jesus lived. In presenting Jesus' way of suffering and his rejection, Mark always places it within the context of the life of Jesus as one who serves. The climax of his teaching on suffering thus includes his way of living: "The Son of Man came not to be served but to serve and to give his life as a ransom for many" (Mk 10:45). The author presents the cross not so much as an atonement for sin, but as the result of obedience to the law of God in life. God mysteriously wills that his Son must suffer and die, so the Son willingly accepts his fate—"the Son of Man must suffer" Mk 8:31). Jesus is patterned after the righteous sufferer in Psalm 22:

> My God, my God why hast thou abandoned me.... Yet thou are holy, enthroned on the praises of Israel. Yet thou art he who took me from the womb, thou didst keep me safe upon my mother's breast. Be not far from me, for trouble is near and there is none to help (Ps 22:1.3.9.11).

Jesus is the model for others in his living and dying, but his actual death offers the deepest insight into Mark's christology. The death of Jesus on the cross lays open a quality of life which patterns what true life means for all people. The authentic follower of Jesus must take up the cross daily and follow the Lord. No optional road, no substitute and no other means exist by which a person can be a disciple. Mark brings his christology into the closest possible contact with the church and the individual believer, and in so doing he reveals the incarnational christology that will pervade his gospel. Mark presents in his gospel an apocalyptic drama in which the author and his community are self-consciously caught up in events they view as the end of history. The gospel portrays this drama in the three acts previously mentioned: John is delivered up (1:14), Jesus is delivered up (9:31; 10:33; 14:41), and finally the Christian is delivered up (13:9-13). The conclusion, however, should not be forgotten. The believers are sad as they experience persecution, but they are also filled with the hope directed toward sharing in the glorification of the Son of Man. For Mark, the cross and suffering stand always in the foreground, but the resurrection remains in the background as the foundation for hope. As the Son of Man must suffer and die and then rise, so he offers the same hope to those who will follow him. The glorified Lord will bring his faithful followers to share in his glory. Mark understood Jesus only in terms of the suffering messiah who asks his disciples to join with him and share in his sufferings so that all can share in his glory.

The gospel of Mark is not the happiest of gospels. The shadow of the cross hangs over the life of Jesus as it will hang over the lives of his followers. The false christology of a divine man who experiences glory is corrected by the true christology that involves a sharing of his sufferings. To a persecuted community, Mark offered consolation by reminding them that all who will follow a thorn-crowned Lord must expect to share in his pain before they can enter into his glory. To this general christology a study of the various titles used by Mark helps to fill out his understanding of Jesus.

The Son of Man

The phrase can mean simply "man" in a generic sense as found in Psalm 8:4:

What is man that thou are mindful of him, of the Son of Man that thou dost care for him?

This also may have been the meaning in the pre-Markan tradition as found in Mark 2:28:

So the Son of Man is Lord even of the sabbath.

The original meaning may have been that everyone makes decisions with regard to the rightful observance of the sabbath since the sabbath was made for all and not vice versa. The use of "man" and "Son of Man" stand in parallelism. The original meaning of the story of the disciples going through the fields of standing grain may have been an effort on the part of Jesus to give "man," simply as a human being, authority over the sabbath. No doubt, however, that in Mark this meaning underlies the more important thought that Jesus as the "Son of Man" is actually "Lord" of the sabbath.

Jesus himself alone uses the title in the gospel and always in the presence of his disciples or the inner circle of Peter, James and John. Certainly whether Jesus ever actually used the title himself and associated it with dying and rising remains unknown. In the gospel of Mark however, this theme predominates. Throughout the gospel the title refers to Jesus as the one who was betrayed (Mk 14:21) and arrested

(Mk 14:41), who suffered (Mk 9:12) and died (Mk 10:45), who was raised from the dead (Mk 9:9) and was seated at God's right hand in heaven (Mk 14:26), and who will come at the end of the age to collect the faithful into the kingdom of God (Mk 13:26). The various uses of the title in Mark is important, but the use by Mark between chapters 2:10 and 10:45 (excluding 9:12) are characteristically Marcan.

Mark's passion introduction (Mk 8:27–10:52), as previously noted, includes in each block a prediction of the passion followed by misunderstanding and a teaching about disciplehood. This central section of the gospel constitutes Mark's concept of discipleship and culminates in 10:45 with the theme of the servant for all. This treatment also climaxes the treatment by Mark of the Son of Man.

A clear progression exists in the use peculiar to Mark from an understanding of the earthly authority of the Son of Man, to the necessity of the suffering of the Son of Man, and finally to the apocalyptic authority with the final dramatization of the soteriological significance of the passion of Jesus. Mark unites all of these themes in his choice of title "Son of Man."

Son of Man—Son of God

Mark used the title Son of Man in a clear pattern in his gospel. He also juxtaposed it with the title Son of God to give a corrected understanding of belief in Jesus. He joined the earthly authority of Jesus as the Son of Man to Jesus as the Son of God. In Mk 3:11 a Marcan summary emphasizes that Jesus exercises his authority on earth as Son of God. In 2:10 and 2:28 Mark stresses the authority of Jesus as Son of Man. In 8:38 the tone is the apocalyptic authority of the Son of Man, carefully linked by a time reference seven verses later to the voice of the transfiguration that addresses Jesus as "my beloved Son." The high priest asks Jesus if he is the Son of the Blessed, and Jesus replies by using the title Son of Man (14:61-62). Mark relates the meaning of Son of God to the meaning of the Son of Man.

The Power of Jesus in Word and Miracle

The preaching and teaching of Jesus, as well as his power to work miracles, form the foundation for the whole meaning of Jesus in the gospel of Mark. The heart of the gospel may be the suffering Son of Man, but the activity of the Son of Man must also be understood to enter into the fuller meaning of the good news according to Mark.

The gospel almost begins with a reference to preaching: "The gospel of God is at hand" (Mk 1:14-15). This opening chapter ends with a sense of compulsion. Jesus had to go about the land preaching (Mk 1:38). Mark does not dwell, however, on the actual content of the preaching of Jesus. Even when Jesus sent out his disciples to preach he does not mention precisely what they were to preach (Mk 6:12). He speaks only of repentance which repeats the actual preaching of Jesus in Mk 1:15 and the very content of the preaching of John the Baptizer in Mk 1:4.

The apparent lack of interest in the actual content of the preaching can be explained by the way Mark identified Jesus with the kingdom of God. For Mark, Jesus is the beginning of God's final and glorious rule. What Jesus said was important but also how he lived and how he died. All form part of the gospel and all are part of the preaching and all are involved with the in-breaking of the reign of God. Jesus was the presence of the reign of God and he himself was the gospel. One choice of vocabulary that seems to have had great import to the author of the second gospel, however, is the word "teaching" or "teacher."

Teacher

Jesus often functions as a teacher of the law, a "rabbi." In Mk 10:17 a man asks Jesus about eternal life and Jesus reacts out of the tradition of the law just as a rabbi or scribe might react. People, whether friend of foe, also address Jesus as a teacher (Mk 12:14.19.32; 9:38; 10:35; 13:1). He taught in the synagogue, beside the sea, or wherever crowds would gather. Also, Jesus identifies his ministry with teaching:

Day by day I was with you in the temple teaching (Mk 14:49).

He also used the title "teacher" when he instructed his disciples to prepare the passover:

The teacher says: "Where is my guest room, where I am to eat the passover with my disciples?" (Mk 14:14).

Mark saw teaching as a regular activity of Jesus, and when the disciples returned from their preaching journey they narrated not only what they had done but also what they had taught (Mk 6:30) even though they were not instructed to teach (Mk 6:7.12.13). For Mark, if Jesus taught, then his disciple had to teach just as his church would teach. The combination of the teaching activity of Jesus and of the church appears clearly in the parables. Mark saw the parables as a principal way in which Jesus taught and then the church could use the parables in its own teaching. As a result, many of the parables were embellished by the early church as they sought new meaning in the teachings of Jesus and as they tried to apply the parables to the present situation of the followers of Jesus.

Miracle Worker

Another example of how the author of the second gospel preserved traditions about Jesus and added to them is his account of Jesus as a miracle worker. The ancient world teemed with magicians and wonder workers. Both Jews and Greeks had their share of those people associated with marvelous deeds. Rabbis healed the sick, conquered evil spirits and even made ugly women beautiful. The Greek world had its magicians and devotees of gods who made the lame walk and the blind see. Jesus as a miracle worker does not set him apart from many of his contemporaries. To perform a miracle does not in itself attest to the identity of the presence of God's envoy or that the miracle worker was the one who would inaugurate the kingdom of God. Even the miracles themselves, as performed by Jesus, are open to various interpretations. If the miracles of Jesus are read from a personal perspective, they appear to be signs of the presence of God with him. To his opponents, however, they were proof that he must be destroyed because he was involved with the power of evil:

> He is possessed by Beelzebub, and by the prince of demons
> he casts out demons (Mk 3:22).

Even his family thought he was mad after they witnessed his deeds of power:

> And when his own heard it, they went out to seize him for
> they said, "He is mad" (Mk 3:21).

With such a mixed background, the survival of the miracle stories in the early tradition is itself a marvel. To concentrate on what Jesus taught and avoid the ambiguity of the miraculous was in fact the tactic of some of the fathers of the church.

But for Mark, this was not the solution. Evidently Jesus did perform miracles, and if they could be ambiguous Mark decided to preserve the stories and give them his own interpretation or at least the interpretation of his community.

Mark adapted and interpreted miracle stories as he had adapted and interpreted the teaching of Jesus to suit the needs of the early church. Both were sharpened to show that Jesus was powerful in word and in miracle in his public ministry.

Jesus still lives in the church; he was equally powerful in word and deed for those who, through their faith in him, joined themselves into a fellowship of people whose Lord he would always remain. Jesus in the gospel of Mark is the suffering Son of Man, the model for all beleivers, who gave his life for others, powerful in word and in miracle.

Matthew

Matthew[66] begins his gospel by carefully presenting Jesus as both Son of David and Son of Abraham (Mt 1:1); the one foretold of old now fulfills all of the expectations of Israel; in him all of the nations of the world are blessed. Jesus stands tall in this gospel as a great authoritative and ethical teacher, part of the tradition of Israel. Like the great leader, Moses, Jesus gives clear guidance and direction to his people. He inaugurates the kingdom of God and, as the final agent and plenipotentiary, he consummates God's purpose in the world (Mt 5:17-18). Jesus in Matthew's gospel is the founder of the new Israel, the church which brings to fulfillment all of the ancient expectations. Matthew has a peculiar interest in the Old Testament and frequently refers to Old Testament prophecies that are accomplished in Jesus. In the infancy narrative alone, five times he refers to the law and uses the passages to demonstrate that Jesus fulfills Israel's hopes foretold by the prophets.

As teacher Jesus' authority commanded respect in Mark (1:27) but Matthew is more interested in giving the content of this teaching in the sermon on the mount (Mt 5:1-7:29). Matthew is concerned in systematizing the teaching of Jesus into a unified body. This tendency agrees with the general tone of the gospel, which presents a community that is clearly organized. The author tries, in fact, to present as orderly a teaching on ethics as can be found in the Old Testament (Deuteronomy and Leviticus).

Apological overtones are heard throughout the gospel, especially in the infancy narratives and in the passion account. These two sections would have been of special interest to Jewish converts, and so Matthew relates the experiences of Jesus in both instances to the Old Testament. He demonstrates that in truth Jesus is the messiah of Israel, and offers explanations that he hopes will convince his readers that the messiah had to suffer.

Following the general pattern developed in Mark, Matthew presents the fundamental messiahship of Jesus but nuances its meaning. He alone among the synoptics adds to Peter's confession of Jesus as the messiah "the Son of the living God" (Mt 16:16). He alone gives the injunction against the sword at the time of Jesus' arrest, which indicates for him that Jesus was not the political and apocalyptic figure of popular messianic expectation (Mt 26:52).

Matthew also deals with the theme of the suffering servant but has a distinctive way of portraying this element of his christology. Mark interprets Jesus' mission in light of the suffering servant by subtle overtones, while Matthew actually identifies Jesus with this figure from Deutero-Isaiah. The author of Matthew's gospel seems to perceive more deeply the mission of Jesus to be the servant of all and to bear the suffering of his passion and death for the sake of the many.

More so than in any of the other gospels, Jesus is also Lord for Matthew. Even when Satan approaches in the temptation narrative he does so with the reverence due the Lord. A sense of adoration pervades his ministry, from the adoration of the magi to Peter falling down and confessing his belief in Jesus as Lord (Mt 2:11; 14:33). That Jesus is the Son of God in a most unusual way, Matthew demonstrates in the story of his origin and exemplifies in his ministry. He has authority and power and commands a sense of awe and adoration. As the Lord, he teaches with authority and gives specific directions to all who will come after him. Finally, as the eschatological Lord, Jesus lives in his church until the end of time (Mt 28:17-20).

The christology of Matthew develops further insights into the meaning of Jesus by presenting him not only as the fulfillment of the old law but especially as the divine lawgiver, the exalted Lord, worthy of worship, present always in the church. He suffers, but his suffering pales in light of the meaning of his Lordship.

Old Testament Influence

The Jewish character of the gospel of Matthew shines forth in every chapter. Although the community was composed of Jews and

Gentiles, the author anxiously preserved the old from Judaism and added the new from Christianity. The genealogy places him in the line of David, and the author finds parallels throughout the Old Testament even in places where no one else might see the relationship. Every word of the Old Testament that might have prophetic significance for Jesus, Matthew seems to discover and to incorporate into his gospel. Perhaps an early member of the Jewish Christian community gathered together possible references to Jesus from Jewish writings, and Matthew used this collection as a source for his gospel. The suffering servant of Isaiah is the servant of the Lord of the gospel who himself has borne our afflictions and carried our sorrows:

> This was to fulfill what was spoken by the prophet Isaiah,
> "He took our infirmities and bore our diseases" (Mt 8:17).

The proclamation of Hosea: "Out of Egypt I have called my son" (Hos 11:1), although referring to the exodus of the Israelites, becomes for Matthew a renewal of the ancient history of Israel in the Son of Man.

The Jewish character is also evident in the attitude of Jesus toward the law of Moses. It almost seems as if the law remains in force without any modification. Some Jewish Christians in the community of Matthew would be anxious to continue the observance of the law, and they would find sure foundation in the words of Jesus recorded by Matthew:

> Think not that I have come to abolish the law and the prophets; I have come not to abolish them but to fulfill them (Mt 5:17).

Possibly to respond to the needs of his Gentile Christians, Matthew also records the twofold commandment of love of God and neighbor and then adds:

> On these two commandments depend all the law and the prophets (Mt 22:40).

The Old Testament is the background for the christology of Matthew but not without a sense of an opening to the Gentiles. Jesus fulfills the Old Testament but the emphasis remains on the fulfillment.

Twelve times in the gospel, Matthew underlines the significance of an event in the life of Jesus by an explicit appeal to an Old Testament prophecy. Each is introduced by the phrase: "This took place to fulfill what the Lord said through the prophet . . ." The twelve incidents are important in the life of Jesus and establish a structure for Matthean christology:

1. The choice of his name (Mt 1:21) and virginal conception (Mt 1:23)
2. The place of birth in Bethlehem (Mt 2:5)
3. The exile in Egypt (Mt 2:16)
4. The threat by Herod (Mt 2:18)
5. The relocation to Nazareth (Mt 2:23)
6. Preaching in Galilee (Mt 4:15)
7. Healing ministry (Mt 8:17)
8. Mission to the Gentiles (Mt 12:18)
9. Preaching in parables (Mt 13:14.35)
10. Entry into Jerusalem (Mt 21:4)
11. Betrayal and arrest (Mt 26:56)
12. Fate of Judas and the acceptance of responsibility for the death of Jesus by the Jewish leaders (Mt 27:9)]

The power of the Old Testament tradition affects every major aspect of the life of Jesus. The Old Testament creates the history and milieu out of which Matthew creates his portrait of Jesus.

Exalted Son of God

In the first four chapters, Matthew treats the person of Jesus and acknowledges that he is both son of David and son of Abraham but that pre-eminently Jesus is the exalted Son of God. His origin is in God, for he is conceived by the power of God, he will shepherd God's people (Mt 2:6), and he proves himself in confrontation with Satan (Mt 4:3-10). But for Matthew Jesus is not Son of God in the manner of ancient kings or angels or even the just. Instead Jesus is the Son of God who will be raised and will reign with God with all authority in heaven and on earth:

And Jesus came and said to them: "All authority in heaven
and on earth has been given to me . . ." (Mt 28:18).

As Son of God, Jesus enjoys a unique relationship with the Father and has been chosen by God to be his exclusive representative among peoples. He shares in the divine authority and confronts his listeners and so reveals the Father to whomever he will. As Son of God, Jesus acknowledges his election by God by living in complete fellowship with God and relying upon God totally by being perfectly obedient to God's will. The so-called Johannine thunderbolt in Matthew expresses this relationship well:

> All things have been delivered to me by my Father, and no one knows the Father except the Son and anyone to whom the Son chooses to reveal him (Mt 11:27).

In the second part of his gospel (Mt 4:17–16:20), Matthew fills out the meaning of the Son of Man by explaining his ministry of teaching and healing. In the third part of the gospel (Mt 16:21–28:30), Jesus as Son moves toward death and fulfillment in the resurrection. The sanhedrin condemns Jesus for claiming divine sonship (Mt 26:63-66); he is ridiculed as the Son of God by the people (Mt 27:39-40), and dies upon the cross trusting completely in God his Father (Mt 27:38-54). But God will not allow his Son to experience eternal defeat. God raised him up:

> He is not here; for he has risen, as he said. Come, see the place where he lay. Then go quickly and tell his disciples that he has risen from the dead, and behold, he is going before you to Galilee; there you will see him. Lo, I have told you (Mt 28:6-10).

God exalted him to absolute and universal authority in heaven and on earth (Mt 28:18-20). Now others will be empowered by the Spirit of God to make disciples of all nations, assured of the abiding presence of the Son of God until the end of the age. The title Son of God appears at his conception, birth and infancy, baptism and temptation, public ministry, death, resurrection and exaltation. It expresses for Matthew the mystery of the person of Jesus as messiah and represents an exalted confession of the Matthean Christian community.

Messiah as Teacher

The ministry of Jesus in Matthew's gospel emphasizes his teaching. He teaches the new covenant much as Moses was the teacher of the old covenant. He has the boldness to proclaim: "You have heard that it was said to the men of old ... but I say to you" (Mt 5:21-22). In the eyes of the Jews Jesus blasphemed by such a claim to authority. As the new teacher he claims an authority that intrinsically requires no credentials other than the obvious rightness and truth of his declarations. He truly speaks about God in a new way. Unlike the scribes, he teaches with authority and the people recognize that a prophet has risen in the land:

> And when Jesus finished these sayings, the crowds were astonished, for he taught them as one who has authority, and not as their scribes (Mt 7:28-29).

Not only does he teach but he lives what he proclaims. The teacher of new ideas remains relatively harmless unless these new ideas are put into practice. Jesus lived what he taught. He has a devotion to the law but interprets this law based on the criteria of love of God and love of neighbor. The scribes and Pharisees frequently offered interpretations of the law but never in the radical way in which Jesus taught and lived. Whatever helped in the fulfillment of the command of love of God and neighbor must be practiced. Whatever hindered these commands, especially the love of neighbor, must be ignored. Love is the foundation of all law, and love alone is the principle by which the law of Moses must be interpreted and judged (22:34-39). For Jesus, love meant an unlimited and unconditional willingness to serve. This command he lived personally, and he called all of his followers to do likewise.

The great teacher proclaimed a new approach to God based upon love but not without its pain. The ancient law of Deuteronomy promised, for the most part, material blessings of harvest, and fertility of cattle, and many children, and a long life. Jesus also proclaims a blessing to his followers, but one which involves a commitment to an ideal, to the kingdom of God. They will renounce personal rights and privileges and willingly serve and endure persecution, even unto death, for the name of the Lord.

Healer

Matthew also presented Jesus as a healer. Jesus knew the need for physical healing. He does not just dispense wisdom like the oracle of Delphi. The exalted Son of God and great teacher touches people with compassion. He overpowers the forces of evil that threaten human society and brings wholeness. In four chapters Matthew gathers together the miracle stories about Jesus in chapters 8, 9, 12 and 14. Most of these miraculous events appear also in Mark, but here in Matthew they are often abbreviated to emphasize the essential elements. The person in faith recognizes that Jesus makes manifest the saving power of God. Miracles result from faith; they reveal the healing effects of God's grace which has been given to the individual because of the person's faith in Jesus. Faith heals the woman with the hemorrhage (Mt 9:18-22); two blind men see because of their faith (Mt 9:27-31). The miracle collection in Mt 14:13-15:39 parallels the miracles of Mk 6–8 with such important miracles as the multiplication of the loaves, the walking on the water and the healing of the daughter of the Canaanite woman. Here Matthew, unlike Mark, used the miracles to invite the people to follow Jesus in faith. In the narrative on the walking on the water in Matthew, the disciples fall down in worship (Mt 14:33). In Mark, the disciples do not understand, for their hearts are hardened (Mk 6:53-56). Jesus bears God's message of compassion, and healing and those who believe, who recognize the saving presence of God in Jesus, are restored to life.

Other Christological Titles

Some of the other titles employed by Matthew relate to his fundamental title Son of God, such as Jesus, prophet, and *Kyrios* (Lord). Others such as Emmanuel, messiah, and son of David fill out the significance of the more essential titles. Jesus means Savior and defines the mission of Emmanuel, God with us. Prophet is a title used more as a reaction of the crowds; while teacher is a role of Jesus in this gospel. This last title was used by Judas and the leaders of Israel and their cohorts, attributing to Jesus a limited level of respect.

The title *Kyrios* however, is significant in the first gospel. It occurs on the lips of persons who address Jesus in faith (the only exception is the accursed in the last judgment scene in Mt 25:37) and has a confessional character. Most often Matthew used this title to attribute divine authority and an exalted station to Jesus (Mt 8:2.6.8.25; 14:28, etc.). The usage, however, was more from the Matthean community than from the actual time of the ministry of Jesus. In Mt 8:25 the disciples in the boat seek the help of the sleeping Jesus and call out: "Lord, save us." The same scene in Mark has the title teacher (Mk 4:38). No doubt Matthew used this Greek expression to denote the exalted position of Jesus as someone close to God, for the title is also used to translate the sacred Hebrew name of God into Greek. *Kyrios* was used by the Matthean community in worship and prayer as well as the title used for the second coming of Jesus in glory. Matthew projects the use of the title backward to the ministry of Jesus, for he knows that Jesus now lives as exalted Lord of all.

Combining all of the titles of Jesus, such as Son of God, son of David, son of Abraham, Emmanuel, messiah, Son of Man, and *Kyrios*, forms an image of Jesus as the divine and exalted one from God, who has returned to God and who has taught and healed as the manifestation of the loving God in human history. Jesus is the presence of the transcendent God and thus demands worship and adoration. He is also the sign of the closeness of a compassionate God through his power to heal.

Many times readers of Matthew note that he lacks the vigor and detail of Mark, but his gospel has a dignity which has made it the source for centuries of preaching on the person of Jesus. Nowhere is this more evident than in the conclusion. This ending of the gospel (Mt 28:16-20) may well be the Matthean summary of the resurrection proclamation rather than the actual words of Jesus. Any believer of the second or third generation also might have used them to express what it means to be a Christian. Whatever the origin of the conclusion, the true believer knows that all authority and power had been given to Jesus. In his ministry Jesus had transformed the lives of men and women and had drawn them away from a life of sin and self-concern into the fellowship of a new creation. Where once people had been divided and separated, now they were united in a common faith. Only a person of extraordinary power could have accomplished such a task. Even the limitations on the relationship between God and people of the old dispensation have been done away with. God has exalted Jesus as Lord. Now the church, as the community of believers can go out into the world and proclaim the sovereignty of Jesus as Lord of *all*. The resurrection and exaltation have made permanent and universally available the presence of the master. That presence in the church as exalted Lord and Son of God was the pledge of victory and of the ultimate fulfillment of the plan of God for *all*. The Jesus of Matthew's gospel inspires awe and worship and gives guidance and direction; he assures the presence of a kind and compassionate God who is ever willing to respond to the human world of suffering, conflict, and pain. Jesus is God with us.

Luke

The gospel of Luke[67] presents an entirely different picture of Jesus. No longer Mark's suffering Son of Man, nor the powerful teacher and Lord of Matthew, Jesus is seen here as the perfect Greek gentleman, filled with the Spirit of God and endowed with the gift of effectively preaching the word of God. Jesus' appearance in the synagogue in Nazareth early in Luke's gospel sets the tone for what follows. Jesus as the teacher is invested with the power of the Spirit. He fulfills in himself the prophecy of Isaiah: "The spirit of the Lord is upon me . . . today this scripture is fulfilled in your hearing" (Lk 4:18.21). In his ministry people are impressed by his authority (Lk 4:31.36-37). He shows his power in his deeds, for he is not only the messenger of the kingdom, but also its messianic agent who reveals the eschatological reign of God through how he acts. This confluence of word and deed gives him power over the forces of evil. Thus he banishes Satan in the course of his ministry (Lk 4:39) and subjects evil spirits to himself (Lk 4:36); he cures by his word (Lk 4:39) and in his role as teacher he heals (Lk 5:17-26; 6:6-11).

Luke's is a gospel of great joy. Jesus brings blessedness to all who respond to him in faith. At his birth the angels proclaim a message of joy for all (Lk 2:11); Jesus rejoices at the return of his disciples from preaching (Lk 10:20) and over one sinner who repents (Lk 15:10).

The Gospel within the Gospel

The christology of Luke captures the mercy and compassion of Jesus. His fifteenth chapter is often called "the gospel within the gospel," for in it Luke presents three central parables: the lost sheep, the lost coin and the prodigal son. In each instance the story illustrates the mercy and forgiveness of God and the joy over a sinner who repents and returns. His compassion extends to the outcasts of society calling them to be his friends. Shepherds, outcasts themselves, welcomed him at his birth. The same pattern continues throughout his ministry. Sinners are always welcome; tax collectors, prostitutes and anyone else who feels left out can find company with Jesus as the forgiving Savior.

Prayer

Luke also portrays Jesus as a great man of prayer. He prayed just before his baptism (Lk 3:21); after he worked miracles he withdrew to pray (Lk 5:16); he prayed all night before choosing his disciples (Lk 6:12); he prayed after the miracle of the loaves (Lk 9:18); he prayed as a prelude to the transfiguration (Lk 9:28-29); he was praying when his disciples asked him to teach them to pray (Lk 11:1); and he prayed in the garden (Lk 22:39-45) and from the cross (Lk 23:46). For Luke, Jesus always remains in close contact with God.

Universalism

Jesus has a universal interest in this gospel. In his prayer Simeon joins together Israel and the pagan world as recipients of the salvation that Jesus brings (Lk 2:31-32). Jesus in Luke calls a Roman centurion and a Samaritan leper models of faith (Lk 7:9; 17:19). Luke also emphasizes the concern of Jesus for women. Jesus treats women with a special compassion. He heals the woman with a hemorrhage (Lk 8:43-48); cares for a woman who is a sinner (Lk 7:36-50), and responds to the need of the widow of Naim (Lk 6:11-17), and women provide for him (Lk 23:55).

This same gospel deals with the special relationship that existed between Jesus and God his Father. He is the Son of God (Lk 3:22; 22:29; 24:49) and, like Matthew, Luke has his version of the so-called Johannine thunderbolt in the synoptic tradition:

> Everything has been given to me by my Father. No one knows the Son except the Father and no one knows the Father except the Son and anyone to whom the Son wishes to reveal him (Lk 10:22).

At his baptism God declared him to be his Son, but previously in the infancy narrative his very conception was an act of God, making him the Son of the Most High (Lk 1:32). The Father who gives Jesus his mission of salvation has decreed all (Lk 22:22) and has given Jesus the Spirit to fulfill this mission. Finally, after Jesus has been raised up by the Father, he too can send the Spirit (Lk 24:49ff, Acts 1:1ff).

Jesus is a Jew, born in Bethlehem (Lk 2:6-7), of Davidic lineage (Lk 11:2; 2:4; 3:31), and raised in Nazareth (Lk 4:16). He was a man attested by God with mighty works (Acts 2:22). The Lucan Jesus is very human, filled with emotion. He responds to the widow of Naim (Lk 7:13), enjoys human friendships with Martha and Mary, and celebrates meals with friends and even with sinners, with Levi (Lk 5:29) and Zacchaeus (Lk 19:2). He seems to enjoy life, and when faced with death he asks:

Father, if you are willing, remove this cup from me; nevertheless, not my will but your will be done (Lk 2:42).

The same dying Jesus will pray to God: "Father, into your hands I commend my spirit" (Lk 23:46). Jesus is the kind and compassionate Savior, filled with human needs and emotions, who responds to people in a warm and forgiving manner. Jesus also lives and dies as the faithful one of God and always in a human manner.

Luke also presents the Jesus who transcends the human condition. His conception is through the power of the Spirit (Lk 1:34-35). His ministry is under the control of the Spirit (Lk 3:22; 4:1.14.18; 10:21). He has a special relationship to God as his Father (Lk 2:49; 3:22; 9:35; 10:21-22; 23:46). Finally, through his resurrection he becomes Lord and messiah through the power of God (Acts 2:24.32; 3:15; 4:10; 5:30; 10:40). All of these elements, taken together with the human dimension of Jesus, comprise Lucan christology. The very human Jesus somehow goes beyond the dimension of humanity and lives and acts in the divine realm without losing the human. Luke connects the human and the divine after the resurrection with his insistence on the importance of the ascension.

Luke and History

Unlike the other evangelists, Luke divides the time after the death of Jesus into set periods. God raised Jesus from the dead on the third day. The other evangelists end here. Then Luke adds forty days until the time when he ascends into heaven to sit at the right hand of God (Acts 2:33; 5:31). Then another ten days pass before the disciples experience the coming of the Spirit on Pentecost. Luke presents ministry, death, resurrection, ascension and exaltation and, finally, the coming of the Spirit as the culmination of christology. Chronology figures prominently in his theology. Luke has had so much of an influence on Christianity that the church uses his time frame for liturgical celebrations. The Easter season continues with the celebration of the ascension forty days after Easter, and then Pentecost completes the cycle, ten days after the ascension. None of the other gospels have such a division. The gospel of Luke ends with a veiled reference to the ascending of Jesus (Lk 24:50), and the Acts of the Apostles opens with Jesus ascending (Acts 1:9-11).

The Return

Although never explicitly mentioned, Luke's christology also includes a return of Jesus as the final phase of his destiny. The angel who appears at the ascension tells the onlookers that Jesus will return in the same way that they saw him go (Acts 1:11). In the gospel Luke has also preserved the saying that Jesus will come in power and glory (Lk 21:27). He also sees the exalted Christ as the one who pours out the Spirit (Acts 2:33) and who stands at the right hand of God (Acts 7:55-56), who is appointed as messiah to come (Acts 3:20-21) and will judge the world (Acts 17:31). Luke divides his understanding of Jesus into four phases: from conception to baptism, from baptism and ministry to the resurrection and ascension, from exaltation to the second coming, and, finally, the second coming itself.

Luke uses many of the same titles as Mark and Matthew, sometimes with the same or similar meaning, at other times with his distinctive nuance.

Lord

Luke used the title "Lord" most frequently for Jesus in both of his books. He used it for both God and Jesus. Pre-Christian Palestinian Jews did on occasion refer to God as Lord, and it was generally used as a Greek substitute for the sacred name of God. Jewish Christians, probably the Hellenists, used the formula in reference to Jesus as a response to the earliest preaching. Such a usage would put Jesus on the same level as God but without identifying him with God. Luke will refer to God as "abba," for example, but never to Jesus as "abba." Jesus is Son. God the Father made Jesus Lord through his resurrection:

> Let all the house of Israel therefore know assuredly that
> God has made him both Lord and Christ, this Jesus whom
> you crucified (Acts 2:36).

In the public ministry of Jesus Luke has retrojected this title and has even used the title in the origin of Jesus. The angels announce to the shepherds that "Christ the Lord" is born in Bethlehem (Lk 2:11). In so doing, Luke has recorded the usage in the early Christian communities which saw Jesus on a par with God. This should not in itself, however, be regarded as an expression of divinity. The title as used by Luke connotes his otherness or his transcendent character, but not necessarily in a philosophical and metaphysical sense. The title, rather, expresses the influence that the resurrection has had on the followers of Jesus. For them, because Jesus has been raised, he has been elevated to the throne of God. Once Luke and the Christian community accepted this position of Jesus, Luke could read back into the ministry of Jesus an awareness of his proximity to God.

Christ/Messiah

Although not used as frequently as Lord, the title of Christ or messiah becomes the most important title for Luke in his two volume work. Luke preaches salvation, and Jesus, the anointed one of God, brings this salvation. The gospel almost closes with the question posed by the risen Jesus: "Was not the Christ bound to suffer all this before entering into his glory?" (Lk 24:26). And it is Luke alone who tells us that the followers of Jesus were called "Christians" (Acts 11:26; 26:28).

The title is used frequently. Sometimes it may be translated as "Christ" to suit the Gentile audience of Luke, and at other times it is translated as "messiah," conveying its basic meaning as one anointed by God. For modern believers the title has become almost the second name for Jesus, and even in Luke something similar has already taken place (Acts 2:38; 3:6; 4:10, etc.).

In its Old Testament usage the title referred to certain historical persons chosen and anointed by God for the service of God's people. The kings of Israel were anointed. Also, at times, the high priest was God's anointed. Even the Persian King Cyrus was the anointed of God destined to return his people to their land (Is 45:1).

At the time of Jesus, messiah indicated either someone sent by God in the kingly Davidic and political tradition, or someone in the priestly tradition. The political overtones for the title would have been known to Jesus and his followers. This would account for the Lucan and Matthean correction to the admission of a messianic role for Jesus as attested before the high priest in the gospel of Mark:

Again the high priest asked him: "Are you the Christ the Son of the Blessed?" And Jesus said: "I am; and you will see the Son of Man sitting at the right hand of power, and coming with the clouds of heaven" (Mk 14:62).

Both Matthew and Luke present the same scene with a refusal on the part of Jesus to respond: "If I tell you, you will not believe, and if I ask you, you will not answer" (Lk 22:67).

After his death and resurrection, the title Christ or messiah became a principal title for Jesus in the Lucan writings. Jesus was crucified as "King of the Jews" (Mk 1:16; 5:26) but for his followers he became the messiah. Within a few years after his death, Christians began to use "Jesus Christ," "Christ Jesus" or "Jesus the Messiah" as an honorific designation that suited Jesus alone. Jesus is God's anointed agent announcing a new form of salvation to humankind.

Savior

A third title important for Luke is "Savior." The title actually occurs only once in the gospel (Lk 2:11) and occasionally in Acts. The meaning, however, takes on a particular significance for Luke. The author of the third gospel presents Jesus as one who brings salvation to the world as its great benefactor. The title itself was used frequently in the Greco-Roman world as applied to gods, philosophers, physicians, kings and emperors. In the Old Testament it is used for individuals whom God has raised up for the deliverance of his people as well as for God himself (1 Sam 10:19; Is 45:15.21). The Christian use of the title may be influenced by both traditions. In the gospel the meaning of Savior denotes deliverance from such evils as sickness, infirmity or sin. In Acts it denotes the complete process: the effect of Jesus on human history and humankind. It is not just deliverance but the actual experience of God's presence in love, seeking out what was lost and bringing the lost home.

Son of God

The title "Son of God" for contemporary Christians usually connotes that Jesus was divine. Such need not always be the case when the title is used in the New Testament. Actually, Luke also uses "Son of the Most High" and in other places just "my Son." Whatever conclusion one might draw from the use of these various titles, Luke does imply a special relationship to God. Like the other synoptics, he recognized the special character of the baptism of Jesus in which a voice speaks:

When Jesus also had been baptized and was praying heaven was opened and the Holy Spirit descended upon him in bodily form, as a dove, and a voice came from heaven, "You are my beloved Son (here some ancient sources add:

'Today I have begotten you'); with you I am well pleased"
(Lk 3:21-22).

The title itself was used frequently in Greek circles and in other
cultures in the ancient near east and can mean divine favor or divine
adoption or even divine power. In Israel, kings were called God's sons
as well as the angels and other individuals who were righteous in the
sight of God. Nowhere can be found either in the Old Testament or in
Palestinian Judaism the title "Son of God" with a messianic nuance.

When Luke used the title he seems to have predicated to Jesus a
unique relationship to God. Gabriel declares to Mary that her son will
be "the Son of God" (Lk 1:35), and when we couple this with the same
declaration that the Holy Spirit will overshadow her (Lk 1:35), the
uniqueness cannot be missed. No one can say much more than this.
Whatever the title meant to Luke and his readers, it surely did not
mean anything on a philosophical or metaphysical plane. Jesus was
Son of God because of his special relationship to God, and he manifested this sonship by his willingness to live according to the will of
God, even to the point of the acceptance of death.

Son of Man

All four gospels use the title with various nuances. It can mean
human being in a generic sense, or in an indefinite sense such as someone. It can mean "everyman" and it can also suggest a heavenly figure.
These meanings have already been discussed. Most times it is found on
the lips of Jesus himself. An exception is Acts 7:56 when Stephen sees
Jesus as a Son of Man standing at God's right hand. As previously stated, originally the title was probably used in a generic sense, such as
everyman. This use can actually be found in Mk 2:28, as already noted,
originally implying that everyone can be Lord of the sabbath because
the sabbath was made for everyone. In the early church the title was
overlaid with the meaning as found in Daniel 7:13, and possibly similar
to the usage in 1 Enoch 46-69. Like Mark, Luke used the title sometimes associated with the passion of Jesus (Lk 9:22.44; 18:31; 22:22;
24:7) and also used it in the sense of future coming (Lk 9:26; 11:30;
12:8.40; 17:22.24.26.30). A tentative conclusion will see the title in Luke
similar to the other synoptics. It refers to Jesus as everyman, as human,
but also as one who transcends everyman. In some ways it is similar to
the title Son of God and might even transcend that title. Luke does not
have the highly developed understanding of John, but recognizes the

manner in which Jesus transcends humanity and used the title to convey both the human and the closeness to the divine.

For Luke, Jesus is the kind and compassionate Savior. He does not offend. He is kind to all in need and responds to specific people with kindness. This Savior is filled with the Spirit and frequently will turn to his Father in prayer: at his baptism (Lk 3:21), in the desert (Lk 4:42; 5:16), before he chooses the twelve (Lk 6:12), at the transfiguration (Lk 9:28) and finally from the cross (Lk 23:46). All of the titles used by Luke support this fundamental meaning of Jesus. He came to bring salvation to humankind and accomplished this precisely because of his unique relationship to God and his possession of the Spirit. Luke makes Jesus most attractive to all, calling all to accept the saving presence of God, especially those in need. Since most people feel left out, at least sometimes in life, a kind and compassionate friend who reaches out to invite everyone inside makes the hurt disappear. The Jesus of Luke is everyone's friend.

Jesus in the Gospel of John

Like the other gospels, John has his distinctive approach to Jesus.[68] In the past, many scholars have searched for the hermeneutical key to Johannine christology that would help in understanding the entire gospel. They studied the titles; they explored the relationship between the human and the divine, history and faith, person and function. But these same scholars never seem to have agreed on a single key. One possible approach focuses on relating christology to anthropology.

John clearly emphasizes the divinity of Jesus. He begins his gospel with a hymn to the Word which relates the eternal Word to the historical Jesus (Jn 1:13). The theology of the prologue relates this Word not only to the incarnation and to God, but also to the meaning of creation and to the response expected from those who hear this Word (1:12). Along with this sense of divinity comes the awareness that the divine finds resolution in a human response. Then the meaning of Jesus is complete.

Jesus is also pre-eminently Son in this gospel, where the close relationship that exists between Jesus and the Father is constantly emphasized; but he is also the son of Joseph (Jn 1:45). As Son, Jesus calls people to believe in him, to recognize him as the presence of the Father (Jn 14:9).

New Testament christology reaches its highest development in the gospel of John. Jesus, the pre-existent Word, always speaks from eternity; he knows the secrets of people's hearts; he knows all that will happen to him and yet allows the drama to be played out. Jesus is divine in this gospel, not only in his baptism, his resurrection and his birth, but prior to all these events. He was with God and, as Word, was God.

Further examination of the relationship of the human and divine in this gospel, as well as a study of the relationship of faith and history and the question of function and person, demonstrates that Johannine christology presents a distinct advance on the meaning of Jesus of Nazareth. The early church has progressed considerably from the earliest formulation. At the same time the gospel does not lose sight of the origins of christology: Jesus is still human and always calls people to faith.

The Divine/Human Jesus

Scholars and readers have long recognized that the fourth gospel portrays a divine Jesus. It begins with a hymn celebrating the pre-existent Word of God, related to God with a closeness of persons: "The Word was with God and the Word was God" (Jn 1:1). The Word became flesh as Son but never left the bosom of the Father: "The only Son who is in the bosom of the Father has made him known" (Jn 1:18). As Jesus of Nazareth, the Word became flesh and possessed supernatural knowledge; he cured with a word (Jn 4:50), changed water into wine (Jn 2:7-9), and gave life through his word to Lazarus (Jn 11:43). He never suffered. With a sereneness that astonished all, he controlled his passion from the moment of arrest to his final proclamation that it is finished.

The contrast to the synoptics makes evident the emphasis on the divinity of Jesus in this gospel. In the earlier gospels Jesus does not know everything. He grows in wisdom and grace (Lk 2:52) but appears to be ignorant of the final day (Mk 13:32); he suffers a painful agony (Lk 22:40-42) and cries from the cross: "My God my God, why hast thou abandoned me?" (Mk 15:34). Jesus experiences temptation (Mt 4:1-11; Lk 4:1-13) and appears defeated by the power of evil in his death. Most people look to the synoptics to study the human Jesus and study the divine Jesus in the gospel of John. In fact, the fourth gospel portrays both the human and the divine Jesus.

Logos (Word)

The author used the title only in the prologue, although the theology of the "Word of God" dominates the gospel. John seized upon a term used in both Jewish and Hellenistic circles and used it as his instrument to set forth a part of the Jesus tradition. The theology of the title is broader than its use in the first chapter. Jesus *is* the Word of God, and thus when he speaks, he reveals God. The words of Jesus, God his Father has taught him (Jn 8:40; 14:10.24). The content of this Word from the Father concerns the person of Jesus and his relationship to the Father and to the disciples. As Word, he reveals the Father and invites individuals to respond to this revelation.

The prologue itself emphasizes the divinity of Jesus. The word pre-exists; functions in creation; gives light and life; reveals the glory of God through the manifestation of grace and truth; returns to the Father from whose side he has never left. The reader can easily picture a divine person with God, descending upon this earth to fulfill a mission and then returning. The Word is divine; Jesus is divine.

The Son of Man

The title Son of Man in this gospel differs significantly from the synoptics. John emphasizes the pre-existence of the Son of Man as well as his exaltation and glorification. The stress lies on the divine. The author uses the title as a characteristic self-designation. The idea in the background seems to be a figure who is archetype of the human race. The Johannine Son of Man descended from heaven and will ascend again.

No one has ascended into heaven but he who descended from heaven, the Son of Man (Jn 3:13).

Then what if you were to see the Son of Man ascending where he was before? (Jn 6:62).

Jesus, as Son of Man, continues his union with God and dwells with God. He is the perfect man, the archetype who epitomizes the true and ultimate relationship of individuals with God. His heavenly origin is the basis for his ultimate elevation and glorification as well as his salvific activity. The Father has already set his seal on the Son of Man (Jn 6:27), and from the Father he has received his transcendent message (Jn 3:11-13). This becomes the guarantee of his future return (Jn 6:62). The title carries a sense of pre-existence, and when people encounter the Son of Man on earth, they face a divine being.

The Son of God

"Son of God" does not appear often in this gospel. The original conclusion to the gospel remarks that the gospel was written to help individuals to believe that "Jesus is the Christ the Son of God" (Jn 20:31). The title also appears in the opening chapter used by Nathanael, and in the trial before Pilate (Jn 19:7). Jesus is the Son of God because God sanctified him and sent him into this world for a mission. Since the title can be used for other divine emissaries, it need not always denote divinity. The close relationship between Jesus and God is better expressed in the use of "Son."

Jesus as Son

Jesus is God's Son. For John, this expressed the close relationship between Jesus and God. The Son does only what he sees the Father doing:

> The Son can do nothing of his own accord, but only what
> he sees the Father doing, for whatever he does, that the Son
> does likewise (Jn 5:19).

Such examples stress the dependence of the Son upon the Father but other texts also imply equality. The Son, like the Father, gives life (Jn 5:21); the Son makes people free (Jn 8:36); the Son gives eternal life (Jn 3:36; 6:40) and the Father has given judgment to the Son (Jn 5:22). The Son seems to stand in equality with God and often cannot be completely distinguished from the Father.

The Son Belongs to the Divine World

The Son lives in the divine world and receives all from the Father (Jn 5:20; 8:47):

> He who comes from above is above all; he who is of the
> earth belongs to the earth, and of the earth he speaks; he
> who comes from heaven is above all. He bears witness to
> what he has seen and heard (Jn3:31-32).

All that the Son reveals depends on his previous participation in the divine world.

The Son as Divine Being

For John, speaking about a pre-existence is not sufficient to understand the Son. He gives to the human Jesus divine prerogatives. As he knows things supernaturally, he also prays differently:

> Father, I thank you that you have heard me. I knew that you hear me always but I have said this on account of the people standing by (Jn 11:41-42).

Instead of a fear of death, as seen in the synoptics, Jesus when facing death offers a prayer glorifying the divine name (Jn 12:27-28). As divine, even his captors fall down before him (Jn 18:6).

The title Son of God may not signify a divine being, but when this title is joined to "Son," the readers learn the intention of the author to teach belief in a divine being.

The Use of *Ego Eimi* (I Am)

The author used this expression nine times without a predicate. Each time, Jesus speaks, addressing a variety of audiences. The exception is found in Jn 9:9. The blind man responds with the expression *ego eimi* when the bystanders question his identity. This example differs from all the other times the phrase appears and will help clarify the meaning.

In the past some scholars dismissed these sayings as of little consequence. More recently scholars have viewed the expression as a theophonic formula representing the divine name or presence. Certainly on the lips of the blind man the expression can mean: "I am the one." But the other uses of the expression open up other possibilities.

Source for the Phrase

Several possibilities can explain the origin of the phrase. Some claim it comes from Hellenism; others hold that it comes from the Jewish tradition in which *ego eimi* is the Greek translation for the Hebrew expression *'ani hu* found in Deutero Isaiah, and that the Jewish practice is to substitute ani for the Jewish sacred name for God.

The phrase *ani hu* occurs six times in Isaiah 40–55. The translators of the Hebrew text into Greek (LXX of Septuagint) chose the Greek expression *ego eimi* to translate *'ani hu.* In Isaiah God speaks and uses the phrase to signify that he alone is God. It presents God as the Lord of history and creator of the world, closely related to other expressions of divine self-predication, especially the phrase, "I am YHWH."

In Jewish liturgical practice the words "I" and "he," by themselves, were sometimes used as surrogates for the sacred name. The expression 'ani hu was used in the liturgy of the feast of Tabernacles, and the expression also appears in commentaries on the Passover service.

The Phrase in John

John seems to have selected this terminology to indicate the close relationship between Jesus and God as well as to indicate that a new age has dawned by his presence:

> I tell you this now, before it takes place, so that when it takes place you may believe that *ego eimi* (Jn 13:19).

> Jesus answered them: "I solemnly declare it, before Abraham came to be, *ego eimi*" (Jn 8:53).

These examples admit of no predicate understood in context. We can compare the first with Isaiah 43:10:

> You are my witnesses, says the Lord, my servants whom I have chosen, to know and believe in me and understand that I am. Before me no god was formed and after me there shall be none.

The author underlines the solemnity of the statement by Jesus. Only he could make it, and only those who believe in him could understand its meaning.

The second example helps in the further disclosure of the meaning of the phrase. When the Jews heard *ego eimi*, "they took up stones to throw at him"(Jn 8:59). A similar reaction appears in Jn 10:22-39. Jesus is in the temple and proclaims: "I and the Father are one." The reaction is the same: He has blasphemed and they seek to stone him. The use of *ego eimi* stresses the unity of Father and Son, God and Jesus.

Implied Predicate

Other examples of the use of this phrase admit of a predicate understood. The use in the Garden of Olives raises much interest. The soldiers, with Judas, approach Jesus and his band of disciples. Jesus maintains complete control and asks:

> "Who is it you want?" "Jesus the Nazarean," they replied. "I am he," he answered. Now Judas, the one who was to hand him over, was there with them. As Jesus said to them, "I am he," they retreated slightly and fell to the ground (Jn 18:5-6).

> I have told you, "I am he," Jesus said. "If I am the one you want, let these men go (Jn 18:8).

The translators chose to add the pronoun "he." The Greek phrase is *ego eimi*, I am. From the context the reader can presume that it means "I am the one." But when Jesus said *ego eimi*, they retreated and fell down. In the presence of the divine, the only appropriate reaction is adoration.

Only one example in the gospel of John finds a parallel in the synoptics. When Jesus came to his disciples walking on the sea he announced: "It is I (*ego eimi*); do not be afraid" (Mk 6:50; Mt 14:27). In Deutero Isaiah *'ani hu* occurs sometimes in association with the power of God over creation, especially his power over the sea. Earlier people often looked upon the sea as an abode of evil spirits, anxious to destroy all who ventured out too far. This may underlie the usage in Mark and Matthew. Perhaps this was the source of the theology employed by John in his use of the phrase.

John used the phrase in an absolute sense in 8:58 and 13:19. The phrase centers on the divine presence in Jesus. People must recognize the unity between God and Jesus. When Jesus spoke: "Before Abraham came to be, *ego eimi*" (Jn 8:53), his listeners and readers today should retreat in awe in the presence of the divine.

Humanity of Jesus

The image of Jesus portrayed in the fourth gospel differs significantly from that in the other gospels. Jesus is the eternal Word of God, the heavenly Son of Man, the Son of God. He alone represents the presence of the eternal God. He appears so divine in outlook that

Christians for centuries have used this gospel to preach the divinity of Jesus and often overlooked the humanity of Jesus. No one can deny the emphasis on the divinity of Jesus in this gospel. But to fail to see how this same Jesus is also very human does an injustice to the genius of the Johannine community, its theology, and the individuals responsible for the gospel. The gospel of John portrays a human Jesus as well as the divine Jesus.

Although the Word existed for all eternity with the Father, no hint at a supernatural origin for Jesus appears in this gospel. Matthew and Luke offer the infancy stories about Jesus and both imply that the origin of Jesus was unlike any other human origin: Jesus was virginally conceived. This gospel, in contrast, refers to Jesus as the son of Joseph:

> We have found the one about whom Moses wrote in the law, and about whom the prophets spoke, I mean Jesus, the son of Joseph, the man from Nazareth (Jn 1:45).

> They kept saying, "Is this not Jesus, the son of Joseph, whose father and mother we know?" (Jn 6:42).

Jesus belongs to a particular family, and, unlike Mark who refers to Jesus as the son of Mary (Mk 6:3), John calls him the son of Joseph.

Chapter 8 offers some evidence that some believed that Joseph was not the father of Jesus and that, in fact, Jesus was illegitimate. While Jesus debates the Jews, he makes reference to God his Father and they reply: "Where is your father?" (Jn 8:19). The accusation becomes clearer as the debate continues. In reply to Jesus' accusation that the Jews do the work of their father, the devil, they reply: "We were not born of an adulterous union" (Jn 8:41). Some saw Jesus as the son of Joseph and Mary; others conclude that somehow he was illegitimate. Perhaps Jesus was born within the first nine month period from the time Mary and Joseph began to live as husband and wife. Some followers concluded that Jesus' origin was divine intervention; others thought he was born out of wedlock. The author of John chose to record the impression of the latter while also maintaining that Jesus was the son of Joseph.

Jesus—His Friends and His Needs

Jesus needed human affection. One of his disciples intimately leans on his breast at the last supper; he enjoyed dinner with Martha

and Mary and Lazarus; he spent time with his mother and brothers
and even attended a marriage celebration. On his journey to Samaria
he grew tired and thirsty. Like thousands before him and after him, he
stopped at Jacob's well to rest and receive refreshment, and changed
his mind. When the disciples ask him if he intends to go to Jerusalem
for the feast of Tabernacles, he declines. Then he changes his mind
and goes (Jn 7:8-10). He does not experience a painful agony in the
garden in this gospel nor temptation in the desert, but the author preserved some hint at these aspects of his life when he remarks:

> When Jesus saw her weeping, and when he saw the Jews
> who had come with her weeping, he was deeply moved in
> spirit so that an involuntary groan burst from him and he
> trembled with deep emotion (Jn 11:33).

> Jesus said to them: "Where have you laid him?" "Lord,"
> they said to him, "Come and see." . . . Jesus wept . . . again a
> groan was wrong from Jesus' inner being (Jn 11:38).

> Now my soul is troubled (Jn 12:27).

> When Jesus had said these things, he was troubled in spirit.
> (Jn 13:21).

The first two examples display the emotion of Jesus as he encounters
his friends after the death of Lazarus. The human Jesus experiences
sorrow at the death of a friend. The divine Jesus utters a word and
Lazarus comes forth. The next examples contain fear and anxiety. He
knows he will die, but instead of seeking release, he gladly accepts the
will of God.

Jesus appears happy in the presence of good friends. He knows
bodily needs and experiences sorrow at the death of a friend. He also
knows fear and anxiety as he faces death and even experiences the
depression of someone betrayed by a friend. Jesus is very human in
this gospel.

Titles and the Humanity of Jesus

Many of the titles used by this evangelist connote a divine being.
In some of these titles some subtle hints appear that the divinity of
Jesus was never separated from his humanity. *Logos* emphasizes divini-

ty but *logos* becomes flesh. The climax of the hymn in the prologue is the relationship between *logos* and flesh. The *logos* entered into the human and earthly sphere. Before *logos* was in the glory of God; now *logos* has taken on the lowliness of human existence.

In Johannine terms flesh (*sarx*) means the earthbound as seen in 3:6; it connotes the transient and perishable as seen in 6:63. Flesh is the typical mode of being human in contrast to the divine and the spiritual. This need not refer to the sacrifice of the Lord, "My flesh for the life of the world" (Jn 6:51), but it might be in the mind of the evangelist. The prologue seems to contain the principal themes of the gospel. Then this central point of Johannine theology might figure here as well. A possible reference to the death of Jesus offers a further indication of the relationship between the *logos* and human existence, destined to death. The flesh assumed by the *logos* is the pre-supposition for the death on the cross. Once the *logos* becomes flesh, the author no longer uses *logos* in the gospel, for in the humanity of Jesus people have contact with the divine.

The fourth gospel frequently contains double meaning words with various levels of thought. The title son of man can designate the ideal person, the ordinary person. Already Mark has shown this. Matthew knows this meaning, for he changed Mark's "sons of men" to just "men" (Mt 12:31). Matthew knew that sons of men is generic for men just as son of man is generic for man or everyman.

John surely knew the Aramaic idiom and was capable of linguistic subtlety. He was also fond of using "man" in reference to Jesus when other more honorific titles could have been used:

Who is the man who said to you, "Lift up your bed and walk" (Jn 5:12)?

You, a man, make yourself God (Jn 10:33).

It is better that one man should die for the people, rather than the whole nation should perish (Jn 11:15).

The maid servant who kept the door said to Peter: "Are you not this man's disciple?" (Jn 18:17).

So Pilate came out to them and said: "What accusation do you bring against this man?" (Jn 18:29).

Behold the man (Jn 19:5).

The Son of Man has a heavenly origin; he possesses divine characteristics. He is also everyman, a man like anyone else. He epitomizes the best in human nature and in him people discover the divine reality.

Jesus is son of God like other faithful messengers with a divine mission. He is "Son" as well, implying a divine existence with God his Father. The human dimension of his sonship, however, appears evident in two passages.

> He who believes in me, believes not in me but in him who sent me. And he who sees me sees him who sent me (Jn 12:45).

> Have I been with you so long, Philip, and you do not know me? He who sees me sees the Father (Jn 14:9).

Jesus reveals the Father because he is the Son. People look upon the humanity of Jesus and see the God of all. The Son reveals the Father in human flesh. Humans learn only humanly. If God chooses to reveal himself, God must do so humanly. The Son revealed the Father by being a human Son.

The unusual use of *ego eimi* relates Jesus to the divine. The author of this gospel, however, also used this phrase to predicate something. Jesus said: "I am the bread of life" (Jn 6:35); "I am the light of the world" (Jn 8:12); "I am the door" (Jn 10:7); "I am the good shepherd" (Jn 10:11); "I am the resurrection and the life" (Jn 11:25); "I am the way, the truth and the life" (Jn 14:6); "I am the true vine" (Jn 15:1). Such self-presentation appears in the Old Testament (Deut 32:2; Eccl 24) as well as in other ancient near eastern texts. Often it connotes the care that the deity has for the created order. The author of John added qualifying adjectives: Jesus is the "good" shepherd, the "true" vine and light. All such predicates and adjectives relate Jesus to human life. As *ego eimi* Jesus is divine; he is also light to people; he is truth and the way, offering guidance and direction; Jesus is bread which supports life and the vine that sustains the branches, offering life. He is the door through which people enter to find security; he is the shepherd who gives nourishment and protection from evil. Finally, Jesus is the resurrection which promises eternal life.

Again, the author moves from the divine level to the human level with his use of *ego eimi*. When Jesus proclaims "Before Abraham came to be, *ego eimi*" (Jn 8:58) all face the divine; when Jesus says he is bread and light and truth, listeners know the divine has come humanly.

Messiah/Christ

Messiah or Christ refers primarily to the humanity of Jesus. The gospel opens with a confession that Jesus is the messiah: "We have found the messiah" (Jn 1:41). The set purpose of the gospel in Jn 20:31 includes belief in Jesus as messiah. Throughout the gospel, however, the title implies a spiritual reality rather than a political reality.

In several passages in the Old Testament, Wisdom replaces the role of the messiah. In their zeal for the law, some scribes even began to identify the law with Wisdom. Two parallel movements converge on Jesus. A prophetic tradition saw salvation and redemption as God's work through a messiah in history. Wisdom literature depicted salvation and redemption already implanted in creation by God. Individuals who live according to their consciences would discover Wisdom and experience the saving presence of God. The former movement centered on the external; the latter on the internal.

Both concepts are united in the fourth gospel. Jesus is incarnate Wisdom. In him people may discover the Wisdom which God has implanted in the universe. Jesus fulfills the law and prophets and is Wisdom incarnate. The title Christ focuses on humanity which expresses divinity. Jesus as the incarnation of Wisdom bears the divine. He cannot be the messiah unless people see a human being who releases all of the possible energies implanted in human nature by a provident God. When the evangelist claims that Jesus is the messiah, the Christ, he proclaims that the human Jesus can lead all to the divine both as fulfilling the prophets and as expressing Wisdom.

The fourth gospel has long been recognized as emphasizing the divinity of Jesus. It also preserves his humanity. The author does not, however, resolve the relationship between the two. The Johannine community preserved a particular sensitivity to the divinity of Jesus but would not fall into the mistaken notion that the divinity eclipsed the humanity. With careful progression the author lead the reader from humanity to divinity without losing anything in the process. The divine Jesus of the fourth gospel is the very human Jesus of Nazareth.

The Many Models of Jesus in the New Testament

Even a short overview of the New Testament demonstrates the many images of Jesus developed from the original experience of the historical Jesus on the part of the early followers of Jesus. He may have been an ordinary peasant from lower Galilee but he spoke eloquently about the kingdom of God. He had received the baptism of John but had changed the message of John from God as an apocalyptic judge to God who was present in everyday life offering reconciliation, salvation, and peace. The ecstatic vision of Jesus brought a message of equality for all, patron and peasant, Gentile and Jew, male and female, rich and poor, slave and free. Jesus challenged the Judaism of his time to become inclusive rather than exclusive. Invite all to table fellowship and forgive all, for God invites all to the fellowship of his table in life and forgives all. So Jesus could be messiah and Christ for them. He could be Lord and Son of God; he could be friend of all and shepherd of all, healer and miracle worker, prophet and liberator, and above all Savior. People looked upon Jesus and saw the kindness and compassion of God decked out not in majesty but in the simple apparel of an itinerant preacher who offered free healing and free fellowship and free grace and free salvation. For Paul this meant free reconciliation and justification and a wonderful future for all, people and things, begun in the here and now. The christology of the New Testament rests upon the faith of many believers in many communities. Reading what others believed of Jesus in the early church helps in understanding Jesus today.

STUDY QUESTIONS AND TOPICS

Mark

1. How is Jesus as "Son of Man unto death" in Mark related to contemporary Christianity?

2. Mark adds a mysterious character to his image of Jesus. Why?

3. Does Mark have trouble understanding that Jesus is human?

4. Does Mark have trouble relating divinity to Jesus?

5. What is Mark's fundamental model of Jesus and how does it makes sense today?

Matthew

1. Jesus is a great teacher, and the Lord, and many other titles in Matthew. How do they fit together in the theology of Matthew?

2. Matthew presents Jesus present to all people in need. Is this a good model for today?

3. Matthew presents Jesus as Lord of all who gives guidance and direction to the church. How does this image help members of the church today?

4. Do you like the Jesus in the gospel of Matthew?

5. What elements of Matthew's christology do you find personally helpful?

Luke

1. Luke portrays Jesus as kind and compassionate. Is this his basic model of Jesus?

2. What appeals to people in the Jesus in the gospel of Luke?

3. Jesus prays frequently in this gospel. Is this part of the appeal and is this important in understanding Jesus?

4. The Spirit is also prominent in this gospel. Does this affect the model of Jesus?

5. Compare the model of Luke with the model of Matthew.

John

1. John presents Jesus as divine. What value does this model offer?

2. John also presents Jesus as revealing God the Father. How does this help christology?

3. Jesus is very human but more divine in this gospel. Is the author having trouble making up his mind on a model of Jesus?

4. Do the various titles used help or confuse?

5. What are your favorite elements in the Jesus of this gospel?

PART III

Contemporary
Models of Jesus

Chapter 1.

JESUS AS THE INCARNATION
OF THE SECOND PERSON
OF THE BLESSED TRINITY

Jesus as the incarnation of the second person of the Blessed Trinity has functioned as both model and paradigm for Roman Catholic as well as Protestant theology for centuries. Understanding the origin of this paradigm demands a study of the controversies of the first five centuries of the Christian era as well as an appreciation of scholastic theology. A complete analysis of this extended period of time in the history of theology easily demands a monograph on its own. An overview of the results of these controversies, as well as an uncovering of the theological development that links the middle ages to the twentieth century, makes more sense in this survey of the approaches to Jesus.

The Council of Chalcedon in 451 stands out in history as the high-water mark for the development of orthodox christology. At this council the church reached such a level of clarity that many thought that all subsequent errors in development could be detected by a careful comparison of new ideas with the declaration of the fathers of Chalcedon. Moreover, all subsequent generations could rest secure in the formulation approved by the members of the council. To seek a more profound understanding of Jesus, or a clearer formulation of that understanding after Chalcedon, was often viewed as imprudent and useless. After strenuous debate and much controversy between east and west the church officially settled at Chalcedon a theology of Jesus within which further theological speculation about Jesus would take place. Chalcedon would influence all subsequent developments in christology. From this period on, theological speculation must respect these estab-

lished parameters. The council however did not put an end to speculation as evident in the succeeding centuries.

The statement in 1972 by the Congregation for the Doctrine of
the Faith[69] reaffirmed what Chalcedon had stated. For many, however, such a statement was interpreted as putting an end to continued
speculation. The conviction that the church had already solved the
question of the theology of Jesus in previous councils, and in particular at the Council of Chalcedon, in the minds of some precluded further exploration. What sufficed for fourteen centuries will suffice for
the twentieth and twenty-first centuries. The unanswered question
remains, however: Was Chalcedon the end or the beginning?[70] If the
doctrine of Chalcedon formed a plateau to be used as a new starting
point, then continual development remains possible. If Chalcedon
and its declaration was itself the summit, then the search ended and
theologians need not continue efforts for further understanding and
explanation. Evidently to understand the model of Jesus as the incarnation of the second person of the Blessed Trinity demands an
appreciation of what the fathers of the church said in council at
Chalcedon.

The Council of Chalcedon

The origin of the Council of Chalcedon[71] has roots in the theological controversy in the eastern church on the precise nature of the
unity in Jesus and the relationship between his divinity and humanity.
Were there two natures in Jesus or only one? Did the humanity of
Jesus exist first, to be subsequently assumed into a hypostatic union, or
was the union concomitant with the existence of Jesus? Is person the
same as nature or not? Can one translate Greek terminology into Latin
and vice versa with clarity on both sides?

Since the matter originally centered mainly in the east, Pope Leo
the Great (440-461) did not wish, at first, to be involved. Finally, when
Emperor Theodosius convoked a council for August 449 in Ephesus,
the pope sent legates and presented his famous *Tomus ad Fulvium*. Leo
insisted on the true and integral human nature of Jesus and in the dis-
tinction of natures after the hypostatic union, which was in one person.[72] He also described the properties of the human and divine
natures, always insisting that it is one and the same person who possesses both. Those opposed to this formulation entered the council by
force, rejected the position of Leo and approved their own. In the history of theology this was called the "Concilium Latronum,"[73] the

"council of thieves." Since the matter was not settled at Ephesus, the Council of Chalcedon was called in 451, with representatives from East and West determined to settle the matter.

THE DEFINITION OF CHALCEDON

Following then the Holy Fathers, we all with one voice teach that it should be confessed that Our Lord Jesus Christ is one and the same Son, the same perfect in Godhead, the same perfect in manhood, truly God and truly man, the same [consisting] of a rational soul and body, *homoousios* [of the same substance] with the Father as to his Godhead, and the same *homoousios* with us as to his manhood; in all things like unto us, sin only excepted, begotten of the Father before all ages as to his Godhead, and in the last days, the same, for us and for our salvation, of Mary the virgin *theotokos* as to his manhood.

One and the same Christ, Son, Lord, only begotten, made known in two natures [which exist] without confusion, without change, without division, without separation; the difference in the natures having been in no wise taken away by reason of the union but rather the properties of each being preserved and both concurring in one the person [*prosopon*] and one *hypostasis*, not parted or divided into two persons [*prosopa*] but one and the same Son, an only begotten, the divine logos, the Lord Jesus Christ; even as the prophets from of old [have spoken] concerning him, as the Lord Jesus himself has taught us and as the symbol of the faith.[74]

Among other advances, the council offered clarification on the use of terminology. Previous to this declaration the terminology surrounding the relationship between the humanity and divinity of Jesus was greatly confused. The confusion became particularly evident in the effort to translate from Latin to Greek and vice versa. For some theologians nature was the same as *hypostasis*, which was the same as substance, which was the same as *physis*. For others *hypostasis* was the same as person, and nature was the same as *physis*. The council sought to relate Latin words to Greek words, but unfortunately there still remained nuances in meaning that could not be easily translated from one language to another. General agreement prevailed, but not without some reservations.

After Chalcedon

The question of the relationship between the two natures and one person remained. How can the unity of Jesus be preserved? How might the human and divine natures function in conjunction with each other. This debate spawned Monothelitism (one will) which would be answered in the Third Council of Constantinople. The Council of Chalcedon had stated that there existed two natures, human and divine, in one person, with no confusion of natures. But then how could theology express the unity of Jesus? The answer to this question involved further development of trinitarian theology, with the christological aspect clarified in the sixth century, especially in the works of Leontius, Boethius, Rusticus the Deacon, and Maximus the Confessor. Finally, the matter reached its highest level of development in the scholasticism of the middle ages.

EARLY ECUMENICAL COUNCILS

Nicea 325
Constantinople 381
Ephesus 449
Chalcedon 451
Constantinople 553
Constantinople 680/81
Nicea 787
Constantinople 869-70

Before the development of scholastic theology, however, clarification of the subject reached another plateau in the Third Council of Constantinople in 680-81. The teachings of Chalcedon were reaffirmed in this council with the additional formulation of the belief that two kinds of will operated in Jesus, the human and the divine.[75] With this formulation the church officially rested its case on the expression of the relationship between the human and the divine in Jesus. Further development would come from the efforts of theologians to interpret and explain this definition. For most of these theologians, Chalcedon declared the summit of christological thought beyond which theologians need not speculate.

Importance of Chalcedon

After more than six hundred years of theological speculation and controversy, the church expounded a formula of relationship between the humanity and divinity of Jesus. The terminology was not completely clear, since the various factions had different nuances for the same words, but at least general agreement with greater clarity prevailed. Now theologians could develop their understanding of Jesus based on the profession of faith as developed officially by the Church.

> The formula of Chalcedon preserves the realism of the incarnation. It is a description in non-philosophical terms, of the life and action of Christ as the Word made flesh. The terms "nature," (*ousia, physis*) and "person" (*hypostasis, prosopon,*) are to be taken with minimal philosophical content. Christ is man and God, one person, one reality, one concrete being, living in two realms, the divine and the human, with two consciousnesses (wills) and two fields of action (energies). The core of the mystery is not that one can be two. It is that God can be man and yet remain God. The mystery is not explained by the dogma.[76]

For someone who has read the New Testament, however, these linguistic and philosophical arguments concerning Jesus often caused much confusion. Has the intrigue with formulation lost the reality? Many theologians believed that "the simple, original proclamation of Christ, the Revealer, the Bringer of Salvation, the proclamation of Christ the Son of God can be heard in undiminished strength through all the *philosophoumena* of the Fathers."[77] For others the development of philosophy actually obscured this vision. The study of the theology of the middle ages makes the contrast between the New Testament and the conciliar formulations evident.

Medieval Christology

The declaration of Chalcedon never completely responded to the question of the precise relationship between the two natures and one person in Jesus. In an effort to respond to this question, medieval theologians, followed down into the twentieth century, first studied the Trinity and then situated christology within their understanding of the former doctrine. They would study the Logos, the Son, in his relationship to Father and Spirit and then consider the incarnation. Certain theologians even held the opinion that any one of the divine persons could have become man.[78] The sequence Trinity-creation-fall-incarnation became dominant in theology and lasted for centuries. The great theologians of the middle ages also tended to isolate what came to be known as abstract or ontological christology from concrete or functional christology. The former deals with the Word of God in relationship to the other persons of the Trinity, particularly the origin of the persons—Father, Son and Spirit—and the precise relationship between the two natures and one person in Jesus. The latter concerns the birth, life, death and resurrection of the Lord and the presence of Jesus as the Savior in his church. Such a division concurs perfectly with the Thomistic understanding of the object of theology: God in himself, who is attainable by the creature only in supernatural immediacy. Such must be treated first before theology can deal with the effects of God's action (the incarnation and redemption) on people. This theology derives from an appreciation of the relationship between the Trinity *ad intra* (within itself) and the Trinity *ad extra* (without, in particular, creation, incarnation). All things originate from God, go forth and then return to the trinitarian fullness. In christology, in the Word, all things proceed from God, and all things return to God. Using the terminology discussed in the previous chapter, the model of christology that resulted from the definition of Chalcedon and the scholastic synthesis becomes clearer: all things emanate from and return to the eternal Word of God become incarnate in Jesus. Understanding christology demands first situating Jesus in the presence of the Blessed Trinity, and then the theologian can come to specific conclusions with regard to the actual redemptive qualities of the life and death of Jesus. After all, the redemption remains the means by which the eternal Word brings about the restoration of all things in the Trinity from whom all things originated.

The full implications of this model only become clear in the study of the various aspects of christology. The motive of the incarnation, the entrance of Jesus into human history, the public ministry of Jesus, his death, resurrection and glorification, and the founding of the church—all take on specific nuances based upon this model.

Cur Deus Homo? (Why Did God Become Man?)

"Why did God become man?"[79] God must have had a purpose, some reason which would have motivated the coming of the Word into human history. Was the incarnation prompted by the fall of the human race and the need for its regeneration, or demanded by the sheer desire of God to share the human condition? Would the Word of God have become human even if humankind had not sinned?

A study of Thomas Aquinas shows an evolution of his thought culminating in the *Summa Theologica*. In this monumental work Aquinas follows scripture: "Since in scripture everywhere the reason for the incarnation is assigned to the sin of the first man, it can be said more fittingly that the work of the incarnation was ordered by God as a remedy for sins so that if sin had not existed, there would not have been an incarnation."[80]

Duns Scotus, on the other hand, argues that the incarnation should be considered apart from the need for redemption. The incarnation of the Word was, first and foremost, the greatest work of God and should be seen antecedently to and independently of the prevision of sin. Redemption was predestined so that Christ could be the adorer and glorifier of the Holy Trinity, the reason for all things, the final and exemplary cause of all in the natural and supernatural world order. Finally, the Word became flesh so that Jesus might be the universal mediator and mystical head of angels and men.[81]

Both opinions relate the incarnation to the second person of the Blessed Trinity. While Aquinas derives his opinion in part from scripture, and sees a redemptive incarnation in the New Testament, at a more fundamental level he situates the incarnation in the Trinity of persons in God. In the all-knowing awareness of everything, God had foreseen from all eternity the fall of humankind and then from eternity destined the incarnation as a remedy for the fall. The three persons in God anticipated the fall and provided the incarnation as the remedy.

Duns Scotus taught that God destined Christ primarily to be the adorer and glorifier of the Trinity. The work *ad extra* was an expression of the work *ad intra*. Since the Word was the reason for all things, the final and exemplary cause of all in the natural and supernatural world order, the essential motivation of the incarnation was the necessary fulfillment of a reality in God, not the historical fact of the fall.

Adoration due to the Humanity of Jesus

Worship expresses the appropriate relationship between creator and creature. Thus medieval theologians discussed whether the worship due to God should be afforded as well to the humanity of Jesus. The conclusion, of course, was affirmative. Jesus is the one person who has the Logos as his center of attribution. The Logos forms the foundation for the worship due to the humanity of Jesus.[82] "On account of the hypostatic union of Christ's humanity with the Logos, it [the humanity] is to be reverenced with latria, the adoration due to God, in itself although not for its own sake."[83]

The Ethical Perfection of Jesus

Ethical perfection of Jesus implies freedom from sin and love as the fullness of God's life within him. Theologians discussed the possibility of sin in the life of Jesus and concluded that Jesus was free from all original sin, from all concupiscence and from all personal sin. The arguments often refer to scripture, but at a more fundamental level it would be impossible for Jesus to have the inclinations to sin from within because of the unity of his human and divine natures. With regard to temptation from without, the same argument was used. Jesus possessed "an innate substantial purity illuminating the whole man."[84]

When Jesus remarks in the gospel of Mark that God alone is good (Mk 10:18), this could imply that Jesus recognized inadequacies in his own being. The response came quickly: "But in this case he surely had his eye not so much on himself as upon the infinite perfection of God. And precisely because he was closer to God than any other creature, he saw more deeply than our human eye into the depths of divine holiness. His human feeling was overawed by the sight of this glory which stood like an overwhelming light before his soul. Jesus could see this light more clearly than any other man."[85]

A theology of Jesus from above, an emphasis on ontology rather than function, determines the response to all questions concerning ethical perfection. All questions of sin and temptation must be considered as the possibility of sin on the part of the second person of the Blessed Trinity and the possibility of tempting the Logos. All such consideration comes immediately to naught. When scripture speaks of the cleansing of the temple, the cursing of the fig tree, the harsh words to his mother, Jesus' anger with the scribes and Pharisees, his condescending attitude toward the Canaanite woman, all of these must be explained away. Any sign of weakness or even imperfect moral dispositions cannot be ascribed to the person of Jesus. Apart from sin and temptation, as the second person of the Blessed Trinity Jesus may not do anything that could be construed as less than what might be expected in polite society.[86] Some other explanation must be found, and medieval theologians offered their personal solutions. This model of christology will set the framework within which all further explanations will be found. Jesus had to have the fullness of virtue which was the positive side of his sinlessness. Anything less would be beneath the dignity of the second person of the Blessed Trinity.

The Entrance of Jesus into History

The entrance of Jesus into human history[87] raises many questions regarding the virginal conception, the relationship of Jesus to Joseph and of Joseph to Mary, the role of the Holy Spirit and God the Father as well as the role of the Holy Spirit. In the traditional understanding, Jesus enters into human history through the full paternity of God the Father, without any human paternity. Theologians talk about the transitus of the Son of God from the divine sphere into the human. In the divine sphere he remains the Logos and Son, but by his entrance into the human dimension he becomes man, assuming a historicity, living humanly within human history. The primary source of the activity was God who is Father, but not without the involvement of the other persons of the Trinity. All that was created, and especially humankind, was created through the Word in the Spirit, so that in the Spirit all things participate in the Word. The history of God's dealings with people evolved in historical stages. In these steps the most important moment was the entrance of the Son into history.

Humankind had experienced sin. In spite of human failure God concluded his plan to bring humankind into a holy society with divinity. Thus, the Father sent his Son as the Word of God incarnate. While it is primarily the work of the Father, it is also the *kenosis* (emptying) of the Son. Jesus as the Word Incarnate entered sinful flesh that he might bear the sins of the world and bring forgiveness and salvation.

Since the source of Jesus was God the Father, Mary, the mother of Jesus, was a virgin. That Jesus could not have been God's Son if he had been conceived like any other human being is not immediately evident. If, however, one begins with the thought of the paternity of the Father in the Trinity as the source of the Son, then it is a natural conclusion that Jesus had to be born of a virgin. No need for further paternity existed, since paternity already formed the basis of the *Logos'* relationship to God the Father. The model of Jesus as the second person of the Blessed Trinity gives support to the doctrine of virginal conception, just as the dogma of virginal conception supports the belief that Jesus was the second person of the Blessed Trinity.[88]

Virginal Conception

The doctrine of the virginal conception is very old in Christian tradition. Even before the year 200, the affirmation of belief in Christ Jesus was expanded in the old Roman Creed by a reference to his birth from the Virgin Mary in order to counteract a docetism and gnosticism that questioned the reality of the humanity of Jesus.[89] The Nicene Creed also affirmed a virginal conception. In all of these instances, however, the whole question of the relationship of the humanity and divinity of Jesus was being hotly debated during this period. The church tried to preserve both the divinity and the humanity of Christ in the face of heresies. In such a situation the symbol of the Virgin Mary was ideal, since it allowed one to emphasize "virgin" to preserve the divinity while stressing that Mary was a woman to preserve the true humanity. In any case, the prime model was the second person of the Blessed Trinity, who was the *Logos* that had become man.

The gospels of Matthew and Luke also speak of a virginal conception, even if these accounts need to be nuanced.[90] No doubt exists that the writers of these gospels presented a virginal conception even if they did not write to establish a dogmatic formulation.[91] The controversy surrounding the virginal conception of Jesus need not enter into the discussion there. The use of the model rather than the actual scriptural or theological foundations for the doctrine as expounded by the model forms the content of this work. The second person of the Blessed Trinity as a model for christology easily relates and supports the virginal conception of Jesus. But using a different model may still preserve the virginity of Mary, but with a slightly different understanding of the truth contained in the teaching.

The Activities and Works of Jesus (Theandric Acts)

In traditional christology, all the activities and works of Jesus were considered theandric (divine acts) since all come from the divine person. Many theologians would divide the activities of Jesus into those which are strictly theandric (miracles and prophecies which only God could perform) and the daily activities of his life, which are called theandric acts only in the widest use of that term.

The medieval theologians used Aristotelian principles in their christology. Actions belong to the person (*actiones sunt suppositorum*) and derive from his essence (*actiones sequuntur esse*). As a result of these principles, all of the activities are predicated of the person of Jesus, which is the divine person of the Word. The Word of God, the eternal

Son, raised Lazarus from the tomb, and the Word of God wept because Lazarus was dead; the Word of God prophesied that Peter would deny him three times, and the Word of God washed the feet of Peter.[92]

The activities of Jesus such as eating and drinking, sleeping and walking are truly human, but since Jesus the man is the divine person of the Word, these actions would also be called divine by reason of being acts of a divine person. The model of the second person of the Blessed Trinity in theology views all of the actions of Jesus as divine actions, since all are directed to the person of the Word who gives the foundation for all actions. One conclusion from these premises is the belief that any action of Jesus could be redemptive since any action was of infinite value.

Traditional apologetics often developed to the point of asserting an obligation to believe in the divinity of Jesus. If Jesus performed miracles and uttered prophecies, then these actions manifested to all that they face more than just an ordinary human being. People contact, at least in thought, a divine person.[93] A theologian could read the gospels which speak of the amazement of the listeners: "Never did man speak as this man" (Mt 13:27) and conclude that expressions like these, of which there are many in the gospels, show that those who knew Christ beheld the deeds he performed in his human nature and realized that he was not just human. They realized that his human nature lay mysteriously but firmly rooted in a person who was far above anything human. Jesus was divine.[94] Once an individual realized the presence of such divine activities and nothing the person encountered contradicted human reason, an obligation to believe in Jesus as divine naturally resulted. This theology and apologetics found its roots in the acceptance of Jesus as the person of the Word, which formed the paradigm for any understanding of the activities of Jesus in his ministry.

This tendency to go to the root cause also affects the chief redemptive activity of the Lord: his cross and resurrection. Since the passion and death of Jesus was the activity of the Word of God, it has an infinite value for redemption. God died on the cross but solely insofar as God was man. Only the person of the Word became man, and only the person of the Word died on the Cross.[95]

Further speculation on the value of any activity of Jesus concluded that any act of Jesus would be sufficient to redeem humankind, because all activity reverted back to the person of the Word. The shedding of blood at the circumcision was an activity which, since it was rooted in the person of the Word, could be sufficient for the redemption of all. To die a human death was a decision on the part of the

Word of God, but this activity was in no way necessary for the salvific power of redemption.[96]

APOCRYPHAL GOSPELS

The Gospel of Thomas
The Gospel of Philip
The Gospel of Peter
The Infancy Gospel of Thomas
The Gospel of Pseudo-Matthew
The Gospel of James

The apocryphal gospels demonstrate that Jesus could work any miracles he wished at any period of his life. Theologians saw him as the Word of God walking around in the body of a child, living out a scenario that had been foreseen and pre-ordained. If all is rooted in the second person of the Blessed Trinity, then no other way exists to understand the activities of Jesus other than that of a divine person expressing himself in human actions.

Traditional theology understood all of this through instrumental causality. Again it was Thomas Aquinas who gave the clearest philosophical foundation for these ideas.[97] An instrument which an artist uses produces an artistic result only if it is closely controlled and united to the artist. The control of the instrument by the artist does not deprive the instrument of its own specific activity nor of its contribution to the final effect produced. Rather, the effect comes simultaneously from the principal cause, the artist, and from the instrumental cause (secondary cause), the material used.

Applying these notions to Jesus, his humanity becomes a conjoined instrument. The humanity of Jesus preserves its own proper power in its activities and has distinctive characteristics. The principal cause remains always the person of the Word. This explains the theological understanding of all of the activities of Jesus, even the most ordinary, as theandric. Even if some of these actions are theandric only in a wide sense, all are referred to the principal cause, the person of the Word.

The Knowledge of Jesus

The question of the knowledge and consciousness of Jesus figures more prominently than all of the other factors mentioned in any discussion of the influence of a paradigm on christology.[98] The Third Council of Constantinople defined as a truth of faith the existence of two activities in Jesus, divine and human. As a result, theologians, especially during the middle ages, developed the theories of two kinds of knowledge: human and divine. As God, Jesus possessed the divine knowledge of God proper to each person of the Blessed Trinity; as man, he also possessed human knowledge and the human way of knowing common to all people. By his divine knowledge, Jesus knew God in himself and all other things in God. This divine knowledge, the uncreated knowledge of the Word, existed as equal to that of the Father and of the Holy Spirit.

Divine Nature—Divine Knowledge

Human Person—Beatific Knowledge
Infused Knowledge
Experiential Knowledge

The human knowledge of Jesus differed essentially from the divine knowledge and can be further distinguished. First, from the very moment of his conception, Jesus' humanity enjoyed the beatific vision. This knowledge belonged to his humanity by reason of the hypostatic union. Thus, Jesus had a human knowledge of his divine being and personality; he always had this knowledge, which the saints enjoy in heaven, in the highest possible intensity.

Second, Jesus' mind was also endowed with infused knowledge; he knew, as created spirits know, all that was equal to him and inferior to him as human, and he had, moreover, knowledge about God himself more perfect than any which a person has by nature. Finally, as human, Jesus had ordinary acquired and empirical knowledge, which he gained from his contact with others and his earthly experience.

Some might think that so complete a set of distinctions would reflect a real division in Jesus himself. But since one person remains the source of these types of knowledge, such an analytical approach retains the unity without division. As God, Jesus knew all things, and, as man, Jesus saw all things in God. As recently as 1947 Pope Pius XII wrote in *Mystici Corporis*, "He also enjoys the beatific vision in a degree, both as regards extent and clarity, surpassing that of the saints in heaven."[99]

Historically when some theologians objected that such a vision appears incompatible with the suffering described in the gospels, other theologians often turned to a physical example to help to understand the combination of suffering and a beatifying vision: "A storm can lash the sides of a mountain and let loose on it rain and hail and lightning. But nothing disturbs the peace of the mountain heights."[100]

While the church has never defined that Christ had infused knowledge, this conclusion follows from the model of christology that sees Jesus as a member of the Trinity. Jesus should have infused knowledge since he is the second person of the Blessed Trinity; he should also know more than any angel or any saint or any doctor of the church. Such knowledge would be independent of any human experience. The only limitation placed upon this type of knowledge is the possibility of inadvertence: "His human mind did not always advert to all that it knew and at any one moment of his human life this knowledge must have been, as we say, latent within his mind and available to use when needed."[101]

Thomas Aquinas also took the lead in the discussion of acquired knowledge. He wanted to preserve the full humanity of Jesus and all of his natural activities, and thus Aquinas affirmed a humanly acquired knowledge. He argued that the perfection of Christ's acquired knowledge had to befit his mission, and no doubt the Lord himself set out to acquire such knowledge. The question of resolving this acquired knowledge with infused knowledge was never adequately answered by Aquinas. He referred to the difference between habit and action and offered no complete explanation.[102] Many theologians concluded that Jesus had an encyclopedic type of knowledge. He knew all things in God while he also had acquired knowledge. The infused knowledge was present when he needed it.

In the history of christology since the Council of Chalcedon the model of Jesus as the second person of the Blessed Trinity has had a significant effect on all of theology. If the foundation for the understanding of Jesus is the person of the Word, then the motive for the incarnation, the infirmities and weaknesses of Jesus' humanity, his entrance into history, his activities and works and, finally, his knowledge and consciousness will all be understood only in relationship to the divinity of the person. The theological conclusions and official pronouncements of the church have all been influenced by this overriding model.

Resurrection

The resurrection founds all christology, and also culminates the meaning of Jesus. Although the keystone of christology,[103] the resurrection did not always figure prominently in the christology based on the model of the second person of the Blessed Trinity. If the person of the Word is responsible for all of the activities of the earthly life of Jesus, then, as the Word of God, Jesus raised himself from the grave. This miracle was seen as the greatest of Jesus' miracles, proving to all who would listen that in truth he was the divine Son of God. In the history of christology theologians related the resurrection to his other miracles, and they understood this event which culminated his ministry as the natural outcome of his divine nature. The eternal Word become man was aware of his divinity even as he lived his human life, performed actions which belonged properly to the second person of the Blessed Trinity, understood completely his mission and, finally, after he had finished his task on earth and had been crucified, rose from the dead to prove to all the truth of his mission and person. In this view christology must always take as its starting point the existence of the second person of the Blessed Trinity. Only in this way can believers understand the meaning of Jesus of Nazareth.

For most Christians, and Roman Catholics in particular, the model of Jesus as the second person of the Blessed Trinity has dominated both theology and piety for centuries. The model also has influenced all of the catechisms down to and including the recently promulgated catechism.[104] The developments since the Second Vatican Council have not completely altered this position. Official Roman Catholic Church pronouncements also bear the imprint of this model of Jesus. The same remains true for many believers.

For Protestant theologians, however, this has not always been the case. The last hundred years have witnessed many models for Jesus, which have been explored in a plethora of books. Often enough the individual Protestant theologian chose among the many approaches to Jesus that were presented in scholarly circles and developed a christology accordingly. At the same time, the earlier conciliar definitions continue to have an important influence on the majority of Protestant theologians, especially after the period of liberal Protestantism in the nineteenth century.[105] Karl Barth, for example, in his *Church Dogmatics* relies heavily on conciliar christology. Thus, the model can be evaluated with implications for all of Christian theology and not just the Roman Catholic tradition.

Advantages

No doubt, such an approach to christology has had clear and distinct advantages in the past and will continue to influence church teaching in the future. Fifteen hundred years of tradition may not be lightly forgotten.

First, for Roman Catholics, this model has been the official posi-tion of the church, witnessed in recent documents and traced back to the early councils. Since the Roman Church, unlike its Protestant counterparts, claims that its distinct teaching authority is founded on divine revelation, for any member of that communion to maintain a different position from what official teaching affirms may cause con-cern. As a result most will not question the clear christology which results from this model. This christology can be easily presented in official documents with the firm support of centuries of tradition. In times of great social upheaval and of new developments in all aspects of life, the believer feels comfortable in subscribing to a christology which has such a strong historical and authoritative backing. Even if a Roman Catholic theologian would like to take a new look at such a model, any critique could prove embarrassing when compared to unequivocal church statements. The model also has frequently result-ed in a uniformity in understanding the meaning of Jesus. Even in the study of Jesus in scholarly circles such a model imposes a sense of order, and sets the parameters within which the theologian may devel-op new ideas.

Jesus as the second person of the Blessed Trinity remains clearly theandric. As a second advantage, the model preserves the divinity of Jesus and protects it against any attempts to denigrate or discredit it. Over the course of centuries individuals have attempted to rethink the meaning of Jesus in ways that resulted in a loss or, at any rate, a lessen-ing of any sense of the divine. The period of liberal Protestantism in the late nineteenth century and the modernist crises of the Roman Catholic tradition at the turn of this century both demonstrate how certain kinds of rethinking of christology can lessen the sense of the divinity of Jesus. The death of God theology has led to similar results. If the model is the second person of the Blessed Trinity no possibility exists for the divinity of Jesus becoming lessened, forgotten or lost.

A third advantage is the theological elaboration that can be built upon this model. Everyone tends to seek unity in life and in thought which is particularly true when trying to deal with a sense of mystery. With Jesus all believers continue to face inexhaustible intelligibility. If somehow a cohesive model can order this intelligibility, then all can be more secure in theology and in belief. The model of the second per-son of the Blessed Trinity gives a cohesiveness and stability that clari-fies the mission of Jesus, his miracles and prophecies, his knowledge and resurrection as well as his entrance into history. If all is rooted in the eternity of God, then all of the minor aspects of the life of Jesus can be ordered according to one principle. This abstract christology becomes the basis for the concrete christology of the gospels and gives a theological principle that can be applied in every case.

A fourth advantage of such a model is the actual expression of piety associated with the christological spirituality of the seventeenth century French school. Pierre de Brulle, Jean-Jacques Olier, and Vincent de Paul had a profound influence on seminary education through the founding of the Society of Saint Sulpice by Olier and the Congregation of the Mission by Vincent de Paul. Their spirituality was based on this model of Jesus, and through their influence on seminary education throughout the world, but especially in the United States, the ordinary piety of clergy and people often centered on the Trinity with a special emphasis on Jesus as the second person of the Blessed Trinity. No one can deny the profound effect and power for good in the American church over the past two hundred years with its devotions and commitment. All this flowed from this particular spirituality.

The model also influences other questions of theology, for example, those related to the institutional church or to principles of morality. The model of the second person of the Blessed Trinity offers an omniscient God/man directing things to his purpose. An ecclesiology based on this model tends to share in this omniscience, giving clear, objective principles of belief and of moral conduct. Jesus spoke authoritatively to his church for all times and circumstances since he spoke from the eternity of God. Jesus foresaw his Church with its sacramental system and positions of authority and affirmed the entire process based upon his decision and knowledge as the second person of the Blessed Trinity. The church's theology followed suit. In an age of indecision and confusion, people welcome clarity in religious expression. This model offers such clarity.

Limitations

Without discounting the advantages of such an approach to Jesus, it must be admitted that it also labors under several liabilities. No one model can ever offer a response to all questions. Nor can one approach fulfill the needs of all peoples of all times.

In the first place, in spite of efforts to prove the contrary, the model has only a meager basis in scripture. Certainly the gospels present Jesus as the Son of God, but not as the all-knowing, beatified Christ of later theology. While the New Testament does speak of God as Father and Son and Spirit, it does not become philosophical in trying to distinguish persons and nature. The Jesus in the gospels appears more like a man of his own times and very unlike the Jesus of this model. The New Testament gives a foundation for the approach in its teaching on the special relationship to God as Father that Jesus experienced, but the differences in the various New Testament christologies are often lost in the effort to spin out the theories of the relationship between humanity and divinity.

Second, the model tends to eclipse the meaning of the humanity of Jesus. No longer do we have an individual with human feelings, with hopes, expectations and needs, but the embodiment of the eternal Word. The "person" who is acting, the second person of God, is important rather than what is said or done. The notion of instrument can create the illusion that the Logos used the humanity of Jesus much as an artist would use a paint brush or a piano to create a picture or music. With the tendency always to go to the divine source of all in Jesus, the reality of the human life of Jesus falls into shadows. Functional christology becomes lost in ontological christology. Who Jesus is in relationship to God overshadows what Jesus actually accomplished for humanity.

Third, such an approach often stifles theology. For some, theology becomes an effort to give support to the statements of the official church teaching rather than an attempt to explore new avenues. A heavily metaphysical construct in christology tends to impose its conclusions on other areas of theology as well. If the answers are already known in christology, and these conclusions control other areas of theology, how can a theologian possibly break new ground? This christology gives a foundation for attitudes within the church which are not in keeping with the entire biblical tradition nor with the understandings that have developed since the Second Vatican Council. Theologians must be free to think, and this model limits that freedom. The model also limits the development of theology through new situations and circumstances. The model pre-supposes that Jesus has already revealed all that is in any way necessary for the church and the individual believer. It does not take into account the development of the behavioral sciences and their effects on theology. Rather, it tends to close doors on areas of discussion instead of facilitating the efforts of theologians to grow in the understanding of faith and thus fulfill their responsibility in the church.

Fourth, this model is sometimes detrimental to Christian piety, since it can easily create a situation in which the ordinary believer cannot identify with Jesus, when always faced with the immediate claim that he functioned as the second person of the Blessed Trinity. If Jesus is the model for other fallible human beings to emulate, the model cannot be so separated from ordinary human experience that leaves no hope for imitation. Jesus, even as a man, is elevated into the realm of the transcendent God, with little or no effect on the lives of believers other than to make them conscious of their sins.

Finally, this approach is not in tune with the developments in theology and in the church in recent times. In an age of dialogue not only with Christian traditions but also with other religions, at a time when in need of a Savior who can be part of the human experience and who presented himself as the humble carpenter of Nazareth, who came not to be served but to serve, who offered a sense of personal worth in his dealings with people, the emphasis on the second person of the Blessed Trinity as the paradigm for all christology has little impact. When people are concerned principally not with the God question but with the question of the meaning of human life, at a time when this life has become more precarious, an eternal "Logos" descending and living a seemingly unreal life does not help. Any hope of attracting ordinary people to see their value in the light of this man's life seems hopeless. The second person of the Blessed Trinity may prove interesting to scholars in the history of Christianity, but offers little reason for enthusiasm to the person who lives in the throes of anxiety, searching to eke out some personal worth and meaning in a world often gone mad with power.

In the minds of many believers the model of Jesus as the second person of the Blessed Trinity has become less in importance in personal devotion. Other models have more appeal. In the study of theology, however, this approach will have sustained interest. Theologians can never overlook the traditions, and Chalcedon with its declaration forms a significant part of those christological traditions. The model of Jesus as the second person of the Blessed Trinity may remain a paradigm for theology even if it no longer offers an acceptable paradigm for preaching, for religious education and, for many, personal piety.

In every age the church maintains its traditions and still strikes out into new areas. The church should not shrink from a task that calls out for new approaches and models. This does not mean that the church throws out the advantages of this model of Jesus. The sense of mystery can keep the notion of Jesus as the pre-existent second person of the Blessed Trinity within its proper bounds and can see to it that other models are not lost. Many approaches to Jesus enrich the Christian tradition, while taking only one approach impoverishes understanding.

In spite of the strong emphasis on this model in the official teaching of the church, other approaches were never completely forgotten. Even now the church finds itself challenged to respond to the new models that are being offered by various theologians, which have grown out of their particular life experiences. These approaches affect the meaning of Jesus as the second person of the Blessed Trinity. The strong reaction to the humanizing of Jesus in the past thirty years and thus a swing back to the more numinous christology emphasize the second person of the Blessed Trinity. Other models, however, have entered the scene with a vigor that cannot be overlooked. To these models must all believers turn to appreciate more of the inexhaustible mystery that is Jesus of Nazareth.

STUDY TOPICS AND QUESTIONS

1. Theology is faith seeking understanding. Why is this important in studying this model of Jesus?

2. What is the difference between Jesus as the Son of God and people being sons and daughters of God?

3. Can you explain in your own words the theology of two natures, human and divine, in one divine person?

4. What have the councils of the church contributed to christology?

5. If Chalcedon is not an end, how should it be accepted in theology?

6. What interested you in the study of medieval christology?

7. Does it make any difference that Jesus could not sin?

8. What are your thoughts on the entrance of Jesus into history?

9. The knowledge of Jesus continues to arouse interest. What makes more sense to you?

10. Why is the resurrection important in the study of Jesus?

11. Should this model be a paradigm in theology? Is this model actually preached in your parish?

Chapter 2.

THE MYTHOLOGICAL CHRIST

Over the centuries, many have questioned the authenticity of Christianity and its founder, Jesus of Nazareth. Questions of faith always pale under the scrutiny of factual and scientific investigation. The methods are different. The foundation and outcomes are disparate. Usually believers and most Christian scholars will just dismiss the criticism of skeptics. Such thoughts have little value to the true believers and Christianity. A careful examination of these critics, however, reveals some important insights. Upon careful examination they may offer some healthy hesitation in the presence of enthusiastic Christianity.

Over the past thirty years many have unearthed previous critiques of Jesus and Christianity. The careful scholar has listened anew to what these critics say. As a result, since the publication of J.A.T. Robinson's book *Honest to God* in 1963,[106] many scripture scholars and some theologians have readily accepted the mythological character of some aspects of traditional Christianity and christology. They do not reject the historical Jesus, but they have re-examined some of the tenets of traditional christology. The portrait of the historical Jesus has been colored by the faith experience of the early followers, and thus no one need feel alarmed if some aspects of this historical Jesus have been lost in the Christ of faith. The study of the mythological Christ is an effort to ask the real Jesus of Nazareth to stand up.

Over the two thousand years of Christianity there have always been skeptics who have claimed that the Christian religion is more the result of human ingenuity or imagination than of any divinely inspired founder. Often the skeptics reject Jesus as an historical figure; at the most, they consider him as a real person who suffered from illusions.

107

For others, his historicity is not as important as his meaning. In the opinion of these people, Jesus of Nazareth, a good man, like the Greek gods of old, performed a function as a representative person, which is more important than the question of his historical reality.

Some time ago a group of Anglican theologians published a collection of essays examining traditional christology. They pre-suppose that by now Christians have overcome the outdated notion that Jesus was in truth the incarnation of the Son of God and they try to discover the reason that gave birth to such an idea. The book, *The Myth of God Incarnate*,[107] uses the word myth in the sense of something that is not true. Thus, they try to get to the real meaning of Jesus, discarding the accretions that have overlaid the historical Jesus.

In the course of centuries, the word "myth" has developed both positive and negative meanings for different thinkers. This chapter shall combine many different approaches to Jesus under the rubric "the mythological Christ." In some instances, as shall be clear, myth is something positive and truthful; in other instances myth implies just the opposite. The common element that binds these various theologies together is the conviction that the Jesus presented in traditional christology is not the real Jesus of Nazareth. Biblical criticism over the past two hundred years has laid the foundation for this new critique of Jesus and Christianity.

Biblical Criticism

Until the end of the eighteenth century the gospels were accepted at their face value as a description, written by eyewitnesses or their associates, of the person, life and teachings of Jesus of Nazareth. The gospels are historically accurate and could be accepted as authentic and truthful. In 1774, however, G.E. Lessing published posthumous selections from the manuscript of a colossal work by H.S. Reimarus, who had died a few years previously. Thus began the controversy which has yet to lose any of its force.[108]

Reimarus believed that Christianity rested upon a fraud. According to his theory, Jesus was a Jew, steeped in Jewish tradition and thus anti-Gentile, who did not wish to found a new religion but to deepen the old one. He may have healed some people, but he never performed any prodigious miracles. He was a messiah who expected a popular uprising that would allow him to lead the revolt against the pro-Roman Pharisees and sanhedrin. Unfortunately for Jesus, this uprising never materialized and he was condemned to death. Then came Christianity.

The disciples of Jesus, according to Reimarus, created Christianity out of their sense of disappointment. Jesus himself had expected the kingdom of God to come in his lifetime and never said anything about dying and rising. As a result of his death, the disciples fell back on the secondary aspect of Jewish apocalyptic hopes and transferred the kingdom to a supernatural sphere as found, for example, in chapters 7 and 9 of Daniel. They gathered followers who believed that Jesus was the Davidic messiah and invented the resurrection. To give substance to their claims they stole the body of Jesus, waited fifty days for it to decompose, and then declared him to be the awaited messiah. Christianity rests upon a fraud. Jesus Christ is mythological in a negative sense, since he never existed as presented in the gospels. He did not preach the good news as recorded by the evangelists; he did not rise from the dead and is surely not the Son of God. Since the time of Reimarus, individuals periodically have proposed one or many of these same opinions.[109]

The interest in rationalism in the nineteenth century continued the interest in this skeptical attitude toward Jesus and Christianity. Many Christian thinkers, influenced by rationalism but eager to maintain the value in Christianity, re-examined the gospels as well as the history of Christianity and tried to preserve what was most essential to Christian faith. At the same time they were open to some of the critique coming from rationalism and historical criticism. Once again, christology was most greatly modified.

D.F. Strauss was the first to deal specifically with the question of myth, and gave his own definition.[110] For Strauss, myth was the clothing in historical form of religious ideas, shaped by the unconsciously inventive power of legend and embodied in an historical person. Before Strauss, certain rationalists had labeled the birth and resurrection of Jesus as legend and myth, but with Strauss a consistent theory arises. He suggested that miracles also derive from legend: the stories of the transfiguration and resurrection, as well as the birth narratives and much of what is extraordinary in the gospels, can be attributed to this human tendency to glorify a man after death. Theologians must study Jesus to remove the mythological elements and then discover the true Jesus. Myth is negative, a hindrance to true faith that should be examined and discarded.

A third individual of the same period who drew certain of the premises of his predecessors to their logical conclusions was Bruno Bauer.[111] His ideas developed in three stages: first an ultra Strauss period in which he deals with the concept of myth but replaces the term with "reflection"; a second period characterized by a questioning of the historical Jesus with the conviction that it is the thought of Jesus that is important, and not the man; finally, an outright denial of the historical person of Jesus. Bauer concluded that Christianity is a compromise rising from the interchange between Jewish and Roman culture.

In the first period he studied the gospels beginning with John, working his way back to Mark and the historical Jesus. For Bauer the gospel of John was a work of art, not an historical document, and was thoroughly dominated by creative reflection. Even Mark, the first gospel, could be considered a literary rather than an historical work: thus the possibility that one person invented the entire system of teachings. Matthew and Luke are expansions of Mark, and John is the result of the influence of Philo on the same basic tradition.

In the second period of his development, Bauer realized that it was necessary to free the theology of Jesus the messiah from the Judeo-Roman idol created by his followers. Whether Jesus existed or not is of no consequence. Bauer suggested that the higher religion associated with Jesus is of value in itself. Christianity has merit because it encouraged the overcoming of nature, not by self-alienation, but by penetrating and ennobling human life through a living out of the teachings of Christianity. Myth figures prominently in the gospels and in the portrait of Jesus, but this should not denigrate the importance that Christian values offer to life. Whether Jesus lived or not is of little consequence; what is important is the effect that Christianity can have on a person's life. Eventually, Bauer came to believe that Jesus never existed. He postulated the idea that some first century thinkers cleverly created the Christian faith as a response to human need.

Rudolf Bultmann

Today when people who are marginally acquainted with contemporary theology and scriptural studies hear of the word "myth," the name of Rudolf Bultmann immediately comes to mind.[112] This German hermeneute stamped twentieth century biblical criticism with his own clear mark, and his thought will continue to influence developments for the next hundred years. Before Bultmann arrived on the scene (he was a prolific writer from 1920 to 1976) the stage had been set for his theories. He presented a new approach to the study of the New Testament by seeing "myth" not as something negative, but as something positive. Many people recognized the mythological elements in the gospels, but now, for the first time, an interpreter of the New Testament saw a value in the myth as expressing a truth. Bultmann recognized the creative power of the early community; he questioned, on philosophical grounds, some of the supernatural elements of the New Testament; finally, he had become disturbed by the inability of Christianity, so understood in his own days, to minister to his contemporaries, especially during the World War. These influences formed the background for his lifelong study.

Bultmann studied the influence of Hellenism on the formation of the early preaching of Jesus and was eager to use some of the findings of contemporary philosophy, namely the existential approach of Martin Heidegger, in his study of the New Testament. All of these influences, as well as the development of the use of form criticism in the New Testament, laid the foundation for Bultmann's theology.

Immediately after the First World War, K.L. Schmidt and M. Dibelius along with Bultmann applied a new method to the study of the synoptics.[113] They were impressed by the efforts of H. Gunkel, who had re-examined the Old Testament to discover the various literary forms contained therein, and they sought to offer a similar study of the New Testament. Their theory postulates a period of oral transmission of the material contained in the synoptic gospels before it reached a written stage in Mark and in "Q" (the postulated written source used by Matthew and Luke in their composition). The oral tradition connected with Jesus assumed various literary genres or forms, each of which had its own history and its own life situation (*sitz em leben*) in the early church, whether in Palestine or in the diaspora. The primitive community did not merely transmit the sayings of Jesus and his deeds; it adapted them to its own historical situation, created new ones and expressed them in particular literary forms. Hence the gospels are not accounts of what happened, but kerygmatic documents projected back into the life of Jesus. They tell us little, if anything, about the biography and personality of the historical Jesus.

Bultmann's theology is complicated and deals with many questions involving the use of philosophical principles of interpretation, the meaning of the Christian life, sin, faith, etc. Two distinctive features of his thought need examination: his concept of demythologizing and his understanding of christology.

Demythologizing

Many people have their own peculiar understanding of myth, as evident in the various proposed descriptions. The same is true for

Bultmann. For him, meaning was more important than scientific understanding. Bultmann claimed to use myth in the historical and religious sense of the word, but with his own nuance.[114] Myth is the way of presenting things so that the other-worldly become worldly, the divine is seen in the human. Its meaning is positive and implies a direct activity of the divine, supernatural, superhuman, within the historical order. Divine or other-worldly activity is presented in analogy with human earthly activity.

An example of this application can be seen in Bultmann's interpretation of miracles. According to Bultmann, a miracle is a happening among other happenings, and can be understood as the presence of the divine in human history only through the eyes of faith. When one believes, he or she can see the event as myth and recognize it as an act of God in human form. There may be a natural cause, but the event itself is interpreted from a theological perspective precisely because it is mythological.

Myth, as understood by Bultmann, speaks of God in human terms, especially when it depicts the use of power. In first century culture there were clearly mythic elements that would have influenced Christianity. People viewed the universe as an edifice having three stories, with God in the heavens, people on earth and demons under the earth. This provided a basis for movement back and forth from earth to heaven, and from heaven to earth as well. The three story universe formed the framework for the entrance of demons into history, the exorcisms of Jesus, the atonement for sins which pleases a heavenly God, the Spirit of God coming from heaven to earth, and the birth and resurrection of Christ.

Bultmann soon recognized the mythological elements that were prevalent in the first century and which colored the New Testament writings. He saw that in order to recognize the truth that was present in the myth, one had to get beyond the mythical reality to discover its meaning. He called this process "demythologizing." Such a process is not the denial of the truth or the value of the myth, nor is it a quantitative reduction of mythical representations; rather, it is a qualitative reinterpretation. Bultmann disagreed with Strauss, who had thought of myth as an allegory and differentiated the shell from the kernel, the latter being the great moral values that are contained in the myth. According to Bultmann, when Strauss and others applied this concept of myth to the New Testament, they actually destroyed the *kerygma,* since the preaching of Jesus is not found beside the myth but in the myth.

The *kerygma* is the saving act of God in Christ, expressed in the myths of the New Testament, such as miracles and the resurrection. Demythologizing, then, is interpretation with no attempt on the part of the interpreter to eliminate the myth, but with an attempt to give an existential meaning to it. The true value of myth consists in the recognition that this world which lies before us is not its own ground and end. Powers, forces and values exist that cannot be communicated in any other way than in mythical language. What is significant is how individuals respond to the meaning that is expressed in the myth: how a person believes in Jesus and finds personal value in a commitment to him. What is communicated in myth is often much more than what can be communicated in strictly scientific language. That is the distinctive advantage of the mythological Christ.

Christology

In the thought of Bultmann, Christ is the event of salvation, but this does not necessarily include the historical Jesus. Jesus proclaimed the kingdom of God, but actuality the proclaimer became the proclaimed.[115] Christianity takes its value not from the how or the what of Jesus, but that Jesus was. Jesus himself has been mythologized into the Christ of faith. There was no point, for Bultmann, in trying to create a life of Jesus, since this has no relevance to the *kerygma*. He did not deny the historical Jesus, as other authors did, but it was clear that, in his thinking, the historical Jesus was not as important as the Christ of faith, the mythological Christ, an other-worldly reality that is being expressed in this-worldly terms, in a poetic and creative fashion.

This mythologizing embraced both Hellenistic as well as Jewish thought patterns, and so when reading the sayings of Jesus in the gospels three strata must be distinguished: the latest, which is Hellenistic; the Aramaic stratum, which is part of the experience of the earliest followers in an oral tradition; and the oldest, the pre-Aramaic stratum, from which most of the authentic sayings of Jesus arise.

Jesus of Nazareth, according to Bultmann, was an ordinary man, a Jew, not a Christian. What he preached was not identical with the earliest *kerygma* of Christianity. This primitive preaching was about Jesus as the Christ and depended on the experience of the resurrection. This does not mean, however, that no continuity existed between the historical Jesus and the *kerygma*. Paul did not make up Christianity, as some have claimed, nor did anyone else. Jesus and Paul and other early Christian writers and preachers had the same basic teaching. Both Jesus and Paul appealed to people as sinners, asking for a decision about their personal existence. Bultmann proposed that scholars must do away with all messianic titles in the ministry of Jesus, since these are the creation of the early church. There remains, however, an implicit christology in the teaching of Jesus, even if it is not the *kerygma*. For Bultmann, this approach was actually legitimized in the New Testament. Paul and John, for example, are not interested in the historical Jesus, because they themselves are concerned with the *kerygma*. The same can be said for the synoptics.

If someone asked Bultmann what is the difference between the teaching of Jesus and the *kerygma*, he would have replied that the *kerygma* changes the one-time event of the historical Jesus into the once-for-all Christ event: the story of Jesus is considered globally as the definitive eschatological event. Jesus preached the coming of salvation and the *kerygma* preached the salvation of God as already come in Jesus the Christ.

To return to the meaning of demythologizing: the meaning of Jesus as the Christ is translated into mythological events and narratives which are meant to bring people to a personal decision. The believer must move beyond the myth in order to appreciate the personal presence of the saving God in his or her belief. In this perspective, the resurrection is the principal myth. It has no historical value and it is not historically verifiable, nor should anyone wish to verify it. What is important is the meaning that the resurrection myth implies: God has given life to Jesus and made him his Christ; God will give life to anyone who responds in faith to the saving presence of God in history. The objective event in faith is the Christ-event, in which individuals come to understand that when they are weak. Then God will act for them as he did for his Christ. The cross signifies God's love and grace not as an emotion (since people already know that God loves them) but as an act of grace from the almighty judge, for the sake of the individual. The essence of the saving act is the grace of God, which makes believers surrender any attempt to realize themselves on their own. This surrender is symbolized by Jesus' death on the cross and permits a new existence (resurrection). The resurrection then becomes fact, not in the historical sense, but only insofar as the individual person is changed by it existentially. The resurrection does not mean the return to life of a dead person, a resuscitated corpse, but involves faith. Believers accept the resurrection as a sign of God's concern for them. For Bultmann the individual's self-understanding and the recognition that Jesus is the Son of God were one and the same thing.[116]

Christ as mythological means several things, from the acceptance of Jesus as an historical figure, though mythologized into the Christ of faith, to the denial of Jesus as historical. Those who take the latter position define the myth as a complete fabrication. Bultmann remained somewhat suspended in his judgment here, maintaining the historical reality of Jesus but emphasizing how little import this has to faith. In Bultmann's opinion, the early writers of the New Testament and the preachers of the *kerygma* actually used another model: the gnostic redeemer myth. The gnostic redeemer myth cannot be explained succinctly because of the various expressions of gnosticism that were prevalent in the early centuries of Christianity.[117] A summary of the myth as constructed by Bultmann includes the following: the primordial light had been dispersed among human beings and the only way these particles of light could be reunited was through the revelation of the truth, the *gnosis*, which was accomplished by a particular individual who knew the truth and introduced the initiates into it. With this as a background, Bultmann believed, the early Christians adapted this myth to fit the historical Jesus and thus the proclaimer of the kingdom of God actually became the proclaimed. The only fly in the ointment is the inability to discover such a myth prior to Christianity.

As should be evident, Bultmann used myth in a specific way that differs from the popular understanding of myth, which seems to equate it with what is false. Bultmann recognized the mythological dress of the *kerygma* and sought to recover the preaching of Jesus for twentieth century believers. He turned to existentialism for the appropriate epistemological and phenomenological categories to interpret the *kerygma* and placed his emphasis on the Christ of faith because the Jesus of history has been so overladen with mythological interpretation that it is difficult to recover any accurate information about the history of Jesus. Bultmann disavowed, then, any desire to recover the Jesus of history. To do so, he believed, would reduce faith to dependence on some kind of viable objective evidence, and this in turn would destroy the very meaning of faith. Christ is mythological for good reason.

The Myth of God Incarnate

The Myth of God Incarnate speaks of myth in a different sense from Bultmann. These writers return to a negative understanding of myth, which calls into question the central affirmation of christology: Was Jesus in truth the incarnation of the Son of God? The reason for such a question goes back to the concerns of the nineteenth century rationalists, who concluded that no serious thinker could assume that what their ancestors believed was in fact a truth that could hold its ground in the face of philosophical and scientific progress.

Michael Goulder, in this collection, begins his essay with an anecdote which deserves a smile from even the most traditional of christologists:

> A few years ago the philosopher in my department, who delights to pull the theologian's leg, asked me if I had heard the one about the Pope being told by the cardinals that the remains of Jesus had been dug up in Palestine. There was no doubt that it was Jesus—all the Catholic archaeologists were agreed. "Oh," said the Pope. "What do we do now?" "Well," said the cardinals, "there is only one hope left; there is a Protestant in America called Tillich; perhaps you could get him on the phone?" So Tillich was telephoned and the position was explained to him. There was a long pause, after which the voice said, "You mean to say he really existed?"[118]

Similar anecdotes have been heard even in the cloistered halls of Roman Catholic as well as Protestant seminaries and universities. The amusement does not mean that people who had believed no longer believe, but rather that their belief is in need of rethinking. After the years of questioning, every serious thinker has to deal with the problem of the mythological origins of Jesus, and in *The Myth of God Incarnate* various theories are proffered to explain the origin of the doctrine of the incarnation. The writers moved beyond the question of the mythological Jesus to seek the explanation for the development of the myth.

The Myth of God Incarnate concludes that there is no one explanation for the development of the myth of the incarnation. The authors believe that the particular religious, cultural and philosophical atmosphere of society, both Jewish and Hellenistic, was conducive to the development of such an idea. They suggest that the explanation of the doctrine may be found in the general synchronistic state of religion in the period. The authors reached this conclusion because no one has found a single exact analogy to the total Christian claim about Jesus in material that is definitely pre-Christian. Full-scale redeemer myths developed after Jesus and Christianity, but not before. The figure of Jesus was the means of crystallizing elements which already existed in the religious and intellectual milieu. According to F. Young, a contributor to the same work, there seem to have been four basic elements:

1. The use of phrases like "Son of God," with a wide range of implications, was current; these were applied to both human and super-human beings.

2. The apotheosis or ascent of an exceptional man to the heavenly realm was found in both Jewish and Greek traditions.

3. Belief in heavenly beings or intermediaries, some of whom could descend to help humankind and others of whom could act in judgment or in creation, was widespread.

4. A manifestation of the chief of these heavenly beings in an incarnation is found in Hellenism as well as in Jewish theological speculation.[119]

If one studies these elements already found in Jewish and Greek thought, the similarity to the developed Christian teaching on Jesus becomes apparent. There is, however, one element of caution. What is also part of the Christian belief is its staunch adherence to the man who was crucified under Pontius Pilate. The orthodox understanding of incarnation has always been firmly anchored in history, despite the objections of many historical skeptics.[120] No wonder early Christianity had to struggle against docetism and gnosticism and the various heresies that have plagued two thousand years of tradition. As long as the mythological was part of the preaching, it would be difficult to prevent the development of unorthodox christologies. As long as the entire belief was rooted in history, the mythological element could never claim complete ascendancy. Even contemporary skeptics are unable to explain the origin of belief in Jesus as the Word of God incarnate. Myth lives on.

For many people who believe in Jesus, and in Christianity, the mythological, in any sense, is completely unacceptable. The authors who contributed to *The Myth of God Incarnate*, however, claim to be still Christian,[121] as did Bultmann. More recently, a number of American New Testament scholars have returned to the question of the Jesus of history and the Christ of faith.[122] None of these scholars falls within that extreme camp of the denial of the existence of Jesus, but each in his own way separates more carefully the Jesus of history from the Christ of faith. The most controversial work at this time remains D. Crossan's.[123] For example Crossan believes that Jesus never taught the Lord's Prayer to his disciples and did not celebrate a last supper with institutionalized passion symbolism related to the Passover. All of this

comes much later according to Crossan. He also affirms that the followers of Jesus knew nothing about the passion of Jesus other than his
crucifixion.[124] No one knew what happened to Jesus' body.[125] "The
cross gospel attempts to write from prophetic allusions, a first 'historical narrative' about the passion of Jesus. Hide the prophecy, tell the
narrative and invent the history."[126] Much of what has come down within Christianity as historical has no foundation in fact. Following the
lead of Bultmann and others, Crossan examines much of what is closely associated with early Christianity such as the Lord's Prayer, the celebration of the eucharist, and the gospel passion and resurrection
accounts, and presents the development that has taken place in each
of these elements of the historical Jesus over an extended period of
time. Not everything celebrated and accepted as part of Christianity in
the early second century can be traced back to the actual ministry of
Jesus. With strenuous criteria Crossan analyzes many early Christian
documents[127] and concludes with a long list of what teachings and
events meet the critical scrutiny of historical science.[128] While not using
the title "myth" or "mythological," Crossan falls in the category of contemporary scholars who have serious questions concerning the historical Jesus who has been proclaimed in Christianity. Much less history
exists, for Crossan, than what is usually accepted.[129]

To accept the mythological element in christology does not imply
a total rejection of faith. Whether Bultmann, or Crossan, or anyone
else who critically evaluates both Christianity and its founder—each has
a contribution to both theology and to personal piety. Advantages do
flow from using the mythological model for a personal christology.

Advantages

First, the mythological model affirms the close relationship
between Christianity and the environment out of which it arose. The
understanding of the writings of the New Testament depends upon
understanding the writings and the implicit expectations of the Old
Testament and especially the speculation on Jewish Wisdom. The same
is true for Hellenism. There existed a developing matrix in the ancient
near east comprised of a mixture of philosophy, religion and cultural
elements that interacted and modified each other over a period of several hundred years. These concurrent influences did not develop in a
vacuum, but were the result of the contact of the human spirit with
various human cultures. The hopes and aspirations expressed in the
Greek myths were not isolated from the human needs of the times,
nor did the fears and anxieties expressed in the same myths spring out

of a set of theories. When Christianity arose, it found some basis in the expressed hopes and expectations of the mass culture and thus it accepted some of that culture's mythical elements.

Second, the acceptance of this model of Jesus as a "mythical" figure reminds Christians that there are some elements in christology that cannot and should not be taken as absolutes. The Christians of every age have to deal with the meaning of Jesus, and they use the terminology and the experience of the times to express their understanding of the Lord. To recall that there is such a thing as a mythological model of Jesus reminds theologians as well as believers that some interpretations of christology are time-conditioned.

Third, the value of Bultmann's as well as other theologians' approach is that it moves from a theoretical understanding of Jesus to an existential one. Bultmann the pastor tried to adapt Christianity to the needs of his fellow believers, at a time when religion was considered irrelevant. He wanted to care for the needs of believers and thus his method of demythologizing was not meant to downgrade Christian faith but to seek new expressions and possibilities for the contemporary mind.[130] The mythological model gives a fluidity of approach to Jesus that can accommodate various levels of personal perception of the value of Christianity. The scientific mind as well as the philosophical spirit can find comfort in it.

Fourth, the mythological model releases dogma from the rigidity that has often characterized faith formulations. *The Myth of God Incarnate* is direct evidence of the freedom that is afforded theologians if they accept the mythological model, even if, in the present case, this freedom has gone too far in discarding the Christian doctrine of the incarnation altogether.

Fifth, the recent rebirth of interest in the historical Jesus can ultimately contribute to a better appreciation of both who Jesus was and how Christianity developed. This in turn will encourage further evaluation of how Christianity may adapt in the future. What had been thought to be have cast in stone, coming from Jesus himself, perhaps is more time-conditioned than previously thought.

Limitations

The drawbacks of such a model, however, are equally evident. The most serious concern is the attempt to separate the historical Jesus from the Christ of faith. Development took place in the early church's proclamation of Jesus. No one can deny that. But to attempt to completely separate the two should cause much hesitation. Is it possible? Is the Jesus of history not in some way also the Christ of faith? If not, how much of Christianity can be accepted as a revealed historical religion? Is Christianity only a good, alternate anthropological approach to life? Separating the two may cause more problems than it attempts to solve.

Second, the mythological element relativizes Christianity. If Christianity rests upon a mythical Christ of faith, then there are no particular boundaries that can be ascribed to Christianity. Without a foundation, Christianity not only can develop in several directions, but will itself become so diluted that it loses its reality. The fragmenting of Christianity has already occurred in the reformation. Such a model would only encourage greater fragmentation, which would inevitably contribute to a process of internal disintegration.

Third, the mythological model could cause serious problems for the theological enterprise. Theology is the human effort to understand faith. Theology will survive as a contribution to faith only if it takes into consideration the need of the human spirit to seek not only guidance but some element of stability. To rely solely upon a mythological model removes any sense of stability.

Finally, the model of Jesus as mythological figure calls into question the very truth of Christianity. Such a model has actually led to the denial of the historical Jesus and the assertion that Christian faith is founded on a fraud. Certainly this need not be the case since some believers accept the mythical elements and still maintain their Christian beliefs and values. The model, however, does call into question the very foundation of Christianity. While it may help some believers, that percentage remains small. The mythological Christ could never be a paradigm.

Many valuable insights have accrued to the study of the New Testament as well as christology when the mythological elements are accepted. No serious thinker can reject or consider unimportant the work of the critical scholars of the past century, and in particular the work of Rudolf Bultmann and others in the twentieth century. All can learn much from the efforts of these scholars. At the very least, they have made more traditional christologists aware of the relativity that has always existed in the theological tradition. Roman Catholic theologians, who in the past were often too influenced by official pronouncements and traditional approaches, should find the mythological model of particular value. Roman Catholic theology has nothing to fear from the studies of Reimarus, Bauer, Strauss, Bultmann and others. This has become evident in the recent pursuit of the historical Jesus. True scholarship has always included in its purview insights that are considered valuable to the development of theology. The study of the Bible needs the findings of archaeology, the historical-critical approach of the nineteenth century, and the development of biology, anthropology and psychology, no matter how critical. All of these initially caused concern for traditional Christians but eventually benefited theology. For this reason there can never be a complete dismissal of the mythological school. Its truth can be of great assistance to the traditional school, just as the reflective traditional theologian can be of assistance to the more mythological-minded.

STUDY QUESTIONS AND TOPICS

1. What stands out in your mind after reading this chapter?

2. What do myth and demythologizing mean to you?

3. Has modern society grown beyond believing in God becoming human?

4. How much can people trust the Bible?

5. Does biblical criticism help or hinder?

6. Does the search for the historical Jesus make any difference?

7. Can faith be maintained while accepting a mythological Christ?

8. Does skepticism help in studying Jesus?

9. Should theologians be encouraged to rethink the meaning of Jesus without any parameters?

10. In your own words, can you see value in this model of Jesus?

Chapter 3.

JESUS THE LIBERATOR

Liberation theology, has had its ups and downs. Roman officials have waxed and waned, or perhaps have tolerated and then critiqued and sought to control.[131] For more than thirty years liberation theology theologians had labored to introduce non-Roman and non-European theology into the forum of theological discussion. Following the lead of the Second Vatican Council, they explored an ecclesiology based upon the church as the people of God. L. Boff and his fellow liberation theologians, E. Cardenal, J. Sobrino. G. Gutierrez, J. Segundo, and a host of others, responded to the experience of suffering humanity, especially in Latin America by offering Jesus as a liberator. They attempted to offer a universal theology that would link the gospel to social injustice. They taught of the liberating power of Jesus that could break down the barriers that had limited the human potential of countless millions.

In this country countless other theologians immediately recognized the importance of this model of Jesus and enthusiastically supported the efforts of these theologians in developing countries. The third world was teaching the first world in christology and people were listening! The school of the poor, the marginalized and the oppressed reached out to the entire world, and many became more sensitive to human suffering, and thus more human.

Liberation Theology Movement

In the early 1980s the liberation theology movement seemed destined to replace or at least modify significantly the theological enterprise throughout the world. Such early promise, however, has not materialized. The often close connection with Marxist philosophy associated with liberation theology, mostly false but still perceived as true, compromised the thought of these theologians in the minds of many. The church became cautious and then, in the words of Boff, "My personal experience of dealing these last twenty years with doctrinal power is this: It is cruel and merciless. It forgets nothing, forgives nothing, it exacts a price for everything."[132]

Liberation theology within the Roman Catholic traditions has not received a universal welcome. The contribution, however, of this new "universal, non-European theology" can never be overlooked.[133] The church still maintains its "option for the poor," and no true follower of Jesus can ever hide from the face of the poor, and shut one's ears to the cry of oppression. The Roman Catholic bureaucracy of Rome systematically began to exercise its power, and support for the movement and especially for the theologians began to wither. An ideology seemed to have more effect than an ecclesiology. For in the United States, the 1980s with the emphasis on prosperity, selfishness and greed, and with an administration hostile to all things Marxist, left little room for liberation for the oppressed.

Decline of Marxism

The collapse of communism and the decline in the interest in Marxist philosophy and economics have also contributed to the pushing of liberation theology from center stage. Free market economies have become the hope for all countries. Capitalism won the war over a controlled economy, and now everyone is supposed to join the parade of triumphant free enterprise. The eschatological hope in theology with a good future for all, being pulled into the present, has replaced the apocalyptic theology of suffering millions.

Perhaps liberation theology, however, is not finished, just chastened. Jesus as a liberator still makes much sense even for the capitalists of the first world. Oppression has not taken a permanent holiday from the face of the earth, and so Jesus as liberator still remains a viable model for millions of people, and is not limited to the suffering humanity of Latin America.

Some fifteen years ago Ernesto Cardenal offered an overture for the meaning of liberation theology in Nicaragua. Although the Sandinistas no longer control the country, many of the problems remain. What Cardenal wrote then still makes sense today.

Sin Is Physical

Every Sunday a group of Christians gathered to celebrate the liturgy of the eucharist in a poor village in Nicaragua. Instead of a homily, there was a dialogue after all listened to the word of God. This Sunday the people had listened to Matthew 11, the story of the messengers sent by John the Baptist to Jesus. One of the listeners responded, "I say that it is also possible that John, in a deep depression in his prison, might be doubting that Jesus was the liberator."[134] Later in the discussion someone objected that Jesus was concerned about freedom from sin and not physical freedom. Another replied:

> Freedom from sin and physical freedom are the same thing. To keep ourselves in poverty is a physical slavery, right? And it's sin too. Then what's the difference between physical freedom and freedom from sin? Sin is physical too, and to save ourselves we also need physical things.[135]

To someone suffering the oppression of economic, social and political control, Jesus brings freedom. He liberates. Salvation includes liberation. Sin is not just personal but also social. From the mountains of Peru to the rain forests of Brazil, to the coffee and cocoa fields of Colombia to the black theology in the United States, in all of the third world countries and for any group that suffers oppression, Jesus has taken on a new image. The model is not mythological, nor does it focus on the second person of the Blessed Trinity: rather, Jesus is the liberator of the oppressed. The mission of Jesus today is a political, social, economic task. To understand the origin and meaning of this new model for Jesus demands an appreciation of the scriptural studies on Jesus the revolutionary, but, more importantly, it requires a deep study of, and concern for, oppressed peoples. Different from the classical model of Jesus as the second person of the Blessed Trinity, liberation christology focuses on the human Jesus who personally experienced oppression and who lived compassionately in the midst of that oppression. The humanness of Jesus not only attracts people in need but also gives them courage to live as he did with hope.

Christology

Latin American theologians in particular have developed a christology that provides a basis for the concern about liberation.[136] In the 1960s and 1970s when liberation theology was discussed, it was often dismissed as a passing fad, based more upon economic need and political pressure than upon any sure foundation in Christian tradition. With the publication of several books on theology by Latin American theologians, however, the movement took on a different hue. Still, critics claimed that the movement lacked any clear christology. This objection was answered with the publication of works on christology.[137] More recently the criticism especially by Rome within the Roman Catholic tradition, and the general collapse of many totalitarian regimes, have caused many to wonder if liberation theology can survive. The careful study of what liberation theologians have said and continue to say must force any systematic theologian to pay attention.

The liberation theologians base their theology on the historical Jesus. J. Sobrino states that two reasons explain the current consensus among Latin American theologians: "First of all there is a clearly noticeable resemblance between the situation here in Latin America and that in which Jesus lived."[138] He does not claim that there is an anachronistic resemblance, but that in Latin America, as opposed to other historical situations, the present condition is acutely felt and understood as a sinful condition.

His second observation concerns the meaning of theology and the origins of christology: "They [the first Christian communities] did not possess a fabricated Christology."[139] The theology developed around two poles: the historical Jesus and the concrete situation of each community. The resurrection made faith possible, but in the development of a christology based upon the resurrection the early Christians had to deal with the features of the life of Jesus and thus had to select those features which would best suit their concrete historical situation.[140]

Today's church faces the same prospect. Those who see Jesus as a liberator compare the present situation in Latin America, or among any oppressed people, with the historical situation of Jesus. By means of this comparison, they seek to express in the most powerful way the faith that is present in the community. In the history of Christianity, each community has to make efforts to discover for itself the universal significance of Christianity that ultimately found its expression in church dogma. Such an effort moves back and forth between the historical Jesus and what happened to him in his situation and what this same Jesus can mean to us in our situation. To return to the historical Jesus demands an understanding of his personal situation as a Jew with two millennia of Jewish tradition, as well as requiring an appreciation of him as the incarnate Word of God.

Freedom and Dignity

Christianity is heir to God's act of liberating the Jewish people from slavery. This figures prominently in the contemporary theology of liberation. The cry of "Let my people go" in Ex 5:1 is echoed in many lands where oppression and faith are yoked together. Just as God once liberated the Jewish people from oppression, so he will continue to grant freedom to those who experience a similar oppression. This part of the Christian heritage forms a part of the actual historical background of Jesus.

The second element of the double action on which Christianity is based is the struggle of Jesus himself. Condemned by the mighty of his day, he sufficiently impressed himself and his teachings on his followers so that, eventually, aided by the Spirit, they became the heralds of a new way of living. People should not live in sub-human conditions. Human dignity belongs as a right to all, men and women, rich and poor. God has so created the human race and all members of the race deserve respect.

Jesus as an historical person embodied the sense of freedom and love and created a new way of life. The first action, which was experienced by the Jews, underlies the historical roots of Christianity; the second reveals the radical consequences of this initial experience of the liberating God. The first action is easy enough to understand. People were oppressed socially, politically and economically, and they were released from their bondage through the leadership of Moses. They began a new way of living that brought them a sense of personal and corporate freedom. Exegetical problems surround the understanding of "Let my people go" in the sense of personal freedom. No one, however, may doubt that the end result was a sense of freedom and liberation, with the possibility of this new people deciding for themselves their personal and corporate destiny.

LIBERATION IN THE GOSPELS

Good News for the Poor
Food for the Hungry
Drink for Thirsty
Light for the Blind
Hearing for the Deaf
Freedom for Those in Prison
Pardon for Sinners
Life for the Dead

The New Testament writings offer similar calls for freedom. Kingdom or reign of God as presented in the New Testament might best be considered a revolution of the old order. Jesus presented it as good news for the poor, light for the blind, hearing for the deaf, freedom for those in prison, liberation for the oppressed, pardon for sinners and life for the dead (Lk 4:18-21; Mt 11:3-5). This kingdom is not reserved for an afterlife, but involves all efforts to transform the present world. Jesus offered a sense of liberation from all that was troubling people in human history: hunger, pain, injustice, suffering, oppression and death—a liberation that would affect not only the human race but the rest of creation as well (Rom 8:22-23). Jesus as the liberator clearly stated that this hope was not some false utopia, but the actual experience of happiness for all. When Jesus began to preach he proclaimed, "The time has come and the kingdom of God is at hand. Repent and believe the good news" (Mk 1:4).

The expectation of a liberator was part of the specific Old Testament message as well as the hope of all hearts. The Jews were led from the land of slavery into a promised land, a land of milk and honey (Is 65:17; 66:22). Isaiah looked forward to the time when all evil and conflict would be destroyed and all creation would be at peace. The lion would lie down with the lamb (Is 11:6). Paul, following Jesus, had a similar hope in his vision of a time when God would be all in all (1 Cor 15:28). As the liberator, Jesus inaugurated this kingdom not as an evolution of the present order but as an actual revolution in the structures of this world. Jesus did not himself create this new world order, but he so liberated his followers internally and so strongly encouraged them that they themselves would share in the revolution of the social order. The new world will be restructured. Then this new order can reveal the glory of God as experienced by people, especially by those who have undergone cultural, political social or economic oppression. This kingdom is not just a future reality, but the presence of the future, now.

Jesus and the Kingdom

Jesus would not regionalize the kingdom of God and limit it to one model. In his lifetime some wished to make him king, thus regionalizing the kingdom to one ideology and one political system. Jesus refused such a limitation. He battled against the current structures, as can be seen in his quarrels with the Pharisees, but he rejected the aspirations for power of his apostles. If he had done otherwise, he would have been attempting to impose particular norms or solutions that would have precluded other possible norms and solutions. Jesus concerned himself with a form of liberation for people that would allow them the opportunity to develop a social order corresponding to the good news he preached. People themselves would be able to translate and make effective the teaching of Jesus in any time and in any place. His openness to many possibilities and his refusal to allow the society of his time to restrict the kingdom of God ultimately led to his death. He was disturbing the established order. He would not allow the Jewish interpretation of religion to be maintained as an absolute. His accomplishments created a new attitude toward God, human life and the future and thus inaugurated a new praxis which would anticipate the new order for which all peoples hoped.

The spirit that Jesus manifested as a liberator was born of a religious motivation, not a humanitarian one. He was aware of his personal relationship to God and sought to bring people into the same free and loving relationship. His understanding of the meaning of God and religion meant being involved in the affairs of people. Thus, what he proclaimed was not divorced from their ordinary experience. The goodness of God included a sense of personal freedom as well as of social freedom. Structures in both civil and religious society were meant to manifest this freedom and not deny its existence nor thwart its power.

The Kingdom of God

The kingdom of God signified all of this. It began in Jesus, but it was not completed. The liberator entrusted his followers to the task of establishing those structures that best fulfill the sense of his preaching. He gave the direction and people must make a response, continuing the building of the kingdom that Jesus began in preaching. The parable of the yeast (Mt 13:33), of the seed placed in the earth (Mt 4:2.29), of the wheat and the tares (Mt 13:24-30), and the dragnet of good and bad fish (Mt 13:47-50) all speak of a future which becomes nevertheless actual in the present. No complete break separates the present and the future; rather, the process of liberation involves the future's breaking into the present. Such attitudes will guard against making Christianity and its founder into some plastic image, since they ensure the perspective of the historical liberating power of the Lord.

KINGDOM

Kingship, kingly rule, reign, sovereignty—the sovereign lordship of God over his people and over the world. The communion between God and his people accomplished in and through Jesus.

The totality of salvation present in the risen Lord does not excuse the faithful from working for the experience of this salvation in a human way. A relationship persists between the kingdom of God and the kingdom which is on earth; faith does not proclaim a flight from the present world, but a renovation of this world. Certainly the field on which the struggle takes place is composed of forces of evil as well as of good, but in this struggle involves more than "religious" questions. Political activity inevitably flows from the concern for justice for all.

Jesus and Non-Conformity

The gospels indicate that one of the characteristics of Jesus was non-conformity.[141] He was a sign of contradiction (Lk 2:34), pointing to a crisis in Judaism (Jn 7:43; 9:16; 10:19). He was not afraid to counteract the senseless casuistry of the purification rites (Mk 2:27), nor the matrimonial legislation (Mk 10:12), nor the use or abuse of power (Lk 22:25-28). He examined the entire law and the prophets and submitted everything to the criteria of love of God and neighbor.[142] He liberated people not just in theory but in practice. Jesus concerned himself with those who were oppressed by the system: women, children, tax collectors, public sinners, all afflicted in body and mind. Jesus openly took their side and identified not with the establishment and the ruling class but with the outcasts, the despised, the marginal people. What he offered them was not a false sense of hope, but an attitude of mind that freed them from the oppression with which they had been unjustly burdened.

When people were scandalized with his liberating stance toward outcasts, he spoke the parable of the prodigal son (Lk 15) or the parable of the workers in the vineyard (Mt 20:1ff), or he told them he was sent not to call the just but the unjust (Mt 9:13). For Jesus the liberator there were no class distinctions: he welcomed prostitutes and heretics (Samaritans); he had a close relationship with Levi, a collaborator with the Romans (Mk 2:15-17), with a Zealot (Mk 3:18-19) and even with people who aspired to use power for their own advantage (Lk 9:46). He broke down barriers and liberated people in their social relationships by ignoring traditional social distinctions. His own attitude demonstrated his sense of personal freedom. He not only had the courage to preach liberation and freedom, but he actually lived what he professed. This alone would have caused great problems for the leaders of Jewish and Roman society.

Universal Versus Particular

Theologians and preachers proclaim Jesus as universal Savior. His life affected humanity; salvation meant a sense of peace, harmony and reconciliation that involved the entire universe. Jesus brought liberation from death and sin and suffering. Theologians used these terms and then spoke of liberation from the painful elements that are part of the human condition. But such a proclamation made sin and death and suffering universal categories divorced from their historical reality. If we accept this approach to Jesus, then it is difficult to understand why the powerful of his day condemned him. Jesus announced the good news by appropriating the words of Isaiah: "He has sent me to proclaim release for the captives, recovery of sight for the blind, to let the broken victims go free" (Lk 4:18).

JESUS AND FREEDOM

Freedom from the Law
Freedom To Ignore Useless Social Mores
Freedom To Speak with Women
Freedom To Associate with Sinners
Freedom To Interpret the Sabbath
Freedom To Overlook Social Classes
Freedom To Eat and Drink

Jesus was not content with a vague and general accommodation to his environment. He did not remain neutral with regard to the inherent contradictions of the society of his day; he actually took sides in the controversies. At the same time, he did not assume power, and thus disappointed the Zealots.[143] He alienated some people, since he attacked the Pharisees and what they considered traditional religion. He shocked the priests by rejecting their position of authority and privilege. Jesus' liberation of people was more than just a spiritual liberation. He attempted to release individuals from restraints here on earth so that they could be free before God. Liberation was particular as well as universal. Jesus refused to preach a sense of freedom that was divorced from historical reality. To be truly liberated meant freedom from all oppression. Liberation existed not in some general way, but in concrete historical circumstances of an individual's life. People do not live abstract, universal lives, and so the freedom that Jesus offered would not take refuge in false hopes. Liberation was for the individual and it was particular.

Political Versus Spiritual

Jesus as a liberator refused to assume power or to use force or violence to transform his society. The gospels do not present a political messiah, because Jesus rejected this possibility. When the crowds wished to make him king, he fled (Jn 6:15). At the same time, a purely spiritual interpretation of his ministry would misrepresent the meaning of Jesus. Jesus saw the kingdom of God in conflict with the powers in this world and would not run away from the battle. Nor is the kingdom only a future eschatological reality. The resurrection of Jesus did not mean that the struggle for liberation was over, nor did it mean that the promise of freedom was reserved for the end of time. Easter was a sign of hope and an experience of freedom, but one which included struggle. Jesus as the liberator struggled against the powerful in favor of the oppressed, but he also frustrated some of the oppressed. The Zealots of the time sought to discover in Jesus the leader who would guide them, banishing the Roman occupation, and who would re-establish Israel as a significant political force. Some of the disciples of the Lord seemed to share this viewpoint, even after the resurrection (Acts 1:16). Jesus would not accept the role of a political messiah either during his ministry or after his resurrection.

This political refusal, however, should also be seen as a political act. As messiah, he refused to change the societal relationships by freeing people from being subject to a powerful minority. Such a decision was politically active, since Jesus as liberator gave to the people the right to determine for themselves their own history and society. The refusal on the part of Jesus to be a political messiah did not preclude his followers from subsequently engaging in political activities. People have a right to establish their own politics in their own society. Social relationships are never just natural facts which Jesus could re-establish

after they had been abused or denied for a period of time. Social relationships are historical. In producing social relationships based on justice, according to the needs of the times, people demonstrate that they
can take the demands of the kingdom and the good news of Jesus seriously in their own moment in history. Jesus is the liberator since he
recognizes that in politics people can develop their social relationships
according to the prophetic demands whose champion the messiah had
become. The proclamation of the kingdom makes more evident the
historical struggle necessary if people are to be truly liberated.

To fail to see Jesus as ethical liberator causes some Christians to
retreat into a spiritual skepticism. Oppression in history and the struggle of peoples is real. The necessary resolution of social relationships
demands a commitment to the order that will accomplish this. The
Thessalonians who waited for the heavens to open to reveal the coming of the Son of Man in power and majesty, and meanwhile lived as
parasites (2 Thes 3:6-11), have counterparts throughout the history of
Christianity. Some spiritual writers may turn to the death and resurrection of Jesus as the once-for-all victory and on this basis put up with
any injustice. But this denies the reality of Jesus as the one who liberated people in more than just a spiritual sense. The tension between the
spiritual aspect of the kingdom and the physical, material dimension
that is so necessary for human life will remain. No theologian can
retreat to the domain of the spirit in an exclusive sense and still be
faithful to the teaching of Jesus.

The Present Versus the Future

Jesus did not offer any blueprint for the structures in society that
would be necessary to usher in the kingdom. He did not advocate the
overthrow of the contemporary political regime. Jesus accepted the
present situation, but not in the sense of passive acquiescence; his followers were told to develop for themselves the structures in society
that would encourage human development and thus hasten the final
coming of the kingdom of God. The absolute presence of God in Jesus
did not annihilate human history. Only in history are futures made.
The preaching of God's reign by Jesus offers the meaning for living
with the present reality. As people continue the earthly struggle for
the future, social relationships and social structures will be based upon
the good news of the gospel. Jesus as liberator frees people from the
past, not by creating a new present nor by destroying the present, but

by allowing and encouraging people to create for themselves the future they desire.

Jesus opens people up to their own future. In the Old Testament God took sides with the oppressed and led them to a new future. The exploited became the liberated as they moved out from under the yoke of social, political and economic control to set a destiny for themselves as free persons. God did not establish for them the social structures in which they would find their freedom, but gave them the impetus to work toward a better future.[144]

SALVATION[145]

Experience of Peace and Harmony
Saved from Powerlessness
Saved from Meaningnlessness
Saved from Cynicism
Saved from Self-Estrangement
Saved from Cultural Estrangement
Saved from Social Isolation

In the New Testament we can also say that God took sides in Jesus, but as was true in the Old Testament, Jesus did not deliver humanity from the task of creating its own history and its own social order so that all people could stand in his presence in freedom. In Jesus the goodness of salvation encouraged and impelled people to create a social order which would correspond to the injunction to feed the hungry, clothe the naked and shelter the homeless. If the kingdom of God was to become a reality on earth, then exploitation must be abolished. Since Jesus liberated people, those who have been freed must experience the liberation of the social order as well. "Sin is physical too, and to save ourselves we also need physical things."[146] Salvation does not mean some vague sense of feeling good or some spiritual "high." Salvation consists in the realistic awareness that the future is created in the present. No freedom exists for anyone unless all are liberated from every oppression.

Apocalyptic and Eschatological

Jesus as a liberator did not offer a panacea or an unrealistic utopia. The historical struggle continues in which temporary solutions may be all that can be expected at any one moment. But the failure to achieve total liberation need not cause the movement to disintegrate into a spiritual opiate. Actions are necessary to destroy false bonds. Actual accomplishments of liberation are essential to present the hope of that full liberation which will be accomplished only at the end of time. The presence of the spirit of Jesus delivers his followers from any mythical character of liberation, since it makes the reality present, even if only in an inchoate way. With such an understanding of liberation, various actions may be accepted as necessary—even if some are presented in Marxist categories. If no activity follows, then Christianity remains but an ineffectual cry, leading to resignation or to the rejection of Christianity itself.

Apocalyptic theology recognizes the continuation of the power of evil with little hope for change in an immediate future. It often encourages resistance that would include violence as seen in the apocalyptic literature of the Old Testament. The eschatological theology also refuses to accept the present condition, but with hope pulls into the present the ultimate fulfillment of the future. Jesus the liberator and the actual movement to create the future in liberation theology flows more from an apocalyptic theology than from an eschatological approach. Both are present in the New Testament. Liberation theology will often appropriate the apocalyptic rather than the eschatological. This will become more evident in the critique of Jesus as liberator.

Interpretation

This overview of Jesus as liberator[147] sets the scene for a further development that will involve a hermeneutical quest. The true theologian cannot be satisfied with an exegetical enterprise that remains self-enclosed, without concrete application.[148] We have already noted that the theology of Latin America comes out of praxis. The same is true for the black theology of the United States. It is the experience of oppression over the past several hundred years that has formed the matrix for Christian thought, an experience of human suffering not unlike that experienced at the time of Jesus, as these theologians understand the gospel.

Former christologies turned to the scriptures and read the images of Jesus found therein in the light of his words and deeds and within the apocalyptic framework and sociological and cultural background of the times. Such an approach is not an end in itself. This interpretation must be joined to the hermeneutical approach that seeks the meaning that Jesus conveyed. Some will seek the "very inten-tion of Jesus," just as more traditional theologians refer to *ipsissima verba* Jesus.[149] This hermeneutic is discovered in the words and deeds of Jesus. The reader, however, must carefully sift out the meaning on the basis of an appreciation of the experience of Jesus as well as of the experience of the one who actually does the sifting.

To know the meaning of the kingdom of God in Judaism and to Jesus himself is insufficient; to discover the meaning of the blessed-ness that is given to the poor in relationship to the words of Jesus is equally unacceptable. Rather, what is the meaning of the kingdom of God at its deepest level and how does this influence and affect the continual quest for its presence? The message of Jesus must be discov-ered anew. No one may be content to say that it involves the coming of the Son of Man in glory, the resurrection of the dead and the inau-guration of the new heaven and earth, without relating this message to present history.

What must be asked is: What is the message of the apocalyptic imagery of Jesus? For the theologians of liberation, the kingdom of God and the apocalyptic message of Jesus find expression in the theol-ogy that they have experienced in the suffering of oppressed groups. There is a difference in time and space and language, but careful analysis shows this new image of Jesus as liberator to be the expression of the heart of the Christian message. The kingdom of God is a total structural revolution.

Faith proclaims this kingdom to be the hope of all generations, but the gospel does not espouse any particular means to achieve it. No definite program is advocated. The gospels offer an attitude based upon the intention of Jesus as seen in his ministry. If Christians decide to take power because this appears at the present time to be the only alternative to continuous oppression, the seizing of power is done not in a spirit of vengeance, but as a reconciling response to a particular problem of social structures. If other Christians at another time renounce power and preach non-violence as the only action accept-able, this too can be the expression of a decision in accord with the intention of Jesus.

Liberation forms part of the kingdom of God and the preaching of Jesus, but cannot simply be identified with that kingdom in the gospel. The kingdom, after all, is the presence of God in a total and complete way which encompasses the entirety of creation. On the other hand, anything that can prepare the social order for the pres-ence of God, so that God can be all in all, is not only a possibility for the Christian, but an imperative.

Faith gives the assurance and guarantee that the future of the human race is the full liberation by Jesus. Already Jesus accomplished this in the resurrection. But Jesus neither in his ministry nor as risen Lord gives the key to solve all of the political, economic and social problems Christians face in history. Christianity is not an ideology and thus does not have a set pattern to impose upon the social order. Nor can anyone say that one approach is valid for all times and places and people. Rather, the presence of the liberating spirit of Jesus gives the believer and the church the opportunity to judge wisely the signs of the times. Then with the guidance of the Spirit, believers in the church will seek out those actions which will be effective in bringing some of the social structures into conformity with the gospel. Jesus desires believers to be creative and imaginative through the analysis of the present scene and in the service of a liberating ideal. The Christian should never fear to make a definite decision and risk failure in an effort to continue the mission of the Lord. Christians pray daily, "Thy kingdom come." What will be the concrete shape of the Christian response cannot be pre-determined. The believer attends to the call of the situation. The follower of Jesus seeks any expression in which the eschatological kingdom can be made manifest in this moment of time. Then people may actually experience something of the freedom that Jesus himself promised to all his followers. Jesus was the liberator and continues to effect what he once preached through the activities of his present-day followers.

Transformation Through Suffering

True transformation takes place on every level: the political, social, economic and cultural. The kingdom is present where justice prevails over injustice, where oppression accepts defeat, and where a wider sense of freedom stands firmly in history. Thus no believer can neglect the present for the sake of some future experience of salvation. Any struggle toward freedom from economic, political or social oppression is not merely a political imperative, but an imperative based upon an understanding of Jesus as the true liberating force in human history. Faith impels working for the transformation of structures.

The actual quest for the liberation of all people will also involve suffering. The cross of the liberator is not far from the backs of those who are trying to maintain their faith and continue this liberating force in the world today. Oppression by the ruling class, imprisonment, torture and even death were the experience of the liberating Lord. His followers will experience the same in their efforts to accomplish the vision that he offered.

Advantages

The Christian theologians of Latin America, as well as the black theologians of the United States and, increasingly, the theologians of third world countries in general, see in the model of the liberator a powerful response to questions that plague their societies. They also recognize that such a model allows them to move beyond the western European type of theology that has characterized much of Christian theology for centuries. The advantages of such a model will prove important for many future generations of theologians, as well as for church leaders.

First of all, this model corresponds to a felt need in developing countries and among the oppressed in any society. Some claim that the traditional Jesus stands for death in Latin America and that "Che" Guevara represents life and destiny.[150] The model of Jesus as liberator offers to Latin American Christians a sense of Jesus that counteracts this false image. Christianity becomes not an ancient artifact, but a reality that is concerned with the problems of everyday life. Jesus lives as part of the struggle that people experience; he gives not only the encouragement but the impetus to overcome this oppression and strive for more just social structures.

Second, the model brings to the fore the sense of social justice that has long been part of the Christian message but has been all too frequently overlooked.[151] Popes may write encyclicals on social justice, or council fathers proclaim an "option for the poor." This helps. But when Jesus himself becomes the liberator, the one who destroys class distinctions, the one who actually strikes out against a prevailing social order, then believers easily subscribe to the doctrine of social justice. Using the image of Jesus as a powerful liberator convinces fellow believers and religious leaders who are not yet awakened to the demands of social justice.

Third, the model speaks not just to those who are experiencing oppression on an economic and political front, but to anyone seeking a sense of personal freedom from the oppression that modern society imposes on its members. Jesus is not a weak-willed messiah, but a strong man of deep conviction who allows people of all persuasions the opportunity to throw off the shackles that have kept them in darkness for centuries. He calls all to rejoice in the sunlight of freedom. Women, the elderly, gays and the young—all need to believe in a messiah who liberates from injustice.

Fourth, the model speaks to the actual structure of the church and its self-understanding. If Jesus is the liberator, then the church cannot function in theory or practice as an institution that contributes to oppression, whether in social, moral or dogmatic matters. If people are freed from unjust restraint, then the church itself cannot impose such restraints.[152] The believer has been liberated and should feel liberated in the community of faith, the church. Liberation theology involves more than just Latin America, underdeveloped nations and the American blacks and their struggle for freedom.[153] Any group that has been victimized has a right to be liberated and to experience the freedom of God and know that they are supported by the church both in theory and in practice. Whether that group is composed of third world people or the black community in the United States or women throughout the world or the gay community or children or the aged, the church that upholds Jesus as a liberator of all people must seek positive ways to offer the sense of that liberation to anyone. Any group that has been unjustly denied a rightful position in society should feel welcomed in the church. If christology is the foundation for an ecclesiology, this model has much to say to the understanding of the church as well as church practice. The advantages are numerous for ecclesiology, as are the implications.

Finally, this model has implications not just for ecclesiology, but for all of theology. Jesus as the liberator will affect social theology and the whole question of Christian morality. Too often in the past morality was identified with sexual morality, and even in that area there was often more oppression than liberation. Morality is also involved with the social dimension of human life. Social theology will be the result of the interaction of the concrete need for liberation and the traditional understanding of Christian theology. If the church is also a liberator, it cannot impose sanctions on thinkers just because their conclusions are not clearly in accord with traditional theology. Freedom to think and express an opinion, even publicly, must be part of the liberation that Jesus offers. Otherwise the liberator is concerned with the false bondage of the human body, but is uninterested in the equally false bondage of the human spirit. Jesus of Nazareth was concerned with every aspect of the human person that might experience oppression and bondage.

Limitations

While the advantages of this model are as exciting as its many possible applications, there are also some notable drawbacks. These, however, should not vitiate the positive effect of this model of Jesus on contemporary theology.

Liberation christology often seems to make Jesus a revolutionary and to lose sight of the Christian belief that has seen him primarily as the Son of God. As they emphasize the liberator, the concern that the oppressed be freed in every way can diminish appreciation of the divine element in Jesus of Nazareth. He becomes an earlier Che Guevara, rather than the Son of God who expressed in his life the presence of the divine, even in the midst of unjust social conditions.

Second, the model tends to be reductionist. A future seen exclusively in social and economic terms short-changes the true future. Within a social and political system, the future also involves the religious, and the cultural, and includes the interactions of diverse peoples from diverse viewpoints and ways of life. The world has grown too complex to be viewed totally in terms of economics and social reform. The interplay of many disparate elements that will never be completely reconciled must co-exist within a creative tension.

Third, the political actions endorsed by liberation theology can be misunderstood. Because Jesus used violence in the temple does not mean that the Christian must turn to violence in the name of Jesus to overthrow an unjust system. Even non-violence can in itself be a form of violence. How must a believer decide what actions are to be used in trying to fulfill the destiny that Jesus has offered? So many other considerations must be weighed to ensure that the good outweighs the evil in any course of action. This is particularly true when Christians become involved with a Marxist approach to life. Marxist theory can be accommodated to the Christian gospel, but the extent of that accommodation is limited. The limitations become patent particularly because the Marxist system, as presently expressed, attempts to exclude any sense of the presence of the divine. Humanism is not the same as Christianity.

Fourth, the model of Jesus as liberator does not deal sufficiently with the power of evil in the world and in every individual. The kingdom of God will not be realized as a result of human efforts alone. The struggle will be resolved not through human power, but through the intervention of the divine, just as that kingdom was inaugurated by the intervention of the divine. The future—the harmony and peace promised by the gospel and by the liberation theologians—does not stand just around the corner, precisely because of the existence of evil. Liberation theologians may appeal to those who seek power to do so in a controlled way. Unfortunately, those who seek and actually seize power are subject to the same temptation to abuse it as those from whom they took it in the first place. Sin abounds even as grace abounds.

Finally, the chief weakness of the concept of Jesus as the liberator lies in the inability to describe "liberation" empirically.[154] What does it mean to be liberated? How can these theologians move from the level of rhetoric and sweet-sounding words to the level of everyday living? Does this mean that all the wealth of the world is to be redistributed so that everyone has the same amount without any distinctions? How would this affect the creative aspect of the human spirit? Does liberation mean that rules and regulations, especially within the church, have no place? How can liberation be practically experienced by an indigenous people in Latin America, or by a corporate executive in New York controlled by the demands of his multinational conglomerate? How would liberation, as defined by such theologians, be a guarantee of a better social order?

Certainly the New Testament gives impetus to the model of Jesus as ethical liberator; it also offers to contemporary Christianity some correctives to its social doctrine that long have been overlooked and even at times have been rejected. The contribution of liberation theologians who deal with the historical Jesus and at the same time seek to relate this Jesus to the needs of the present time can never be banished to the backwaters of theology. For too long theology has been hampered by the limitations of European philosophy without those limitations being recognized. Now an independent movement has arisen out of need which corresponds to the best of the Christian theological tradition. The interplay of the various theological approaches may be the only hope that theology has of making a contribution to a world content to ignore its reflections.

At the same time it would be highly dangerous to erect this model into the new paradigm that will seek to respond to the various questions troubling not only the Christian church but human society itself. People live in a very complex world that cannot function without the interaction of many disparate, belligerent and even essentially contradictory groups. Theology cannot afford to be so unrealistic as to offer solutions that fail to take into account the complexities of life in a day when a decision made in a small Arab state or a black nation can set off tremors throughout the world in a matter of moments.

Liberation is part of the Christian experience because it is part of the teaching of Jesus. That much cannot be gainsaid. Liberation as the paradigm of christology, as the instrument that Christian theologians will use to respond to the demands of the contemporary church and the contemporary world, is another matter. As in the case of the previous models, Jesus as liberator has definite advantages and definite disadvantages. How can theologians and people of faith understand the meaning of the life and death and resurrection of Jesus? How can all apply this understanding to the needs of today while at the same time preserving the insights of two thousand years of Christian faith? Liberation christology corresponds to the experience of some people but may not be applicable to the experience of Christ by all peoples of all times. Liberation christology forms part of the answer, but not the whole answer.

STUDY TOPICS AND QUESTIONS

1. Does Jesus as liberator fit within American society?

2. Should this model also affect the understanding of the Church?

3. Sin is physical too. Why? How?

4. "Let my people go!" What people, and let them go to do what?

5. Are all people suffering unjustly?

6. Was Jesus a fanatic?

7. Can violence be accepted within Christianity? If so, are there any limits placed on how violence can be accepted?

8. Preaching about accepting suffering is often part of Christianity. How does this affect this model?

9. Should not Christians just accept the spiritual realities without becoming confused with this world's affairs?

10. Does the apocalyptic and eschatological make any sense?

11. Who ascribes to this model?

Chapter 4.

THE MAN FOR OTHERS

The publication of *Honest to God* in 1963 by J.A.T. Robinson,[155] Anglican bishop of Woolwich, caused a reaction throughout the entire world. In this provocative book Robinson did for systematic christology what he also tried to accomplish in the study of the New Testament when he published *Can We Trust the New Testament?*[156] Both books generated so much discussion on every side that they cannot be disregarded. The former produced its own progeny in numerous articles which eventually led to a book called *The Honest to God Debate.* Robinson freely admits his dependence on two twentieth century theologians, Paul Tillich and Dietrich Bonhoeffer. Tillich's *Systematic Theology* was published in English in 1953,[157] the same year that witnessed the publication in English of the *Letters and Papers from Prison* of Bonhoeffer.[158] The publication of *Honest to God* became a climax of much of the theological debate waged in Protestant circles for the previous decade.

No doubt the provocative bishop of Woolwich had much to say to contemporary Christianity that needed to be said. Now, thirty years later, the book has perhaps been pushed to the sidelines, but there are still many elements of the bishop's theology that have found their way into the mainstream of Christian thought. The book fertilized the thinking of the church far more than was expected. Robinson entitled his fourth chapter "The Man for Others." He created this expression by abridging a phrase in Bonhoeffer's *Letters and Papers from Prison:* "man existing for others, hence the crucified."[159] Since that time the phrase has been used frequently in Christian discourse, even by Pope Paul VI and Pope John Paul II.

142

Bonhoeffer

The examination of models of Jesus must include the study of "the man for others."[160] The writings of Robinson, but even more so those of his source, Bonhoeffer, need to be included since both authors turned to this model as an antidote to a prevalent christology that overemphasized the divinity of Jesus. Robinson perceived an urgent need to rethink the relationship between humanity and divinity precisely because it had tended to be one-sided:

> To use an analogy, if one has to present the doctrine of the person of Christ as a union of oil and water, then the early Church made the best possible attempt to do so. . . . But it is not surprising that in popular Christianity the oil and water separated and that one or other came to the top.[161]

Traditionally, as Robinson pointed out, an overemphasis on the humanity tended to lead to positions that the church labeled as heretical or at least as offensive; an over-emphasis on the divinity led to positions which were comfortably accommodated within orthodoxy, but nevertheless shortchanged the humanity of Jesus. To counteract such a tendency, Robinson chose to follow some suggestions of Bonhoeffer[162] and spoke of Jesus as the man for others.

Torn Humanity

Bonhoeffer was the chief architect of the model, and to understand it as more than a clever slogan demands an appreciation of Bonhoeffer's thought. Bonhoeffer sees the origin and continuing presence of evil in the world as the breaking of the link between God and ourselves, which led to the tearing of the very fabric of humanity. The human race has been wounded interiorly by the presence of evil. People live and die painfully experiencing the sense of incompletion and the rending of what was meant to be whole. The Savior would restore the torn fabric of humanity through the reconciliation of everyone with God. For Bonhoeffer, the church is the focus where the fabric is restored and where people experience the reconciling presence of Christ.

For Bonhoeffer, the meaning of Jesus was not to be found so much in the study of his being, or through an ontological analysis of his relationship to God; rather he must be seen and understood in a functional way as the one by whom reconciliation is accomplished. He is Savior, then, primarily as the man for others. Applied to the church, this model identifies the Christian community as a group within which the man for others continues his work of reconciling and restoring. The corollary of the view of Jesus as the man for others accomplishing the reconciliation and restoration is a church continuing this mission through the activity of its members.

Church as Community

Bonhoeffer saw the community element of the church as essential, since the result of the activity of Jesus as the man for others was the building of the sense of community. Christians now belong to each other in Christ; the individual believers need each other. The one who believes in Jesus relates to others just as the individual himself discovered Jesus through others. The church is more than a place where the word is proclaimed and the sacraments are administered; it is also the place where the members of the community live in forgiveness and communion with each other precisely because of their understanding of Jesus as reconciler. Unless those who have been personally healed continue the mission of Jesus and see him as the one who offered himself to others, Christianity has no meaning. This model intimately relates the mission of Jesus to the mission of the church.

Religionless Christianity

Many people associate Bonhoeffer with the notion of "religionless Christianity" and the end of the church.[163] These ideas come from a letter he wrote to a friend while he was in prison. The letter is largely made up of questions. No doubt his thought was in turmoil as he wrote, but he did not abandon his earlier view on the church. He could not do that without abandoning his viewpoint on Jesus himself. Rather, in his personal conflict he asked questions that are legitimate for the church of every generation. He was led on by an instinctive feeling for the questions that are bound to emerge rather than by any conclusions already reached. Robinson refers to the thought of Bonhoeffer as a "tantalizing intimation."[164] Bonhoeffer had planned to write a book on the questions he proposed, but his execution by the Nazis prevented it. What he envisioned was a church different from the one he had experienced. He wanted a church that would be the expression of Christ in the world, an incarnation that envisioned Christ not as the all-knowing divine second person of the Blessed

Trinity, but as the man who gave himself in his total existence for others. Practical theology always had more of an interest for Bonhoeffer than dogmatic theology. The formation and development necessary for the Christian—conformity to Jesus, who was made man, crucified and raised from the dead—forms the foundation for his thought. The key verse for Bonhoeffer was Romans 12:2: "Do not be conformed to this world but be transformed by the renewal of your mind that you may prove what is the will of God, what is good and acceptable and perfect."

> **Conformed with the incarnate—to be really man**
> **Conformed with the crucified—to be man sentenced by God**
> **Conformed with the risen Lord—to be man before God.**[165]

God first creates human beings. Believers do not slavishly imitate Christ so that they become spiritualized; people first become human because God became human in Jesus. Christ recreated the human form before God, and he accomplished this in his attitude toward others.

The Church and Human Need

The church that flows from this model bears the form proper to humanity. The community shows a human image. The church concerns itself with the whole person and with all of the implications of human life. Religion as the external expression of faith matters little, but Christ shaping a community of people matters much. When people are conformed to the incarnate one, they become what they really were meant to be. Really free people allow themselves to live as the creator's creature. When people refuse the conformity to Jesus they fail in their very being. Such thoughts recall the remark of Camus that "Man is the only creature who refuses to be what he really is."

Conformity to the crucified one emphasizes that every person must be declared just by God and can do this only by dying the daily death of the sinner. Christians learn to die to their personal will and accept the suffering entailed. This experience of suffering, which is intrinsically bound up with the service of others, enables one to die to one's personal will by gladly committing oneself into a stronger hand.

Finally, the conformity to the risen Christ declares that every

believer must be a new person before God. Bonhoeffer understood
this in strongly biblical terms. In the midst of death, the believers live;
in the midst of sin, they are righteous; in the midst of the old, they are
new. The world notices none of this, for the new person lives in the
world like any other person, apparently undistinguished from anyone
else. The difference lies in the internal conformity to Jesus, which
makes his followers more human and more closely bound to each
other.

Ethics of the Cross

Like Luther, Bonhoeffer teaches the ethics of the cross rather
than that of glory. People do not become God; rather God became
human, and thus believers become human in the church, provided
that they see Jesus as the man who existed for others and that they in
turn fulfill a similar mission. In common with the reform tradition,
Bonhoeffer finds Jesus in word and sacrament, but especially in the
community.[166] Bonhoeffer accepts a functional rather than an ontological christology. He concerns himself with who Jesus is in relationship
to others, rather than with trying to explain just who Jesus is in himself. The German theologian could live with many unanswered questions, unlike those who have taken more traditional approaches to
christology, precisely because he studied Jesus in his relationships.
When asked where Christ is, he responded:

> He is at the border of my experience, where he gives mean-
> ing to my existence.
> He is at the center and is the meaning of history, giving to
> history purpose and hope.
> He is at the heart of nature, giving to an creation meaning
> and hope.[167]

Everyone who believes in Jesus discovers the presence of Christ in personal existence, in the movement of history and in the meaning of creation. All three become meaningful in Jesus because his existence was
for others.

The mature thought of Bonhoeffer remains unclear. He never
had the opportunity to develop his thinking beyond a rudimentary
stage and his experience in a Nazi prison limited his perspective even
more. Very often, however, the seeds of mature thoughts can be found
in the earliest writings of a person; some of Bonhoeffer's earlier con-

cepts give a clearer perspective on his christology. Such a procedure often occurs in the history of theology. The secretary of Thomas Aquinas finished the *Summa Theologica* based on earlier writings. As with those of Aquinas, these thoughts of Bonhoeffer remain incomplete, but they give a clear enough indication of the general direction.[168]

Christology

In 1933 Bonhoeffer delivered a series of lectures on christology which he claims to have had more trouble preparing than any other lectures he had delivered. These presentations marked the end of his regular academic work, since with the rise of Nazi Germany in the succeeding years he would be more and more involved with the survival of the confessing church.

The fundamental theme of the christology in these lectures was the presence of Christ. With Harnack and others, he found it impossible to make the traditional notion of the two natures the basis of his approach. For Bonhoeffer, such a stance did not deal sufficiently with the attempt to relate the meaning of Jesus to the contemporary scene. A retreat to past responses would never satisfy this theologian's need to break new ground. Also, his reform tradition reached beyond the more traditional approach to christology and allowed him to develop some modifications in what has come to be called functional christology.

Bonhoeffer chose not to use the historical Jesus as the basis for his approach. The recent studies on the relationship between the Jesus of history and the Christ of faith had caused so much confusion that only with difficulty could he base his approach on the actual historical figure. Instead, he chose the only possible point of departure that would fit his purpose. He returned to the "for me" of the reform tradition.[169] Christ-for-me does not involve dogma nor literary-historical research into the gospels, but focuses on the church as the experience of Jesus in relationship to others. The Christ remembered, systematized, analyzed, historicized, actually becomes present and continues as the one whose existence is determined by his relationship to others. The lectures were divided accordingly: present Christ, historical Christ and future Christ. Unfortunately, the final section remained unfinished.

Jesus for Me

The analysis of traditional christology can cause the theologian and the believer to get bogged down in metaphysical speculation. To know Christ, said the reformers, is to know his blessing. Bonhoeffer believed firmly in this adage. He was aware of the eternal mystery that surrounds the historical manifestation of God, but believed that the understanding of this mystery is not found through philosophy, but rather by the theologian asking the questions "What?" and "Where?" rather than the question "How?" What is Jesus for me? Where can I find him? These questions carry greater significance than the how of Jesus' person. The response to these two previous questions clarifies the mystery better than the question of how, since no one can ever come to grips with the question of how in an adequate sense. Even with the limitations placed upon the response to these questions, the possible answers can lead to a deeper personal understanding of Jesus and his relationship to the individual believer which is more important than any effort to try to settle the question of how the mystery is possible.

REFORMERS

Jesus Lives in the Word in the Church
Jesus Lives Through the Sacraments in the Church
Jesus Expects a Response to the Word
Jesus Is the Sacrament Offered, To Be Received

Bonhoeffer believed that Jesus discloses himself in word and sacrament and that he also lives in the church. As the Word, he is God's address to people and hence demands a response.[170] No communication exists unless the receiver listens and responds. The word of God addressed to humankind implies a relationship that will bind Jesus as the expression of the thought of God to those who have learned of God from Jesus in his church and have responded. Anyone can talk about Jesus as the revelation of God, but that revelation remains incomplete until people accept it.

Word and Sacrament

Bonhoeffer also sees this word present in the continuing life of the church. The community proclaims the Word of God and expects a response from the listener. Believers in Jesus speak the word of God now, even though the ultimate human expression of the word of God was in Jesus. Followers of Jesus must identify this human word as the word of God and can do so only in the context of the church. There exists one right question and one right answer. The question is found in the proclamation of the church and the answer is found in the personal and individual response of the person who hears.

Christ is also sacrament.[171] Bonhoeffer demands that all ask the question: Who is present in the sacrament?" The response: Jesus Christ, the God-Man, in his exaltation and his humiliation is present in the sacrament. Jesus is really present, not just represented in the sacrament; only one who is absent needs to be represented. Bonhoeffer's thought joins Jesus' presence in the sacrament to his presence in the church. As the Word he speaks to create the church and as sacrament Christ assumes a bodily presence in a ritual meal, but only because the church already exists as his body. Just as the word demands a response to complete the relationship, so too with the eucharist. The celebration of sacrament presupposes the presence of the church and of Jesus as the one given for others. Only in this way can he be present in a ritual meal, again defining his mode of being as one whose existence is for the sake of others. "Who is Jesus of Nazareth?" must of necessity point also to the question "What is Jesus? Jesus is the Word that is offered to others; Jesus is the sacrament that is offered to others; Jesus is the church that exists as the result of the acceptance of what is offered."[172] This thought develops further not by asking the question "How?" but by asking "Where?" Further analysis will help to understand just how well Robinson's use of the title "the man for others" sums up the particular theological perspective that both Bonhoeffer and Robinson consider to be necessary for a model of Jesus.

Jesus and Personal Existence

Jesus stands on the border of my existence, beyond my existence and for me.[173] Jesus offers to people the possible discovery of their authentic existence and forms the boundary of that existence. As the mediator Jesus restores the torn fabric of humanity and accomplishes a reconciliation between God and humankind. When individuals turn and seek a sense of peace and unity with God they experience reconciliation. Authentic human existence can be discovered only when forces within and without an individual allow for a healing of the internal spirit as well as of eternal relationships. Jesus as the one who offers himself for others in his ministry and fulfills his mission of mediator in his death and resurrection offers the possibility of accomplishing in individual lives and in personal human experience a similar sense of well-being and healing. He has already fulfilled the one true law of human existence in relationship to others, which people had been unable and unwilling to fulfill. Jesus stands eternally as judgment on the human failure to meet the demands of the law of human existence through an acceptance of the law of love. He stands at the border of existence, calling all to seek and find fulfillment; he stands beyond, since all still struggle with the forces that are alien to human life; and he stands before to help people achieve the human possibilities that are present in every life. He lives for others and for their existence.

He Is the Center of History

History expresses the universal expectation of a messiah, someone who would come to heal all of the broken dreams, and fulfill all of the shattered promises, who would bring a sense of hope and a longing for a future which is more than just a repetition of the unhappy past.[174] Jesus fulfills and at the same time destroys all human expectations and hopes. He destroys them, since the visible and triumphant messiah who would accomplish all of these hopes and expectations failed to come; he fulfills them even though the sense of perfection and completion lies hidden in the human possibility to learn from Jesus and accomplish in individual and communal lives the power of healing and reconciliation that creates the only true meaning of human life. This has already happened, since Jesus has already given himself to others. God has truly entered human history and the expected one remains here, calling people to accept their personal responsibility to live the life based upon a common and interdependent human existence.

This Christ, the center of human history, offers himself in word and in sacrament and in the church. The church thus becomes the center of history, since in this community we have the actual experience of people who are following the example of Jesus, who gave himself for others.

He Is the Center of Nature

In the original plan of God, nature was created to be the word of God, but it has been enslaved through the guilt of human beings.[175]

Nature does not need reconciliation, but is in need of liberation. Christ in his church announces the liberation of nature as seen in the sacraments, for elements of the old and fallen creation have now become part of the new creation. The church in its sacramental practice speaks for muted nature and proclaims the creative word to believers.

Human existence, human history and nature are closely connected in the thought of Bonhoeffer. Human life is always history and always nature. As the fulfiller of the law, of human hopes and expectations, of the demands of love, and as liberator of creation, the mediator performed these tasks for all of human existence.

Jesus lived first as the mediator for all people, but in so being he accomplished the purpose of human history through reconciliation and healing; he is the end of the old world and the beginning of the new world in God. Jesus frees nature from the bonds of human sin and guilt, and nature then becomes the additional means to proclaim the word of God. Existence on behalf of the human race also includes a personal offering to human history and the liberation of all of creation.

Bonhoeffer criticized the obsession of the "how" christology of traditional definitions, but he admitted the need for dogma in Christianity. He set out to study the various heresies in Christian history and concluded that a once-for-all univocal declaration about Jesus Christ is illegitimate: theologians should not speak of the divinity and humanity as objects. The question "how" raises too many problems with which it cannot cope, but it will lead inevitably to the more pressing questions of "Who is Jesus for me?" and "What does he do for me?" Still, Bonhoeffer appreciated the need for dogma. Through his reflection on the New Testament, he found two most evident and most demanding themes which can form the basis for the Christian dogma of Christ: the incarnate one and the humiliated and exalted one.

The Incarnate One

Theologians may describe Jesus as God, but they must go beyond the divine essence in which Jesus participates when they attempt to explain this concept. They cannot try to study his omnipotence or his all-encompassing knowledge or his eternity, but rather must speak of the man among sinners; the incarnate one whose life included the manger and the cross.[176] The study of christology involves the entire historical Jesus, and in this perspective theology declares that Jesus lived as the presence of God among people. In him the created recognized the creator among themselves. The understanding of Jesus as the presence of God depends upon his human environment and relationships. As a human creature Jesus attained his glory, but under the veil of the cross. To take seriously the incarnate one demands an insertion of Jesus into the earthliness of human history. In that experience God manifested himself and creation glorified him. Incarnation rests upon an existence for others.

The Humiliated and Exalted One

If the incarnation involves a sense of humiliation, then exaltation can be interpreted as a return of Christ from the human sphere to the eternal life of God.[177] But in this dichotomy, theologians often lose an appreciation of the meaning of Christ. The humiliation and the exaltation cannot be separated into two moments; they both must be predicated of the same incarnate one. Jesus is not exalted only in his resurrection. As the crucifixion brings to a culmination the life that is offered to others and for the sake of others, so the resurrection completes an experience of exaltation in humiliation. When Jesus forgives his betrayer, prays for his persecutors, and overlooks the abandonment by his apostles, God exalts him in his lowliness. Following the example of Jesus, all who actually lose their lives save those lives, not only in the future but in the present.

The church also lives by the power of his humiliation and his exaltation. Daily it re-enacts God's gift in Christ, receiving the forgiveness of sins through the real presence of the incarnate, humiliated and exalted one. In him God enables the church by faith to see the meaning and purpose of life. The one who gave of himself on behalf of others and in so doing brought about the glorification of God and his own personal exaltation continues to fulfill the same function in the church. Jesus is the man for others, found in word, sacrament and church, who calls individuals as members of that holy community to continue his mission of being the incarnation of the self-offering God in human history. Jesus promises that in following his example men and women will discover the meaning of human existence when they care for each other, feed each other, clothe each other, share a common life that rejoices with the happy and sorrows with the burdened. Then they will experience the sense of exaltation in the actual living of the life of humiliation as they await the final exaltation on that last day, when the sense of the interrelated and interdependent will be manifested finally and irrevocably. Then God will be all in all. The man for others is indeed a model that speaks eloquently to the torn fabric of humanity and offers a possibility of restoration and healing.

Bonhoeffer certainly offers to the reflective believer much thought. But whether or not anyone knows of Bonhoeffer and his writings, Jesus as the man for others continues to make sense. Jesus appeals to people precisely because of his efforts to respond to the needs of people. No one need go any further than the reading of the gospels to find in Jesus an example of how to live, apart from any theology. Whatever his origin, his destiny, his knowledge or consciousness, his ministry as someone who reached out to others attracts people. Jesus was a good person who responded to human need, experienced rejection and died. He lives on in those people who find personal meaning in imitating him and his teachings. Among the many appealing aspects of the man for others in the New Testament several stand out.

Universalism

In a world which categorizes and divides and sets limits on people, Jesus stands for all belonging. The destitute and the disposed belong. No one has to live on the periphery but all can join the circle of people together. Feeling good about life and self and others does not depend upon money or position. Everyone can feel good about life. Jesus showed the way. The little people belong as much as the big people. Men and women, old and young, children and elders, black and white and oriental and red, rich and poor—happiness and peace and contentment belong to all.

Forgiveness

Everyone has also sinned, failed, messed up, lost out, gone astray, forgotten, overlooked, been blinded, selfish, proud, envious, jealous, lustful, greedy, angry, lazy. Everyone is forgiven and everyone can forgive everyone else. Grudges just do not help. Reconciliation with family and friends and even strangers makes life not only happier but probably longer lasting. Jesus the man for others was never turned off by sinners. Rather, he turned to sinners and proclaimed that forgiveness belong to them. Therefore reach out and forgive someone else.

Kindness

The man for others treated people kindly. A kind person will always emphasize the good aspects of another. A mean person always picks out the bad, the weak, the not so flattering. The man for others could always find something good in a person whether that was a public sinner, a prostitute, a tax collector, or a boastful disciple. Kindness could dismiss certain personality quirks or habits. Kindness could always overlook the unseemly in favor of the nice. The man for others made people feel good about themselves precisely because he could find their good qualities.

Compassion

A kind man for others picks out the kindness. A compassionate man for others enters into other people's experience and life. When that experience is good, then both enjoy it more. Celebrations only make sense when they are shared. Good times need people and bad times need only oneself. Compassionate people help others to have a good time. They also help others when the times are painful. Sorrows borne by more than one seem less painful. Jesus entered into the sorrowing aspects of human life, whether the widow who lost her son or a noble whose servant was ill. The man for others never separated himself from human life, whether good or bad.

Advantages

Christology gains much in this model. In the history of Christianity people sometimes have lost sight of the actual meaning of the gospel and how it affects their personal lives. Jesus, viewed as the man for others who calls his followers to imitate him and to be for others themselves, makes clear the essential purpose of Christianity. A functional approach to Jesus allows the individual believer to live in such a way that the teaching of Jesus actually affects and is seen to affect the human condition. Francis of Assisi, Vincent de Paul and Mother Teresa of Calcutta are but a few of those whose faith has made them live for others.

Such a model also emphasizes the present reality as a reward for a life well lived, instead of emphasizing the eternal life to come. If people live their earthly existence oriented toward a relationship with others, then the present is stressed and future rewards flow from it as the natural consequence of what has already taken place. Incarnation implies that God has taken an interest in human history and is present not only in the future but today. Jesus the incarnate one has dignified the human enterprise with his presence, so the daily task of living carries with it a spiritual value that should be appreciated and enjoyed.

The appreciation of Jesus as the man for others also gives to Christian ethics its proper perspective. Believers do not live life accumulating merit; they live lives in relationship to others who are trying to better the human condition. An ethics of the cross will be the price paid, but the cost will be more than compensated for by the result—the continual discovery of true human existence. The experience of Bonhoeffer during the period of Nazi Germany helped him to appreciate the need for a determined Christian ethic that would encompass not only the experience of practical living for others but the discovery of authentic existence as well.

This model also helps to disclose what it means to be human. People are forever searching for a personal meaning in life. They ask the question often: "What does life mean?" Jesus, as the man for others, assures those believers who follow him that they will arrive at the discovery of the true human existence. This involves more than a concern for the spiritual aspect of the person; true human life involves all dimensions of the human personality.

Physical, psychological, emotional and spiritual aspects must be appreciated and allowed to develop. Such a model enhances the potential already present in the lives of people and expands the field of human activity within the Christian economy. The new life of a person finds its fulfillment after living for others, just as the resurrected Lord found his fulfillment after a life and death offered for the sake of others.

To see Jesus as the man for others gives proper place to the meaning of Jesus in scripture. The gospels portray Jesus as the one who frequently explained the meaning of his life in relationship to others. He concerned himself with the poor, the sick, the oppressed. He offered not only a healing of soul but a healing of mind and body. Jesus responded to every aspect of a person's life and in each instance took people as they were and tried to offer himself in service. "For the Son of Man has come not to be served but to serve and to give his life as a ransom for the many" (Mk. 10:45).

Jesus as the man for others serves well the interest in the social needs of human life so common today. Both within and without the church a new awareness postulates that the survival of the human race depends upon individuals becoming actively interested in each other, particularly in those who experience economic, social or cultural oppression. The haves must care for the have nots. The tendency in the past to live in isolation has been shaken by the sudden awareness that the human race lives precariously on this planet and that only through cooperation and concern for every individual can the human race hope to survive. Jesus, the individual who cared for the oppressed in every way, gives an added impetus for Christians to become involved in the critical needs of society. At the same time this model as lived effectively by Christians shows those who do not believe that the Christian church concerns itself with social problems and has taken an active role in trying to alleviate oppression. If Jesus had been seen as a man for others, perhaps some of the atrocities that have been perpetrated during the present century would have been resisted, if not wholly prevented. Christianity cannot retreat to the safety of the sanctuary, precisely because Jesus himself would allow no concern for personal safety to interfere with his service of others. With such a model in mind the Christian church must reach outside of itself and embrace those who cry out in need, even if at times this may mean an experience of pain and suffering for the church itself.

Limitations

The weaknesses of the model are also clear. Bonhoeffer, Robinson and those who accept Jesus just as a good human being tend to overlook the history of theology and the contributions that have been made in the past by great Christian theologians. A functional approach has value, but cannot be separated completely from an ontological one. All must ask not only what does Jesus mean to me and do for me but also what does he mean for himself and for God. Christians must search out who Jesus is and how he is the Son of God and the Savior of humankind. Theology before the middle of the twentieth century contained insights which should not be denied or overlooked. The emphasis of a more functional christology tends to overlook these insights.

While this model emphasizes the role of Jesus as servant, which is surely present in the New Testament, it does not deal sufficiently with other lines of thought in the New Testament. Jesus is also the Son of the Father. He made clear that his relationship to God was different from the relationship that others had to God. The New Testament has not one christology, but many. The approach of Mark, where Jesus is seen as the suffering Son of Man who does not seek personal vindication, remains as true as the approach of Luke, where Jesus appears as the perfect Greek gentleman, calm and compassionate, dedicated to God and filled with his Spirit, testified to by his life of prayerful contemplation. The views of Matthew and John must also be included. They both set forth in various degrees the servant theme, but they also see Jesus as the exalted Lord of all, who demands reverence and homage. The present model picks up one biblical theme but overlooks others. Even in the use of the New Testament for this model those authors could have benefited from a closer study of the scriptures to include other aspects of the servant theme, thus giving a fuller appreciation of its meaning. To be servant means to be united with those whom one serves. This sense of unity with those in need, as described in the New Testament, could have been used as a firmer foundation for the model of Jesus as the man for others.

After the widespread concern for the poor and the oppressed in the 1960s and early 1970s, theologians judged social ethics to be much needed but at the same time one-sided. Christianity must be involved with the poor, but it has no ready answers for the social problems of the world. The poor shall always be present, and even in the midst of poverty the gospel can and must be preached. Those who believe in Christ are not fundamentally social workers, but preachers of the good news. Seeing Jesus as the man for others can encourage certain believers to see the mission of the church primarily, or even exclusively, in terms of social justice. The tension that will always exist between the mission of the gospel to proclaim the good news of God's saving presence in human history and the mission to alleviate the plight of those who are suffering because of a lack of justice is healthy and ought not to be eliminated. The Jesus who is found in the poor is also celebrated in the eucharist, and they are not two different entities. Only when the model of Jesus as the man for others is joined with other models can this creative tension be sustained.

A further problem with such a model is that it tends to obscure the meaning and reduce the importance of the institutional church. If any person who lives his or her life for the sake of others in imitation of Jesus lives the full meaning of discipleship, then an organized Church has little purpose. Not without basis do some cite Bonhoeffer as a basis for rejecting organized religion. His own comments on "religionless Christianity" fit in here with his theology of Jesus as the man for others. But without some support from an organized body, the impetus to fulfill the mission of Jesus as the one for others can often become dissipated and actually die. For survival in this cruel and often evil world, Christians need the sense of community that comes only in the commitment to an organized church.

No doubt the model of Jesus as the man for others has much to say to the contemporary believer. It offers insights into the meaning of Jesus and helps translate his meaning into the practical elements of human life. After years of an over-emphasis on the divinity of Jesus, the model of the man for others offers a corrective. At the same time it should not be seen as the paradigm. It answers some of the questions and responds to some of the problems, but it can by no means encompass the wealth of insights that have been part of the Christian tradition. Jesus still remains, however, the man for others, his life given for the many. The true believer must learn from this model and put into practice its implications. The strength of the model is also its weakness: it presents an often-forgotten dimension of christology, but one that can obscure other aspects.

STUDY TOPICS AND QUESTIONS

1. Jesus was a "good guy." Why can't we just leave it at that?

2. Being for others helps in life. Jesus is a good model for ordinary living.

3. Religionless Christianity makes sense.

4. "What is Jesus for me?" makes the most sense.

5. How does one restore the torn fabric of humanity?

6. Humiliation comes with being for others. Is it worth the price?

7. Universalism in Christianity makes Christianity better even if it also weakens it. Correct?

8. Being like Jesus means practicing ordinary human virtues.

9. A model without much theology appeals to most people.

10. How does this model interact with theology?

Chapter 5.

JESUS LORD AND SAVIOR[178]

On June 5-7, 1992 seventeen thousand Catholic charismatics gathered in Pittsburgh to celebrate the twenty-fifth anniversary of the Catholic charismatic movement.[179] The conference attendees gathered near the spot where during a weekend retreat in 1967 a group of faculty and students of Duquesne University experienced the baptism in the Holy Spirit. From that beginning, the power of the Holy Spirit spread out to eventually affect millions of Roman Catholics through the world. The organizers of the conference expressed the hope that this return to where it all began would energize the movement out of its current slump. Such a declaration does not augur well for the charismatic movement among American Roman Catholics.

Present difficulties, however, should not detract from past accomplishments. Over the past twenty-five years the charismatic movement has involved more than ten million Catholics in the United States and some fifty to sixty million Catholics throughout the world. Presently there are approximately five thousand prayer groups throughout the United States, and, although hard to pin down, perhaps half a million Catholics participate in these prayer meetings. For each of them, Jesus has become a Lord and Savior, offering salvation to all.

During these past twenty-five years the millions of faithful followers of Jesus within the Roman Catholic tradition benefited significantly from the charismatic movement. Presently, some just grew out of their initial enchantment with this unusual approach to Jesus. For others, inertia may have robbed them of continued interest. Whatever happened over the past quarter century in the United States, however, should never be seen as limited to a particular time and place. The effects live on.

159

In recent years, many of the large charismatic groups, such as Word of God in Ann Arbor which at one time had over 1,800 members, have experienced splits over leadership differences. Many other groups have experienced similar problems. The leaders at the conference in Pittsburgh noted that in the first ten years the movement had unprecedented success but the past fifteen years have seen loss of attendance and division especially with regard to leadership.

The recent work by Kilian McDonald and George Montague, *Fanning the Flame*,[180] became a chief topic of discussion at the conference. The book seeks to make the movement more understandable and acceptable to non-charismatic Catholics. Using sources from the fathers of the church and general Roman Catholic tradition the authors attempt to demonstrate how the experience of the Holy Spirit associated with the charismatic movement was common in the church for the first eight centuries. How this will affect the general movement and understanding of the charismatics in the church remains to be seen. The conference closed with 17,000 members singing in tongues, interspersed with prophecies and spontaneous prayers. But all hopes for a new rebirth of the movement by returning to where it all began seemed unrealized.

No doubt the movement has experienced a decline. Yet such an experience of the power of Jesus and the Holy Spirit may well be the only means to hold on to Catholics in third world or developing countries, who increasingly leave the church of their birth to profess faith in evangelical or pentecostal churches. Jesus as Lord and Savior continues to remain strong for millions of Christians and is appealing to people in developing countries. The success of the Billy Graham crusade in Moscow this past year is but another sign of the power of this model of Jesus.

The experience in Pittsburgh calls to mind that which took place in Rome in St. Peter's Basilica on Pentecost in 1975. Ten thousand Christians gathered in one place and sang together: "Jesus is Lord." Believers from all over the world, Roman Catholic and Protestant, people from main-line denominations as well as from evangelical groups, gathered in Rome at St. Peter's and expressed in an enthusiastic outburst their personal and communal conviction that they had experienced the presence of the Lord in their lives. Jesus was their Lord and Savior. The Spirit had been given and they had been baptized in the Spirit to declare the wonderful insights and blessings of the Christian faith to all. In Rome, the singing stopped the Sistine Choir. In Pittsburgh, people left with a hope for what might yet come.

Beginning in the late 1960s this enthusiastic movement swept across the United States and other countries and carried with it a host of devotees. Lives were changed; decisions were made for Christ; commitments were forged; personalities were altered; barriers were broken down; hopes and expectations were fulfilled. Millions shared in the new outpouring of the Holy Spirit and came to know Jesus as their Savior. Whether described as pentecostals, charismatics, born-again Christians or evangelicals, there can be no doubt that a new phenomenon had hit the church and that, for the first time in recent history, what had previously been associated with an evangelical fundamentalist type of Christianity had found a place in Roman Catholic circles as well as in the main-line Protestant churches.

People gathered weekly or daily to express in communal prayer their conviction that they had experienced the wonders of God. Seminars were conducted for the uninitiated on the meaning of baptism in the Spirit, in reading of the word of God and on the ministry of healing. The conviction of the group that the Lord lives among them led them to see his presence in all of their decisions, both personal and communal. Enthusiasm for Jesus and for faith and for life in the Holy Spirit spread quickly as more people gathered to express their faith openly and with vigor. Even if the movement within the Catholic Church has decreased in membership, those who remain base their faith on Jesus as the Savior of all, coming into lives through the gift of the Spirit and making a radical change. The person makes a total commitment to the reality of the gospel of the Lord.

The study of Jesus and his acceptance in faith in the late twentieth century will always include some appreciation of the charismatic movement. The image of Jesus expressed in the lives of charismatic Christians has affected not only the church but politics and social life as well. That the movement has experienced some fragmentation, some decline and dispute over leadership, comes as no surprise to the student of history. These movements have always had similiar experiences. What people think of as proper to a particular time and pace in history has always been part of the fabric of Christianity. Over the centuries, the church has repeatedly experienced an ebb and fall of enthusiasm.

The Meaning of Enthusiasm

In 1945 Ronald Knox published the book *Enthusiasm*.[181] In the first chapter he writes of the choice of possible titles for his work and claims that he has settled for *Enthusiasm*, "not meaning thereby to name (for name it has none) the elusive thing that is its subject. I have only used a cant term, pejorative and commonly misapplied as a label for a tendency."[182] Knox's purpose was to offer an understanding of a recurrent theme in the history of Christianity whereby certain individuals choose to live a less worldly life, or seek to restore the earlier experience of the church, or allow the full presence of the Spirit of Jesus to guide their lives.

In the history of the church very often these movements attempted a fresh approach to religion. What had been an external and often empty form of observance now became an affair of the heart involving the entire person. Tired of what passed for formal religion, these enthusiasts wanted something else. Their religious personalities suited them well for an experience of the Holy Spirit.

> Sacraments are not necessarily dispensed with but the emphasis lies in a direct personal access to the Author of our salvation with little intellectual background or liturgical expression. . . . . An inward experience of peace and joy is both the assurance which the soul craves for and its characteristic prayer attitude.[183]

Knox then treats some of the characteristics of the movements that have recurred in history; often there is ecstasy, prophecy, people breaking out into unintelligible utterance, identified at times by expert evidence as a language unknown to the speaker.[184] Although written in 1945, any contemporary charismatic will identify with these same characteristics.

Throughout the book Knox examines the enthusiastic movements that have recurred in the Christian tradition, but it must be admitted that his personal position toward them is not one of "enthusiasm." In the last paragraph of his final chapter, Knox affirms that the institutional perspective of the Roman Catholic Church does not mean that it lacks all spiritual initiative. The church maintains the new as well as the old. Then he admits the danger in such an institutional position:

> Where wealth abounds it is easy to mistake shadow for substance; the fires of spirituality may burn low and we go on unconscious, dazzled by the glare of tinsel suns. How nearly we thought we could do without St. Francis, without St. Ignatius. Men will not live without vision; that moral we do well to carry away with us from contemplating in so many strange forms the record of the visionaries.[185]

His final line is a quotation from *La Princesse lointaine*:

Frere Trophime: Inertia is the only vice,
Master Erasmus: and the only virtue.
Erasmus: Why?
Frere Trophime: Enthusiasm.[186]

Jesus as Lord and Savior creates enthusiasm. Throughout history the Jesus of personal salvation remains as an integral part of Christianity. This model needs to be retained and explored because for many the Savior is most personal and thus most important. Unlike theological discussions, personal Savior reaches into the depths of the human soul, and the individual, open to this power, feels the effects. The change brings a becoming, newness of being in faith.

Redemption

The New Testament itself shows no great interest in the meaning of redemption, but the Old Testament background of this notion colors any sense of salvation and savior. Redemption in the Old Testament refers principally to the "buying back" of the firstborn dedicated to God (Ex 34:20; Num 18:15). Later, it refers to the action of God in redeeming Israel from the slavery of Egypt (Dt 7:8; 24:18). In the later writings of the Old Testament redemption is transferred to the individual whose redemption equals liberation (Jer 15:10).[187]

The writers of the New Testament continue to use this Old Testament image, but with even greater emphasis on the aspect of liberation. The implications of buying back are almost never referred to, with the possible exception of Mk 10:45: "The Son of Man also came not to be served but to serve and to give his life as a ransom for many." Matthew takes this saying from Mark and incorporates it exactly into his account in 20:28. Perhaps the early church had some notion of the buying back which then quickly fell into disuse. Jesus did not need to buy back humanity, for humanity always belonged to God. Even the above passages, however, lack the notion of ransom that is often found in the medieval writers. For some, redemption was the buying back of humanity from the devil. But even for the most rudimentary of theologians, such a notion deserves no position in Christian theology.

Redemption was part of the background of the New Testament writers, but they were not overly concerned with the notion. The writers of the New Testament interested themselves and their listeners with Jesus as Savior. The notion of liberation, however, persists because Jesus redeemed people from sin, from the "principalities and powers," from the law and death (Rom 3:24; 1 Cor 1:30; Eph 1:7; Col 1:14; Heb 9:16). The one additional note from the New Testament congruent for the discussion on Jesus as Savior is the conviction that Jesus died and rose for all. Jesus accomplished universal redemption (Phil 3:10; Rom 4:25; 1 Cor 6:14; 2 Cor 4:14). Instead of "buying back," redemption in Christianity came to mean preserving and then surpassing the goodness that God had planted in creation which had been marred by sin.

Salvation

The New Testament, however, frequently speaks of salvation and Jesus as Savior. Jesus preaches salvation by the proclamation of the kingdom of God. With him God established a communion with his people which means that now they are saved. The gospel itself is the message of salvation: "To us has been sent the message of salvation" (Acts 13:26). It is the way of salvation: "These men are servants of the Most High God who proclaim to you the way of salvation" (Acts 16:17). It is the power of God for salvation: "For I am not ashamed of the gospel; it is the power of God for salvation to everyone who has faith" (Rom 1:16).

The actual content of salvation in the New Testament offers a wealth of meaning. The death of the Lord created present salvation for all with its liberation from law, sin and death (Rom 6:1ff; 1 Tim 1:15; Eph 2:1-10); God offers divine adoption (Rom 8:17); grace justifies people (Rom 3:24). Believers already experience the saving presence of God in their lives through Jesus even as they await the full expression of salvation (Heb 9:28; Rom 8:24; Phil 3:20).[188]

The authors of the gospels present Jesus as the one who offered salvation. The angels proclaimed it to the shepherds (Lk 2:30). Jesus himself extended it to all who would listen: the upright and the sinner, the rich and the poor. Each person had to make a personal commitment to the Lord as Savior in order to experience the saving presence of God. Jesus broke the power of evil. Satan fell like lightning from heaven (Lk 10:18). No longer might people think of history's outcome as either good or bad. Goodness is the only response. An irrevocable communion has been established between God and humankind. Evil and sin can never totally overcome the fundamental sense of goodness and unity that every human being has as a gift. Humanity is already graced in its fundamental orientation to God. This gift then becomes actualized in the graced individual who has responded in faith to the Lord. Jesus as redeemer and Savior offers the assurance that God and goodness have already triumphed. Peace and harmony and truth have become not only possible, but actual. The blind have seen; the lepers are cleansed; the lame walk; sinners have turned from their sins and people can walk in dignity because they have responded to Jesus as their personal Savior. He offered not only a salvation for the future, but a present reality. The New Testament teems with references to what was accomplished within human lives. As Savior he preserved them physically, psychologically and spiritually; he was a presence that healed mind and body and soul. He fulfilled Israel's expectations and longings for someone to restore the torn fabric of its covenantal history.

Contemporary enthusiasts turn quickly to scripture and find in that record of revelation the fullest meaning of Jesus as Savior. Throughout the gospels individuals come to Jesus and express their commitment to him in faith and thus experience his saving power. Jesus enters into their lives and they become whole. Life makes sense as they profess faith in Jesus as their Savior. The same must be true today.

Evangelicals have long emphasized this model of Jesus. The history of Christianity in the United States demonstrates this concern. Traditionally, thousands of "born-again Christians" continue to make their personal affirmation in faith after a moving presentation by a powerful preacher of God's word. Most Americans have witnessed, at least on television, the magnetism of evangelists such as Billy Graham. Many have participated in Protestant revival meetings or in the missions that used to be conducted regularly in American Roman Catholic parishes; these evoked a similar sense of repentance and commitment. Through these missions Roman Catholics often experienced a call to return from the ways of sin to receive the healing forgiveness of Jesus in the sacrament of penance. The parallel evangelical approach would have appealed to the sinner to change his or her way of living and make a permanent and personal commitment in faith to the saving presence of Jesus.

Saved from Sin

As Savior, Jesus was concerned principally with the healing of the soul, the spiritual dimension of human life. Jesus saved people from sin and helped them to overcome their evil tendencies. Even when he did not always accomplish the total conquest of sin, a person believed that the Savior would overlook individual failings, provided that the person had made a personal faith commitment. Jesus in his lifetime told people to sin no more; he continues to echo this same refrain throughout human history. The soul, the spirit, needs the saving presence of God. Jesus responded by giving people a sense of fulfillment in their spiritual lives. They could turn their backs on a life of sin and walk away from the darkness of evil into the light of goodness and truth. The evangelists preached the same theme, and it finds its expression in the charismatic movement today. Jesus continues to call his followers to make a basic commitment so that they can turn away from sin and become his holy people.

Baptism in the Spirit

For many people who have become part of the charismatic movement, baptism in the Spirit initiates this spiritual moment.[189] People record how they have experienced the Spirit in a most intense and personal way through the instrumentality of others. While part of a prayer group, and often aware of personal resistance to the movement, the individual experiences a sense of God never experienced before. All of a sudden individuals know that their lives have been affected by the presence of God through Jesus the Savior and there can never be a return to a former way of living. Because of his born-again experience Charles Colson faced his prison term from Watergate calmly and afterward decided to devote his life to the spreading of the gospel of Jesus. Renewed in the baptism of the Spirit, his life purpose became a testimony to the presence of Jesus as his Savior, and the Savior of all.

For others the experience of Jesus as personal Savior has not been so foreign to a previous way of living. Many good Christians have experienced the baptism of the Spirit and found their Christian faith taking on an element that was previously lacking. They become enthusiastic about what they believe and grow in their personal commitment to the gospel message. Faith existed previously, but now it has been kindled to a new brightness. They begin to see everything in the light of the gospel and live accordingly. Again, often enough, these people were at first reluctant to get involved, but once part of the movement they too have become apostles who want to lead others to a similar commitment. They have been healed in soul by the presence of Jesus as Savior and will never again be the same.

Healing

The model of Jesus as Savior does not stop at the healing of the soul. Jesus concerns himself with people and thus with the bodily aspects of human life as well. If Jesus is the personal Savior, he must also be interested in the physical ills of his people, just as he was concerned with the physical needs of the people of his own time in Palestine. Thus, healing is closely associated with the charismatic movement.[190] The preacher will announce the presence of a sufferer with a particular malady and will declare that the illness is now cured. Or an ill person will come to be healed through the laying on of hands by the leader or by the entire group. Scores of people have attested to healings through contact with the healer or through the ministry of a group of believers. Jesus as Savior continues his healing ministry through the activity of the believing community. Once again, the lame walk, the blind see, the deaf hear, all through the power of Jesus present among his people. The Savior promises and fulfills his promise.

For the first time in recent Roman Catholic history, priests preach healing. Thousands will travel for miles to attend a healing prayer gathering led by one of several Roman Catholic priests. Not unlike traditional American pentecostals, people with illness experience a healing through the laying on of hands. Jesus the Savior, through the ministry of priests, reaches out to suffering humanity and brings physical healing.

When an individual believes in the power of Jesus as personal Savior, then that person can lay claim to the power of the resurrected Lord. This belongs to the Christian community by right—not because of anything anyone has done, but because of what Jesus has done for them. With such a claim, God will of necessity respond because God has so promised. Whatever is asked in the name of Jesus will be given. The enthusiasts will not excuse God from working miracles. Rather God must work miracles because God has bound himself to heal in Jesus his Son. The Savior must be interested in the sufferings of his people and must help them. All the believer has to do is turn to the Savior with complete confidence. Indeed, an incredible number of people seem to have been cured, and this has not been confined to what was once called the evangelical churches. Lutherans, Episcopalians and other main-line churches join the Roman Catholic community with charismatic leaders who bring the healing presence of the Lord to sick and troubled persons.

Healing of Memories

Finally, the experience of Jesus as personal Savior also includes the healing of the psyche, the emotional and affective part of the human personality. Very often people need psychological healing, even more than spiritual or physical healing. In many instances the psyche prevents the person from knowing the saving presence of God, so it must be healed first. The Savior concerns himself with how people feel and offers solace and comfort. People especially need the healing of memories. The contemporary charismatic movement has helped us to appreciate that. People do not need to carry forever the burdens of their past. They can experience the presence of their savior, whose presence heals the wounds inflicted by the past.[191] People crippled emotionally need not continue in such a condition. Too often the bad moments of the past reach into the present and prevent a person from enjoying the blessedness of life. The Savior knows the needs of his followers and responds generously to those who have trust and faith in him. Memories are healed. People can walk away from the pain of their history and live in the sunlight of God's love.

As a result of the experience of Jesus as Savior the believer will want to become an evangelist and lead others to experience the same saving presence of God in their lives. The contemporary experience shows a blurring of denominational lines among those who accept this model of Jesus. Whether one is a Roman Catholic or a Baptist or a Lutheran matters little. The faith dimension that has led an individual to know Jesus as Lord is everything. Many can be united into the one band of believers who have made their personal commitment to the Lord.

Community and Life's Meaning

This enthusiasm also creates a powerful sense of community among believers. Christianity, no longer limited to Sunday observance, colors every aspect of a person's life. The word of God becomes important as the vehicle for the Spirit and people become devoted to its expressions. Savior takes on a meaning that will be present in the ordinary details of human life and not restricted to the confines of textbooks.

People who have accepted Jesus as Savior find new meaning in their lives. Life is not absurd, because the commitment to the Lord and the service of the brethren gives direction. The courage to live for others after experiencing the presence of God in Jesus gives a value and a purpose that cannot be adequately described unless the individual has experienced it. All people should live as Jesus lived, through the gift of the Spirit.

Believers are assured in the depth of their being that God holds their personal future and the future of the human race in his loving hands. No dark and mysterious force manipulates us. God's loving care controls our destiny and gives us the possibility of doing something with our lives.

Cynicism has no room to exist. Christians will never emphasize what is wrong or evil or bad or sinful, nor will they mock the presence of goodness. Christians are not the losers in life, but the ones who actually have achieved something of the peace and harmony that all desire. They have found themselves, for they have found their Savior; they already experience benefits from his life even as they look forward to a better future.

The Savior knows that all have failures, even when they have committed themselves to him. The Savior redeems from all personal failure by telling his followers that in spite of sin the person has value in the eyes of God the Father. A new possibility exists. People can be more than they are at any one moment; they can always bring some sense of goodness to the fore and come closer to living the way that will bring peace. Even in the midst of personal failure those who have been saved know that they still remain precious in the eyes of God, of Jesus and of his holy community. Whoever has been saved knows no sense of isolation. Jesus is the friend who will never fail, the faithful one who will never be lacking in fidelity, even when people are unfaithful to him. The isolation and aloneness that often characterize human life find no place among those who have come to know Jesus as Savior. They always have the Lord, and they always have around them other believers who have also experienced his saving presence. Jesus as Savior redeems and saves his people with a richness often lost in words. Jesus saves his faithful ones from the power of evil and sin and gives them moments of peace. Far too many Christians experience each other as forces of damnation rather than of salvation. If people come to see and accept Jesus as their Lord and Savior, the power of evil will be lessened in this world and in the lives of people. The Savior will be the one who heals and restores, not only in theory but in fact.

Advantages

On a personal level, the advantages of this model are legion. First, scripture establishes the foundation. Jesus came to heal people in mind and in body. He called for a change of heart and a change in living and promised to be with his followers and to give them the presence of his community. Everything that Jesus accomplished in the lives of his contemporaries he continues to fulfill in the world today. The model thus recaptures an understanding of Jesus found in scripture and often overlooked in some of the theology and religious practices that have developed in the Christian tradition.

Salvation is concerned with the healing of the whole person, not just the soul. This model embraces the totality of the human being and relates the presence of God to that totality. Christianity as a religion is concerned not only with individuals' souls, but at the same time with the maladies of mind and body that mar that soul. The model relates Jesus to the many facets and the many needs of human life and presents him as someone who is concerned with all these facets.

The model depends on a personal commitment in faith to the Lord. Many Christians belong to a church but never have made such a commitment. Just because people have grown up with Christianity does not necessarily mean that they have ever accepted Jesus. The call for a commitment in faith to Jesus as Lord and Savior emphasizes the role of individual faith as the foundation of Christianity. No one can go through the motions of being committed to faith without the personal relationship to the Lord.

The model also emphasizes the community aspect of Christianity. Those who are committed to the Lord join together in a life of fellowship and mutual care. Isolation and alienation should never be a part of Christianity. Those who have come to believe in Jesus as personal Savior create a spirit of commitment to each other. Groups of charismatics manifest a genuine concern for each other that often astounds those outside the movement. The bond of faith in the Lord blossoms into a sense of mutual love of the brethren which the gospel of John claims as an essential characteristic of the Christian community.

This model also has a definite effect on believers, since they tend to become evangelists themselves—people who proclaim the good news of salvation to others. These believers do not hide Christianity under a bushel basket, but proclaim it from the rooftops. They become enthusiastic preachers of the Lord, calling people to experience what they themselves have known. From a small movement, the charismatic community in the United States grew to include hundreds of thousands throughout the world. The modern-day evangelists offer someone to believe in, someone who is concerned with every aspect of human life. They preach and bring the good news to others with a sense of dedication which rivals that of the earliest preachers of the gospel and the most effective heralds of Christian history.

This model also contributes to a sense of well-being for the believer. If Jesus is Savior, then there is nothing to be ashamed of in human life, no need to harbor the bad dreams of the past; belief banishes the sense of guilt that sometimes plagues every believer. Jesus has died and risen and has brought forgiveness and peace. No matter what a person may have done or failed to do, no matter what a person may do in the future, the Savior never abandons his faithful ones. Sin can never destroy the fundamental sense of union that exists between the believer and Jesus:

> For I am sure that neither death nor life, nor angels, nor principalities, nor things present, nor things to come, nor powers, nor height, nor depth, nor anything else in all creation can separate us from the love of God which is in Christ Jesus (Rom 8:38-39).

The commitment is too strong; the love of God too powerful. Such faith offers the believer no license to commit evil; rather, it helps an individual to rise from sin and failure without having to bear the damaging burden of guilt. The one who called sinners will always call sinners and will always offer forgiveness and peace. He does not hold grudges against people, but as Savior he promises pardon to those who will turn to him in faith. Salvation is real for anyone who seeks it and accepts the offer.

This model also unites various Christian bodies in a unity of faith that has rarely been experienced in history. The denominational differences that have characterized the history of Christianity, especially during the last four hundred years, are not nearly so important as the bond of faith and love that should exist among people who have accepted Jesus as Savior. The common bond of unity in Jesus creates a larger Christian community. The differences remain, but can never obliterate the presence of Jesus as Savior gathering his flock into one fold.

The richness of this model can be seen in the lives of those who have come to accept Jesus as Lord. People seem dramatically changed; minds, bodies and souls are healed; people are united with each other; lives become more interesting; peace and harmony now characterize the human story; Jesus is real in personal lives. No wonder that so many have turned to this model of Jesus.

Limitations

Although well in accord with scripture, the model does not embody the full picture of Jesus as presented in the gospels and letters. Jesus the personal Savior is also the transcendent one; he is the Word of God made flesh and experienced as Savior, but he still remains the Word of God, the eternal one, present with God (Jn 1:1.18). While the proponents of this model do not deny these dimensions of the gospel Jesus, they seem to fall into shadow. In addition the Savior did not work the miracles of healing that would save all people from all ailments. He raised Lazarus from the dead, but allowed him to die again. The various images of Jesus from scripture cannot easily be reduced to one approach.

This model, especially as evidenced in some of the devotional expressions in the charismatic movement, can tend to create an elitism in the church. Historically, as Knox noted, the enthusiasts have tended to separate themselves from anyone who did not agree with them totally and have taken the stance that anyone not like them falls short of the full living of Christianity to which all are called. The enthusiast considers the exceptional experience of God the norm, the standard of religious achievement. "He will have no almost Christians, no weaker brethren who plod and stumble."[192] A sense of "holier than thou" can develop which, instead of strengthening the presence of God in the community and enhancing mutual love, can tend to divide and destroy.

In their devotion to the word of God, enthusiasts sometimes tend to interpret the word of God in the most fundamentalist sense.[193] The Bible is accepted without limitations, even though it was written by limited human beings. The Bible can become a magic talisman—not only to give direction, but actually to plot the future and respond to all the questions of human life in a definite, clear and simple fashion. Scholarship is ignored as unnecessary or despised as unworthy of faith. Since the charismatic movement involves a broad cross-section of the church, with a special appeal for those who are looking for clear answers, anyone who tries to present a different opinion on the Bible is sometimes seen as lacking in full faith or at least as dealing with issues which do not concern the true believer.

"Jesus as Savior" can so emphasize the relationship to Jesus that the whole sense of the church as an organized community of believers falls into shadow.[194] The sacraments, which are meant to be the outward expression of faith are considered of minor consequence when compared to the baptism of the Spirit and other charismatic gifts. And while the ecumenical aspects of the model are heartening, it can lead to a false irenicism. In this false enthusiasm, doctrinal differences among the Christian churches are summarily dismissed.

Many have experienced the healing presence of God physically and emotionally as well as spiritually, but thousands of believers, many of them in the charismatic movement, seek a healing of mind and body and do not experience it. Is this due to a lack of faith? What of the suffering of the innocent? If Jesus as Savior can perform miracles, is he not discriminating against those he does not heal? Even those who seem most faithful to him experience painful deaths, which seems out of character for his goodness.[195] Does the model deal sufficiently with the power of evil and sin and suffering in life, or are there other components that have been overlooked?

A paradigm responds to more questions than an ordinary model; it allows for greater development of possibilities. According to this standard, the model of Jesus as Savior cannot be the paradigm, for too many important issues remain unanswered, not the least of which is the question of human suffering.

The sense of prayer, the commitment of the people to the Lord Jesus, can never be gainsaid. Historically, the enthusiastic movements flourished at different periods, often in reaction to the rigidity in Christianity and sometimes because of the lack of attention paid to the role of faith. With the passing of time, the groups often became more rigid than what they rebelled against; they tended to cast into shadow certain fundamental elements of Christianity while they stressed others. They splintered over problems of leadership.

The sobering remarks of Ronald Knox should be recalled, however, at the end of this chapter as well as at the beginning:

> Where wealth abounds, it is easy to mistake shadow for substance; the fires of spirituality may burn low and we go on unconscious, dazzled by the glare of tinsel suns.[196]

Because of enthusiasm, inertia is not only a vice but a virtue. Instead all must trust everything to the kindness of a loving Savior. That is the virtue. However, Christians cannot run from the world, refusing to recognize its problems and what can be done to solve some of them. That is the vice. How difficult to unravel the two!

STUDY TOPICS AND QUESTIONS

1. Charismatics make no sense. Charismatics are the only real followers of Jesus.

2. No one should criticize people coming together to pray and experience the Holy Spirit.

3. Enthusiastic movements have always been in the history of the church. What are these movements contributing today?

4. What is essential is belief in Jesus and not a hierarchical and sacramental Church.

5. How do redemption and salvation make sense today?

6. True healing takes place.

7. The healing that takes place is all psychological.

8. Only "unusual" people follow this approach to Jesus.

9. The model helps millions. Why do you think this is true?

10. This is another model without much theology. Maybe theology is not as important as usually thought.

Chapter 6.

THE HUMAN FACE OF GOD

Recent study on the meaning of christology has focused on the humanity of Jesus. Today, the uniqueness and universality of the Lord does not arise from his divinity but from his humanity. Movement back and forth, from an emphasis on the humanity to an emphasis on the divinity, has always characterized the history of theology. The ancient school of Antioch, which emphasized the humanity, and that of Alexandria, which emphasized the divinity, have had their counterparts throughout history. Today the pendulum seems to have swung in favor of Antioch.

Theologians today often present Jesus in the context of anthropology. Jesus is the point toward which the human race has always been directed;[197] or, the humanity of Jesus is a new way of being human;[198] or, the deity does not exclude but actually includes humanity;[199] or, the human in Jesus is the realization of the divine;[200] or, Jesus manifests God as the compassion of God.[201] These new approaches are found in popular magazines as well as in scholarly journals, so the Christian world knows what is being said, even if at times there is little understanding.

The principle that underlies this approach locates the unique universality in Jesus precisely in his being human. This christology is not from above and deductive, but from below and inductive. Theologians do not discuss something that is above or below or beside, but a reality that is within; the human expresses the divine. God chose as revelation the human form, the man Jesus. The mystery of Jesus lies in his humanity. The human becomes the localization of the divine. With this perspective theologians must ask, "What does it mean to be human and what does it mean to be divine?"

The Human and the Divine

At first sight it seems easy to respond to the question "What does it mean to be human?" On closer scrutiny, the answer is not so evident. What characterizes humanity? Is there a difference between being human as a man and as a woman? Does age affect the meaning of humanity? Do circumstances, such as culture or education? Are there limits to what a human being can be? Can what is human be defined as "what humans do"? If so, killing and destroying are as human as love and compassion.

What does it mean to be divine? Everyone has some idea of divinity. Power, knowledge, eternity, authority, control love, mercy—all have been associated with divinity. But what does divinity mean? If God has created humankind in his image, has the human race done little more than repay the compliment? When people accept a divine revelation based upon faith, how much of the content is the result of human projection, offering God-for-humanity but not God in self? Does the unveiling of God imply a further veiling?

Christianity believes that Jesus revealed God. But how is it possible for the human to be the vehicle of the divine? Can anyone really separate what is human and divine in Jesus? If everything is perceived as both human and divine, does such a prospect lose sight of the divinity, or of the humanity? At the very outset the question poses a problem in trying to discover how the human can be the expression of the divine. If people are not sufficiently clear on the meaning of humanity then surely no one can completely delineate the meaning of divinity.

The behavioral sciences in recent years have shown that words like humanity, human nature and human behavior are empty formulas that can be filled with disparate elements. Humans kill and betray, they lie and cause suffering as well as love and forgive. The most noble qualities can be predicated of being human, as can the most debased.

Theologians say that the concept of the divine needs rethinking; God can be in process. This means that the qualities traditionally associated with God can be forgotten. God can become in human history. Change is possible even with God. But does this new process theology also fall into the same trap of creating God in a human image?

The ability to respond to all of the above questions escapes a grasp. Yet, Christians have a faith statement that God is present in Jesus and believers come to know God through Jesus; he is the human face of God.[202] "Philip, he who sees me sees the Father" (Jn 14:9). Since theology is faith seeking understanding, the faith statement remains.

Then the pursuit of the contents of that faith statement is possible, even if the conclusions forever remain limited.

The Foundation

The examination of Jesus as the human face of God involves questions of anthropology as well as of history. Was Jesus, in an historical moment, the fullness of what it means to be human, the definitive and eschatological man, the new man, the primordial image for all of humanity? Do people learn what it means to be human by observing the life and death of this historical person? These questions pre-suppose another faith statement: humankind is created in the image of God. "So God created man in his own image, in the image of God he created him, male and female he created them" (Gn 1:27).

FAITH STATEMENTS

Jesus Is the Image of the Invisible God
All Are Created in the Image of God
All Are Marred by Sin
All Need Faith To Believe in Themselves and in God

Within the Judaeo-Christian heritage all people are created in the image of God; they can manifest God; every person can be the vicegerent of God, manifesting some of the qualities of the divine. The image is not limited to the spiritual nature of the person but involves the totality. An inherent dignity results which is humanity's heritage and destiny.[203]

Christians recognize Jesus to be the image of God in an exemplary way:

> He is the image of the invisible God; the first born of all creation (Col 1:15).

> He reflects the glory of God, and bears the very stamp of his nature (Heb 1:3).

But Jesus is not separated from others who are also created in the image of God. He will always be the firstborn of many brethren and like us in all things but sin (Heb 4:15). Understanding Jesus as the human face of God depends first upon believing that every person is created in the image of God and can thus reflect the same.

To fill out the words "humanity" and "human nature" with content and then apply them to Jesus, however, cannot just mean predicating a way of being human as the final criterion for the humanity of Jesus. There will be differences as well as similarities. Jesus lived, for example, without the influence of evil and sin. In faith followers of Jesus learn that the usual understanding of being human is not accurate. Jesus of Nazareth presented a meaning of being human sufficiently transcendent to apply to every human being. Humanity or someone's idea of what it means to be human is not the measure of evaluating Jesus, but rather his humanity is the criterion by which people not only judge themselves but even come to realize their potential.

Jesus as the human face of God was the revelation in a personal way of the meaning of God. The two elements, the human and the divine, are not disparate or separated, but are united in one historical person. This implies further consequences. This revelation of God took place in a personal way, circumscribed within the finite limits of the human Jesus, this historical person. In Jesus people may experience the presence of a being at one and the same time "for humanity and for God." [204]

Why Jesus Was the Human Face of God

If all people are created in the image of God, if all have the potential to manifest the divine, then why is Jesus singled out to be the human face of God in an exemplary way? What is it in Jesus that differentiates him from millions of others who bear the face of the human and contain the stamp of the divine?

The human exhibits inherent limitations in attempting to express the divine. Believers need not try to measure Jesus against some abstract concept of humanity; no a priori principles need to be established from which deductions will flow why Jesus is the exemplary image of God. Rather, the procedure begins with the human Jesus and relates his experience to all human experiences. Study his life to discover how, in his living, others experienced the divine. This process will discover what humanity means, or at least what humanity meant to the historical Jesus recorded by those who believed he was the presence of God.

Such an attempt involves investigating the self-awareness of Jesus. That immediately causes hesitation. How can anyone enter into the personality of Jesus, seeking to unravel the fundamental way in which Jesus is present to himself as an individual? The task of exploring oneself is difficult enough; how much more difficult it must be to attempt to deal with the self-awareness of another. Yet, the words, actions and attitudes of Jesus as recorded in the gospels can teach much about his self-understanding. The study must always be incomplete, but with careful examination of the impact Jesus had upon others some entrance into his personal life can be gained. This helps to situate Jesus in relationship to his personal life and at the same time reveals his distinctive personality.

Jesus' Concept of God

Most major religions present an image of God as a loving parent, a Father. Judaism recognized the paternity of God, and it was in this atmosphere that Jesus grew up. But Jesus was not content to affirm God as Father in the same way every other pious Jew would address God. For Jesus, God was *Abba*. God was like the loving parent who responds to a small child. There was an intimate relationship between God and Jesus different from that of other people. Jesus always distinguished this relationship. He spoke of my God and your God, my Father and your Father, and never our Father.[205] The universal meaning of Jesus contained in this unique dependence on God was at the very heart of his message and ministry.

The study of the gospels also discloses a keen sense of dependency upon God. Everything Jesus has he has received from his Father; the Father has taught him all and has given him direction; he has been sent to accomplish the mission of the Father; the Father is greater than Jesus and it is the Father's will that Jesus will accomplish.[206] In all of religious experience the sense of dependence and creatureliness is significant.[207] The trace of God present in human life is experienced by some, even though denied by others. The awareness of limitations, of a lack of fulfillment in life, the sense of mortality, can contribute to an awakening of the question of God. Do people live in isolation or in need of others? Can personal relations fulfill the need for persons to move out of themselves, or is there another force, a power, an ultimate person who can give the true foundation for dependence and creatureliness? Evidently for Jesus the sense of dependence and creatureliness is related to his self-awareness of God in his life as *Abba*. Jesus relates to God not with a sense of identity, since he will always maintain the difference between himself and his Father, but in the spirit of revelation. He can reveal God as Father, as *Abba*, because Jesus is God's Son. The union of willing and even of being makes Jesus present where God the Father is present and vice versa.

ABBA

Jesus' experience of the divine is primarily of a creative lover, whose Spirit/power works to save and free and fulfill and enrich, whose compassion is grounded in empathetic understanding of the human condition. But his experience includes also the awareness that this love is directed to himself in a distinctive way; he is *the* beloved, the *agapetos* addressed in the baptism scene; so Abba is not just Father, Abba is *his* Father.[208]

Personal Awareness of Goodness

Everyone experiences moments in life of personal worth and goodness. Jesus had a unique sense of his goodness. He did not live a fragmented life; he possessed a harmony that resulted in a consistency in all of his words and actions. He maintained a tranquillity, even in the midst of the greatest conflicts, that caused admiration. Jesus was aware of his own principles and would not compromise them; he lived what he believed in an integral way. Everyone possesses an awareness of similar qualities, but with a difference. The power of evil and sin waxes strong in the world and in the hearts of people. Instead of contributing to a better environment, people tend to make the evil in the environment ever stronger, which in turn makes the affirmation of this same evil easier by personal sin.[209] Lives that are fragmented, out of harmony, lacking in consistency, filled with compromise in the midst of personal turmoil, such lives have characterized the history of the human race. Jesus lived differently.

He did not repay evil with evil; he did not treat people in kind. Jesus decided how he would live his life and would not brook any interference. Jesus did not retaliate against the people who maltreated him. The environment was evil, but instead of contributing to the strength of the evil, he lessened its power by his manifestation of goodness, which absorbed the evil and transformed it. He lived as the compassionate, kind and forgiving friend, even when he was offered rejection, cynicism and resentment. He knew his God, knew his mission and lived accordingly. His life was remarkable because of his ability to express the power of goodness.

ORIGINAL SIN

Lack of Grace
Sin of the World
Personal Sin

The goodness that people express has to be viewed in relationship to the evil that also exists in the human heart. A lack of consistency characterizes both the inner human spirit and external actions. Paul recognized this tension when he wrote:

> For I do not do the good that I want, but the evil that I do not want is what I do (Rom 7:19).

When faced with goodness, people often react against it. They respond with resentment, or attempt to belittle or deny. When faced with evil, people often accept it, even though they know that evil should be resisted. The war of the members against the spirit is fought on the plains of the human heart, with frequent casualties. Jesus seems not to have experienced this internal warfare. What he did was surely learned from his environment, but what was appropriated was the goodness and what was rejected was the evil. His actions, his words, even his basic attitudes toward human life seemed to have its roots within. Jesus lived by transferring the epicenter of his life to God, to *Abba*, and thus the externals always expressed the internal principle. This does not mean that he found his center of existence outside of himself; rather he discovered his center was in relationship to God and thus he could live a harmonious life in which the outward expression flowed from an inner conviction. The closer a person is to God, the more freedom that person experiences. Jesus, the graced man, lived in freedom and in harmony.

Value and Purpose

Finally, Jesus lived with a definite sense of purpose for his life and with an energy that defies imitation. He was too sure, too definite, too aware of his value and his mission to ever be compared with others. His presence in human history can have a definite effect on every person, especially when it comes to questions about the ultimate meaning of personal life or the meaning of God, for in Jesus the

fusion of principle and practice met. Jesus saw his purpose and meaning in light of his proclamation of the kingdom of God. He knew that
no final response can be given to the quest for meaning unless it
includes the presence of God and unless the communion that should
exist between God and his people is personally accepted.

For Christians who struggle to discover personal meaning and
the overall purpose of their lives, the unique universality of Jesus will
always involve the two poles of his own meaning: his relationship to
God and the way he expressed this relationship in his life.[210] To relate
to God as Abba, the human would have to be elevated and somehow
participate in the realm of the divine, otherwise the divinity would not
become part of personal experience. No one could relate to God as
Jesus did unless God invited such a relationship and created its possibility. All people are created in the image of God, and this abstract
belief becomes concretized in the actual inclusion of the religious element in the human search for meaning. Anyone who seeks to discover
some purpose in life must include the divine, precisely because God
created all in his image. Jesus fulfilled this human destiny. He lived for
God, and all who met him knew it.

JESUS

Dependence upon God
Personal Purpose Found in God
Expressed Goodness in His Life
Sense of God as *Abba*
Without Sin
Mission from Within
Tranquility and Harmony in the Presence of Evil

Comparisons can certainly be made to other human beings who
lived with a sense of dependence, found purpose in the divine or spiritual dimension and expressed some goodness in life, but the life of
Jesus is more than just the sum total of the best of human qualities
that have been expressed in history. He founded his life on his self-
awareness and his sense of God. He appears to be the man without
sin, able to live in the human and sinful environment without feeling
its sting, and without affirming its presence by personal ratification.
His sense of purpose, his mission, is inscribed within and not just from
without. Nor did he seem to struggle to achieve tranquility and harmo-

ny. The level of humanity he reached is the goal that all people seek; he remains, even in his unique universality, the firstborn of many brethren.

If "humanity" and "human nature" can be empty formulas that need to be filled with content, the life of Jesus gives the elements that will make up the content of the human in its highest form. If the divine can be expressed to human beings only in a human way, then the highest example of the human spirit can alone be the vehicle that God uses to reveal himself.

The combination of the human and the divine, and speaking of Jesus as the human face of God, still involve a faith statement, but one that has been somewhat unfolded. The New Testament presents some ideas on why Jesus was the human face of God in an eminent way.[211] It also shows how people can still relate him to the universal human potential of being the image of God. Jesus could be the expression of God in this pre-eminent way, but the question still remains: "How was Jesus the human face of God?"

How Jesus Revealed the Father

It is clear from the gospels how contingent, ambivalent, limited and precarious the human life of Jesus was. He lived as a man, not as a woman and not as androgynous. He lived in Palestine under Roman occupation, with all of the contingencies and limitations that such a narrow mode of existence imposed. He did not benefit from world culture or world knowledge; he did not act and react with people of vastly divergent backgrounds and experiences. He lived an ordinary life in his own historical setting.[212]

The evangelists do not present a biography of Jesus in any sense, but in their writings they offer insights into some aspects of his personality and life that often become overlooked and which are important to understand him as the human face of God. He slept, ate and drank, went to parties, enjoyed the company of friends, was part of a family, lived in a small community; he wept over the failure of people to listen to him, felt frustrated with his disciples, grew angry and disappointed. These aspects of his life manifest his humanity and surely do not demonstrate any great originality.[213] He lived as part of Roman dominated Palestine in an eclectic environment, comprised of many philosophical systems and religious strains. In this world of contrasts Jesus stood out, however, as a remarkable person. He caused his listeners to wonder, to be shocked, to be scandalized. At one point even his own family thought he was out of his mind (Mk 3:21). The evangelists are aware of his uniqueness, but do not deliberately contrast him with his contemporaries. He seems quite ordinary most of the time. He lived a hidden life for many years, became an itinerant preacher for a brief period and finally was crucified. Yet, when these same writers treat of his power and his influence over people, they show him displaying a quality that far exceeds ordinary human expression. Jesus possessed a transcendence, but one that made itself felt in and through the ordinary.

Both the ordinary and extraordinary are evident in the gospels. The ordinary aspects of life, however—his relationships with people, his attitude toward Judaism, his sense of forgiveness, his sensitivity toward others, his openness to people's problems, his delight in human friendships, his pain at the lack of understanding of his disciples, his frustration with the hardness of people's hearts—bear the expression of the divine. As the human face of God, every detail in his life shared in this transcendence. A study of the New Testament should not be concerned with isolating moments of the life of the Lord, but with the manifestations of the divine that shone through the ordinary elements of his human life.

Attitudes

The attitudes of Jesus figure significantly in understanding how Jesus reflected God the Father. The heart of his gospel message is that God as Father is mindful of humankind and cares for all. Jesus bore witness to the indestructible certainty that God offers salvation. This reflects a personal attitude, a conviction that salvation—the making whole of humanity and the perfection of the individual—is possible and that ultimately the meaning in life involves the fullest expression of personal freedom and liberation. Giving oneself to God paradoxically brings personal freedom. Jesus expressed these attitudes in how he lived and also in how he died. In his attitude toward life he maintained a fruitful tension between the contradictory poles of suffering, evil and sin, and salvation linked with final and irrevocable good. In Jesus the goodness outweighed the evil that surrounded him; thus he could give others an example of how to resist the evil and accept and manifest the good. The basis for this attitude was the belief that God, *Abba*, is greater than all suffering and grief and greater even than any ability to accept goodness. Creation itself reflects the goodness of

God. Such a positive attitude revealed Jesus' personal conviction of how God regarded humankind.

The attitudes displayed by Jesus in his personal concern for the poor, the compassion he offered to those who were the outcasts of society, the kindness he manifested to sinners, to widows, to children, to his disciples and friends, these are human dimensions of his personality, but they also express God's concerns. Jesus possessed a universality that included the possibility of the conquest of all personal and social forms of alienation. The sense of separateness, the experience of living marginally, the isolation that causes so much pain can be resolved into a harmonious and fruitful life. Peace does not exist only on the interior plane, nor should it be seen as simply a social phenomenon. Rather, it is a combination of the two. Jesus did not retreat from the marketplace of human life, and thus his meaning, his revelation of the healing of the torn fabric of humanity, had to be accomplished in the domains of both the personal and the social. His personal attitude underlines the interrelationship of the two elements. People will hurt personally in a way that no social or political cure will be able to help, and vice versa. The death of a mother or father inflicts pain personally, just as subhuman housing, lack of education, restrictions on travel and the inability to participate in the destiny of one's country cause suffering socially and politically. Jesus, in his attitude toward human problems and human needs, offered a universal significance that would respond to the various phases and facets of human alienation. He preached and lived universal reconciliation.

Jesus revealed the meaning of God in his attitude toward liberation, freedom and salvation. A feeling of apartness or alienation often causes or contributes to struggle in life, and so Jesus offered an attitude of creative love for all. Based upon the freedom given by God and the salvation promised, Jesus believed that reconciliation was possible, and he actually lived according to this principle. No one was excluded, no one need feel left out. He welcomed into his company prostitutes, widows, tax collectors, sinners. The communion that Jesus preached was experienced in his person and offered to those who would respond to him in faith. Jesus did not offer an absolute principle, but reminded people of a possibility that could be realized. Jesus gave to human history not the final answer to the question of the search for meaning and liberation, but rather the expectation that humanity can be liberated completely, not by seeking something outside of human history, but by seeking something within the human situation.

Freedom and liberation and meaning and God are not to be discovered abstractly nor only within the narrow confines of the human spirit, but outwardly, bodily, involved with others in the same quest, within social structures as well as in the quiet of one's heart and in the depth of the spirit. He had friends, talked with his disciples about his hopes, encouraged them to make their own decisions with regard to law, ignored social customs when they restricted relationships and also retreated to the mountains to pray, alone. The interior sense of freedom is conditioned by exterior freedom. Social freedom always includes the encounter with other free people, and with God.

How Jesus Died

Jesus had a unique personal experience of God. The core of his message depends on the presence of the saving God in his personal history—this God who is mindful of the human race. Understanding Jesus, then, involves an appreciation of God's care for all people in human history. The disturbing point, however, in the life of Jesus as well as in all human lives, is the presence of signs that appear to contradict the loving care of God. How can anyone deal with the suffering and death of the Lord? The attitude of Jesus, his words and actions, how he faced suffering and the experience of his death have caused people to rethink the meaning of suffering.[214] The pain of Jesus, his crucifixion, did not alter his awareness of the saving presence of God and the nearness of his kingdom. This impels all to examine failure and pain.

The Death of Jesus

He not only offered satisfaction for sin, but he enacted and suffered death as death is the expression, the manifestation and the revelation of sin in the world. . . . It is precisely in its darkness that the death of Christ becomes the expression and the incarnation of his loving obedience, the free offering of his entire created existence to God. What had been therefore the manifestation of sin thus becomes, without its darkness being lifted, the contradiction of sin the manifestation of a "yes" to the will of the Father.[215]

In the midst of terrible human suffering, Jesus trusted in the salvation and power and goodness of his Father. The death of Jesus, however it might appear, was not a failure. Jesus died as he lived: he trusted in God and believed that eventually liberation, salvation and freedom would be accomplished.

An alternative to the Christian response to suffering and death considers life itself an illusion and concludes that people die as they live, in absurdity. The early Christians, however, believed that in the case of Jesus the benevolent God had the final word, since they also professed that Jesus was raised from the dead. In his dying the Lord committed himself in trust to God. He did not renege on his teaching. Death was the summation of his life, the culmination of his conscious choice for the sake of others. He died as he lived. The value judgments made in his ministry were all completed in that final decision to trust his life to the hands of his loving Father. The outcome was not yet known, but was accepted in faith. The Father responded by raising Jesus from the dead. With this action the suffering and death did not lose their significance, but were seen as the prelude to the establishment of Jesus in power:

> This Jesus, God raised up. . . . God has made him both
> Lord and Christ, this Jesus whom you crucified (Acts 2:32-
> 34b).

Suffering in life always causes problems. When people accept Jesus, including his pain and death, they know that human suffering involves God. Israel in its sacred books records the divine pathos in its history. Now, in Jesus, God is present in human suffering through the experience of his Son. The sorrow borne brings redemption, since through the faithful acceptance of this suffering the believers can experience aspects of life that are possible only through pain. Love is purified in pain; truth becomes imperative; mortality, limitation and dependence increase in magnitude, loom over the sickbed and stand beside mourners. God knows all pain and sorrow and suffering, for he has experienced the same in Jesus, his Son.

Crucifixion and Resurrection

Happily, the crucifixion culminates in the resurrection[216]—but this final dimension of the meaning of Jesus cannot be separated from the totality of his life. Belief in the risen Lord sees the continuity between this proclamation of God's presence in word and action and the universal significance of Jesus for all people. As risen Lord, Jesus is not only vindicated by God; as risen Lord his relationship to God is brought to completion. In his dying in love and obedience to the Father, Jesus revealed the mystery of his relationship to God, and in the resurrection the Father manifested his relationship to Jesus. Jesus had committed himself to the Father in his life and then in his death. When the Father raised him, the Father manifested his eternal commitment in return.

The resurrection also manifests liberation from earlier limitations, but the content of this liberation depends upon an appreciation of the earthly life of Jesus. The two cannot be separated. A risen Lord separated from his earthly life is mythical; an earthly Jesus separated from the risen Lord is another human failure. Only through the reciprocal relationship between the two realities does it become clear that the resurrection founds all faith in the earthly Jesus as the human face of God.

The followers of Jesus experienced the risen Lord. As a result of these experiences they gathered together to become the foundation of the Christian community which became the church. Properly speaking, the resurrection created faith in Jesus as the human face of God because only in terms of the risen Lord could people speak of the exaltation of the earthly Jesus and appreciate the divine transcendence that was present all through his life. The gospels contain formulas or expressions of faith in which there is some appreciation of the divinity of Jesus, but these must be seen as attempts on the part of the early believers to remember in a creative way what Jesus said and did and then understand the meaning involved. After the resurrection the disciples could see the relationship of many of the events of the life of the Lord which they had personally witnessed. Now they could see him as the human manifestation of the divine. His mission revealed the Father, but this was understood only in the light of the resurrection. Since God raised Jesus from the dead, his earthly life took on an importance greater than what his followers could have understood during their actual experience of his public ministry.

The early believers had to identify faith in the risen Lord with faith in the man Jesus: the raised and exalted Christ of faith had to be seen in continuity with the Jesus of history. The disciples with their Easter faith creatively recalled the major events in the life of Jesus and recognized them as manifestations of the divine. The teachings, the way he treated others, were now related to the presence of the divine. The apostles saw the ordinary events in the life of Jesus through an additional dimension: the human reflected the divine. They looked upon Jesus and recognized the presence of God.

Easter Faith

Jesus underwent an experience of "personal transformation" which enabled him to "live" beyond death. This belief
was coupled with another: this personally transformed Jesus
somehow manifested himself to various of his early disciples (male and female) through a series of actual, historical,
revelatory encounters, which were variously expressed as
"appearances," "revelations" or "conversion" experiences.[217]

This Easter faith, however, was not newly created by the experience of the risen Lord without a support in the historical experience
of Jesus. The foundation in the earthly experience of Jesus by his followers was perfected and understood only through the resurrection.
The faith of the disciples can be compared with ordinary human faith,
which grows from the fundamental intuition to the point of full acceptance. You meet someone; you like that person, feel comfortable; you
talk; you begin to confide; finally you believe in that person and trust
that person with your life. Such a thing occurred with Jesus and his disciples in his ministry, but the resurrection led them to the fullness of
faith in him. The Easter event was the principal basis for his followers'
faith in Christ.

As with faith in Christ, so the understanding of faith in Christ
must be based upon the resurrection. The theological appreciation of
Jesus as the human face of God will depend upon the acceptance of
the resurrection. Christology is founded on the Easter event, which
involves not just what happened to Jesus, but what happened to the
followers of Jesus. The Easter experience lies in the assembling of the
disciples in the name of Jesus and in the power of the risen Lord in
their midst. The resurrection and the assembling are two facets of one
event: Jesus is present to his disciples in a new way—as one who has
been accepted by the Father and thus has been changed in the relationship he has to his followers.

In the light of this experience, the disciples interpreted certain
sayings of Jesus theologically, as well as those of the Old Testament.
The meaning of the death of Jesus was also understood in the light of
the resurrection, and the same could be said of the new appreciation
of the Old Testament notion of the messiah. Even the cosmic theology
of Philippians and Colossians is founded on the resurrection. Only
after his resurrection, when he is Lord in power, does he reign over all
(Col 1:15ff). The resurrection manifests the conviction of the Christian
church that, in Jesus as risen Lord, the divine presence has taken a

human form in history. This human form, the earthly Jesus, has now been accepted by the Father as the final and eschatological manifestation of the Father's concern for humankind.

Human and Divine

The problem that plagues any study of christology is the precise relationship between the human dimension and the divine.[218] Theology cannot allow the loss of any of Jesus' humanness, nor can there be a loss of the divine. With difficulty theologians and the church will speak of two components or two realities. Rather, all should be conscious of two aspects of the one reality. To speak of Jesus as the human face of God does not imply that the human person of Jesus was just taken up into the Logos. Such statements would convey the idea that Jesus was constituted as a human being and was then taken over by the person of the Logos. The problem lies in the inability to find language that can speak about two total aspects of one reality. How can Jesus, as human, also be called the Son of God. Even the use of the "also" gives pause, since it, too, implies a separation rather than a unity in the reality.

In his humanity Jesus intimately lives with the Father and by virtue of this intimacy he is the Son. The center of his being as a man reposes not in himself, but in God the Father. The center, the support, even the heart of his personality consists in his relationship to God. Jesus was constitutively related and oriented to God as Father and was at the same time related to people as brother, as the bringer of salvation and the saving presence of God. Jesus possessed this unique combination, and that is what makes him distinctive and gives him his identity. His autonomy as Jesus of Nazareth is his constitutive total relation to the one whom he calls Father: the God whose special concern is with the human race.[219]

Asking whence this experience arose involves the milieu of Judaism under Roman domination. Every human experience, even if thought original, stands in a tradition of social experience. No individual ever draws upon potential inner strengths alone. The consciousness of Jesus was like that of any other human being who lived within the Judaic tradition in Palestine. His experience of God was nurtured by his Jewish traditions as well as by his human awareness of creatureliness and dependence. Unlike his contemporaries, however, he was more concerned with proclaiming the saving nearness of God than God's apocalyptic judgment. It was this saving presence that he identified with himself. Unless he suffered illusions, the only explanation was that God had manifested in Jesus his saving presence in a final and definitive way. His followers in fact reacted in this way. In Jesus the divine disclosed itself in a creaturely and human way so that all might call this an instance of human transcendence, or transcending humanity or even eschatological humanity. But even here no manifestation equals the reality. Jesus discloses the divine transcendence and also veils God, since the created can never adequately reveal or unveil the infinite.

Philosophical Foundations

This discussion can continue only by involving the various efforts to give a firmer philosophical groundwork to the relationship and the presence of these two total aspects of the one reality of Jesus. The works of K. Rahner,[220] P. Schoonenberg,[221] A. Hulsbosch,[222] E. Schillebeeckx,[223] H. Kung[224] and others attempt to deal with this question on a philosophical ground. The agreement that they seem to have reached accepts as fundamental the model of Jesus as the human face of God, or the sacrament of God, or the human manifestation of the divine, or God in Man. In each instance the theologian tries to break out of the more traditional approaches to christology as already seen in the model of Jesus as the second person of the Blessed Trinity. They try to present other models based upon scripture and human experience as well as contemporary philosophy.

All of these theologians deal with the fundamental model of Jesus as the human face of God. In him, in his own person, is revealed both the eschatological (the final the ultimate, the irrevocable) face of all humanity and the trinitarian fullness of God's being. Jesus, being a man, is God translated for humanity in a human fashion. Existence for others sacramentalizes the pro-existence of God or the self-giving of God to his creatures. God is God for people and with people. His unique universality lies in Jesus' eschatological humanity, as the sacrament of God's love for all. In forgetfulness of self, Jesus identified himself with God's cause, which at the same time was the cause of all people. Thus, Jesus lives as the firstborn of many brethren, since he is the one leaven for humanity which now participates in a different way in the life of the divine.

Jesus did not bring a new system, a new way of being human, a new way of living divorced from the ordinary experience of all people. Every individual has a wealth of possibilities, since in every person there is the potential for manifesting the presence of the divine. Jesus reminded people of this. Nothing that is human is foreign to God. Because of this human richness, the salvation offered by Jesus can never be translated completely into an all-inclusive system. The human face of God revealed in Jesus allows the possibility of many other expressions in other human faces. Everyone has the spark of the divine that the coming of Jesus recalled. Everyone, without exception, is created in the image and likeness of God. Jesus revealed the presence of God in himself, but also reminded all people of their potential to reveal the divine. In him people can see God and also can see their own possibilities.

> —for Christ plays in ten thousand places,
> Lovely in limbs, and lovely in eyes not his
> to the father through the features of men's faces.[225]

Advantages

The advantages of such a model are evident at every turn. It emphasizes the totality of Jesus of Nazareth as the expression and revelation of God. There is no aspect of his life forgotten or unimportant. No one may concentrate on the cross or resurrection or any other single moment without relating that event to the other episodes of his life. Certain moments were, of course, more significant than others, but each involves the full revelation of God.

Second, such a model relates Jesus to the ordinary experience of human life. Because Jesus expressed the divine in the ordinary events of human life, people can identify with Jesus as the messiah and Lord in power. People need not feel divorced from the sacred as long as they can believe that this historical person, in every aspect of his life, manifested the divine. People can study any dimension of his life through contemplating the New Testament and find some meaning for themselves as they try in turn to manifest the divine in their personal history. By reading prayerfully the pages of his history, his followers discover what lies hidden behind the words.

Third, no false dichotomy exists between the human and the divine. Two elements do not make a third; rather, one reality expresses the other. This profoundly influences all levels of theology. If the human can express the divine, then human life has a value that can never be eliminated or forgotten in spite of all attempts to denigrate it. The human face of God affects Christian anthropology as well as questions related to morality and the meaning of the church. Ecclesiology in particular is affected, since there is a parallel in the understanding of Jesus as the human face of God and of the church as the sacrament of Jesus in the world today. This involves every aspect of the church, not just its hierarchy and sacraments. Where the church is, Jesus is. The praying church, the consoling church, the reconciler, the lover of truth, the patron of the arts, the teaching church, the serving church, fulfills its destiny as the presence of Jesus in the world today. The very human church reflects the divine Jesus. This model also restores a sense of balance in Christianity, which in the past often emphasized the spiritual to the detriment of the material. Since it was believed that the meaning of Jesus centered on his divinity, individuals were thought to be more like Jesus the more they concentrated on the spiritual. If the human is the expression of the divine, however, then the material aspect of human life is equally important as the spiritual. Both are vehicles that reveal the divine. The bodily aspect of humanity cannot be disparaged, since it mediates the divine and offers the divine as expression in space and time.

The model of Jesus as the human face of God also prevents the concentration on the future fulfillment of Christianity that would lead to forgetting the present reality. If Jesus is the human face of God in history and if human history bears his stamp, then what is taking place now has great consequences for the human race. Salvation is not something reserved for the end of time. People experience the saving presence of God now in a human form. The fullness to come will ratify and perfect what is already present.

The reading of the New Testament makes clear that the model of Jesus as the human face of God is in full accord with scripture. In the gospel of John, Jesus tells his disciples that he who sees him sees the Father (Jn 14:9). Throughout the ministry of Jesus, people recognized that the power of God was present in his life. He revealed the concern of God for people in all of the episodes that are recorded in the gospels. They could look upon him and come to an appreciation of God. The gospels show the divine element of Jesus, but never apart from its human manifestation. Even the gospel of John, which stresses the divinity of Jesus more than any other of the New Testament writings, always joins divinity to the human dimension. The Logos becomes flesh; God's Son is the son of Joseph; the powerful "I am" is also bread, wine, shepherd.

Finally, such a model has important pastoral implications. If theologians speak of Jesus as the human face of God, they can avoid a great deal of philosophical terminology, which most people do not understand and have no interest in trying to understand. At the same time, the model offers much grist for the mill of those who want to analyze it philosophically, especially in the light of the development of personalism and other approaches to philosophy.

Accepting Jesus as the human face of God also helps believers to relate to and identify with the Lord without having to worry about theories. Christology, then, is not divorced from ordinary life and relegated to the lecture halls of academia. People can relate to it, since it includes in its purview the whole of human experience; as the human face of God, Jesus makes present the divine without ever abandoning human finite existence. For the person concerned with the spiritual life, the life of faith, an appreciation of this model offers vast possibilities for maturing as a Christian. This represents "practical" theology at its best and is sufficient reason alone to pursue and develop this model.

Limitations

Of course, the model also has weaknesses. The great danger is that with the emphasis on the human as the expression of the divine, the signified can be lost in the sign. If the human expresses the divine, and if believers therefore concentrate on the manifestation as very much part of ordinary human experience, then why continue to talk about the divine at all? Why not just see Jesus as a good person who leads people to understand something about their personal lives? Or, granted that Jesus can be considered to be the presence of the divine, how indispensable is the divine, since all anyone can know about it is its human aspect? Might it not be true that the value of Jesus rests on how he lived his human life, apart from any relationship to the divine?

All of these deviations are possible. When the human is over-emphasized the divine will fall into the shadows and concern for the divine can even disappear. Some people, Gandhi for example, can bypass the divine completely and still make a plausible case in favor of the value of Jesus and Christianity. Some will often use as their starting point the value of Jesus as exemplifying the best of humanity. Such people fail to see the intimate link between the human and the divine as fundamental to all life, and specifically to the life of Jesus.

Another problem is the possible loss of the afterlife. Christianity has always presented a doctrine of a future life, not only as a vindication of a life on earth well lived, but as the reward for such a life. To be with God in a complete and total way captures that goal. Now, if

Jesus becomes the human face of God and theology emphasizes the divine reality that is already present in every person's life, the sense of a future life may also fall into the background and disappear.

Such a position avoids the pitfalls of sterile philosophical quests, but it can also, by the same token, become anti-intellectual. Lacking some clearly-thought-out philosophical foundation, all theological propositions tend to become fluid and eventually lose credibility. Most believers may choose to take a stance that avoids philosophy, but this is not possible for the professional theologian, who must seek out responses to fundamental questions. A theology not built on a sound philosophical foundation will soon collapse.

Certainly efforts have been made to give a firm foundation to this model of Jesus as the human face of God (see P. Schoonenberg, K. Rahner, E. Schillebeeckx, etc.) but in no case have they answered all the questions. The present model lacks the clear philosophical response that theologies in the past have given on great christological topics. Disagreement runs too strong. The root question is, of course: Does this position maintain the sense of divinity of Jesus as expressed in the official councils of the church?

Finally, the danger of pantheism looms large in the background of this model. If Jesus is the human face of God, and if every human person can display the divine, then God is present in every person: there is an *en hypostasis* that is part of the human experience. If this is true, what prevents Christians from being pantheists? Can people be identified with God? Yes, with qualifications, but if this would do away with the various distinctions in God and concentrate on a human being as manifesting God, then why not finally settle for the presence of God in the universe, or at least speak of God as the collectivity of that which is present in a limited fashion in individuals?

In spite of its limitations, there is no doubt that this model is most fruitful. It answers more questions and lends itself to more conclusions than any other model discussed. The strengths are too strong and too well documented to be ignored; the dangers, conversely, are probably so unlikely to be realized that they need not cause alarm. If for no other reason, since this theological position contributes so much to the spiritual life of the believer often unconcerned with deep theological issues, perhaps it should be accepted as a paradigm that speaks to the needs of both the speculative and the practical theology of today or at least for preaching and religious education and personal piety. Jesus as the human face of God enriches the Christian life and faith takes on a new glow. The model excites and adds a new element to the Christian pursuit of the meaning of Jesus.

STUDY TOPICS AND QUESTIONS

1. Jesus is a man. Jesus is divine. Christian anthropology is the reversal of the coin that is christology. Is this true?

2. The universality of Jesus lies in his being human and divine rather than being divine and human. Does such a statement make sense?

3. What does it mean to be human? What does divinity mean?

4. Do faith statements help or hinder? How many can you name?

5. What is your concept of God? Is it the same as Jesus'?

6. Everyone is aware of personal goodness and personal evil. What difference does that make?

7. Do value and purpose in life help?

8. How does Jesus continue to reveal God?

9. How does death fit in your life and in this model?

10. Do you like this model or not?

PART IV

Evaluating the Models

The previous chapters have involved a dialectic. Many models exist and each model has both advantages and disadvantages. All have arisen in Christian history and all claim to have some basis in scripture. But each one has come from a different tradition, from a different period of history or from believers who have had different horizons within which they have chosen to judge the suitability of their approach to Jesus. But which models are compatible, not only with each other, but with the general consensus of Christianity as it has been manifested through the centuries? Are the different perspectives and conclusions mutually exclusive or are they complementary? Can anyone state with certainty that one model far surpasses another? Must everyone be content with admitting that each model is equally good and valuable without any attempt to evaluate them in the light of their distinctive advantages and disadvantages? Is each model a help or a hindrance to the understanding of Jesus? Are they relatively opaque, so as to reduce the reality of Jesus to only a glimmer of light, or are they translucent—not so clear as to permit perfect visibility, but still giving a good view of the reality to all those who will use them?

Criteria

The choice of any model will always depend upon certain criteria, but who is to establish the criteria? For anyone to set up a number of criteria can in itself be a choice of models. The person who writes a book filled with personal ideas and then sets out to discover some support for the theories presented is like the person who chooses a model and then sets out to establish the criteria that will support the choice. People who read the New Testament seeking to find support for a particular model of Jesus may assiduously overlook any themes that seem to support a conflicting model, or at least a different one. Certainly the model should be clear and should account for the divinity of Jesus, but it should also respect his humanity. It should be mystical as well as practical. It should be subjective, since that is how people learn, but objective, too, since that will hold on to a firm basis in fact and reality. The model should relate to the experience of the poor, since the church must identify with the poor if it is to be true to the example of Jesus. It also must allow for the rich who also are with the church always. Founded in the New Testament, any model should be appreciated and understood in the history of the church and in the history of theology. If it could be final and definitive, then it would give a firm basis for faith; but it should also be provisional, since the understanding of faith is always developing. How can these paradoxes be resolved?

The spectrum of criteria cannot be reduced to internal considerations of theology, but must cover, as well, personal piety, church teaching, various Christian traditions, the fears and anxieties of those who shy away from examining approaches to Jesus, and a host of other hidden agendas. In any effort to evaluate, the one making the study must be aware of the tendency to emphasize one over the other, or to emphasize the extremes in every position other than the one proposed. A sincere desire to progress in understanding Jesus precludes the choice of criteria that will support only one model over the others.

A number of criteria should already have become evident in the examination of the models in the individual chapters above. I propose for consideration eight:[226]

1.   A firm basis in scripture. In the return to the Bible by all Christian traditions as the authentic presentation of the word of God, there has developed a sense of confidence in being on the right track if a firm basis for theology can be found in scripture. To deal with the models of Jesus then, the principal support must come from the New Testament.

2.   Compatibility with Christian tradition. Christians have understood the Bible in their own historical situation. They have struggled with the question of Jesus and have offered many different answers to the questions that have arisen over the centuries. Since

an image can be accepted as a model and perhaps even as a paradigm, it must respond to many of the facets of Christian understanding of Jesus. Returning to ancient Palestine may not help, but understanding the relationship of the century of Jesus' birth to the succeeding nineteen centuries will.

3. A capacity to help Christians in their efforts to believe in Jesus. Believers do not live in a vacuum. Christians living at the end of the twentieth century need a model that will help them to relate to a world quite different from anything that has preceded it. Developments in science, an awareness of the religious, philosophical and ethnic pluralism in this world, a wider appreciation of religion —all of these will have an effect on the model of Jesus. After experiencing so much world tragedy, the Christian needs a model that will speak eloquently to the heart that seeks to believe.

4. A capacity to direct believers to fulfill their mission as members of the church. A model of Jesus unrelated to the activity of the church in the world is not faithful to the Jesus of the gospels. Every gift contains a corresponding responsibility. The model that impels believers to live their Christian heritage should be favored.

5. Correspondence with the Christian religious experience today. Ever since Cardinal Newman wrote *On Consulting the Faithful in Matters of Dogma,* the church has been troubled by its implications. It has always been the tradition of the church to pay attention to the lived beliefs of Christians in matters of faith, but the church has used this criterion cautiously. To take the principle seriously means that all should be concerned with the model of Jesus that good-living people actually use today. Avoiding theological subtlety, the model should relate to the faith experience of the masses of Christians. How do people view Jesus in their personal lives?

6. Theological fruitfulness. Each model has strengths and weaknesses in their relationship to theology. Old models have given way to new models, some advancing the theological enterprise, others hindering it, still others having little effect. The model that can provide solutions for more of the theological questions that are being raised, and that offers the potential for more development, must be considered of greater value.

7. The ability to foster a good sense of Christian anthropology.

Christology always involves an anthropology: the more people understand themselves, the more they can understand Jesus, and vice versa. If a model can help Christians in coming to a better sense of the meaning of Christianity as actually lived by people, if it can help define such a thing as the Christian self-image, then such a model merits acceptance within the Christian tradition.

8. Support for good preaching and religious education. People learn more about Jesus and his gospel through preaching and religious education. Some models are more helpful for introducing people to Jesus than others. Some models are more conducive for further religious education than others. At a time when Christian preaching often leaves much to be desired and when religious education comes constantly under criticism, the model should help in both of these important church activities.

To evaluate six models by all eight criteria would be tedious. The individual chapters already offer the strengths and weaknesses of each model, and no doubt some readers have already made their decision on the model that best will serve them as a paradigm. The following summary of possible conclusions may also be helpful for the reader.

Second Person of the Blessed Trinity

The model of Jesus as second person of the Blessed Trinity has a weak basis in scripture, but a much stronger one in tradition. It appears to have little direct relation to fostering personal faith today, since it seems divorced from people's ordinary lives.[227] The model also tends to encourage the split between the sacred and the secular, since it often emphasizes the church over the marketplace and the spiritual over the material. It still corresponds to the religious experience of some believers, but fewer than previously. The model has been theologically fruitful, since it has dominated the theology of the church, spiritual theology, and has been the backdrop for moral theology for centuries. At the same time it has not been particularly helpful in the theology that has developed over the past several decades. Perhaps the greatest weakness lies in its tendency to encourage a distorted Christian anthropology rather than a good self-image of the Christian. People have problems identifying with Jesus as the second person of the Blessed Trinity.

Mythological Christ

The mythological figure has some foundation in scripture, depending upon the meaning of mythological. The force of this model has waxed and waned in Christian tradition. It can help some people to believe, since it can eliminate for some certain troublesome aspects of the gospel, e.g. miracles and a literal interpretation of the divinity of Jesus. It encourages believers to ignore certain academic theological issues in favor of getting on with the task of fulfilling a concrete mission in the world. For most Christians, however, it is totally foreign to their experience. Jesus is very real now and in the past. The theological fruitfulness is evident, if not always welcome, since it has generated much discussion and has opened new frontiers. Believers need not look upon the New Testament as absolute. Its ability to foster a sense of Christian anthropology, however, is impaired by the tendency to reduce the value of the spiritual and make the divine appear as only another way of being human.

Liberator

Jesus the liberator has a firm foundation in scripture, provided that Jesus is not viewed as an extreme revolutionary, but as one who indeed challenged the existing social order. This model has appeared occasionally in the history of theology—for example, in the social gospel of late nineteenth and early twentieth century Protestant thought. The model also could be accepted as the basis for the social encyclicals of Roman Catholic twentieth century thought. Most recently, it corresponds to the social-political experience in Latin America, that of the civil rights movement in the United States and those of the women's movement and other minorities. The model certainly helps Christians in their efforts to believe, since it is concerned with the sufferings of millions and moreover impels believers to accomplish something for the sake of others. While the model reflects the religious experience of suffering groups, it is often perceived as unrelated to the experience of other Christians. Its theological fruitfulness, in spite of the efforts to present it as a position firmly based in theology, has been limited, impaired by its narrow purview. Its ability to develop a good anthropology is also limited, since it is based upon the experience of the oppressed in very specific areas of the world and under very specific conditions.

Man for Others

The man for others certainly has a basis in scripture. The model does not appear frequently in the history of theology, but it has achieved prominence in recent times. This approach to Jesus encourages people to believe precisely because it impels the faithful to fulfill their Christian mission. Though not the primary experience of most Christians, many people would like it to shape their experience of Jesus; they would be happy if they could reach out and be of service to others. Theological fruitfulness is limited, since it does not have a broad enough base; understanding of a strong anthropology is evident, since it concentrates on the meaning of the humanity of Jesus for others, which will enhance every person's humanity.

Lord and Savior

The model of Jesus as Lord and Savior also has a good foundation in scripture; it has existed throughout Christian history in both orthodox and unorthodox forms. The model helps some people to believe even as it might hinder others. At times such an approach discourages social involvement, since it tends to be individualistic. Surely this model does not form the experience of the majority of believers. Theological fruitfulness is very limited, since those who ascribe to this model often are not concerned with matters of speculative theology. While it can develop a good self-understanding for some, for others it can also contribute to a sense of self-depreciation in the sight of God.

The Human Face of God

Finally, the human face of God has a firm foundation in scripture as well as in Christian tradition. It fosters belief, as meaningful in the twentieth century as in any other, with each age contributing its own perspectives. However, the model sometimes lacks a strong incentive toward involvement in mission and might also encourage pietism. Accepted in its fullest sense, however (as Jesus was the human face of God for others, so Christians must imitate him and be themselves the face of God today), then it does provide some sense of mission. Although such a model does not figure prominently in the experience of most Christians in theory, it often does in practice. Good Christians know instinctively that when they see and experience Jesus they see and experience God. Theological fruitfulness can be demonstrated by the divergent opinions that such a model can sustain. This approach surely emphasizes a good Christian anthropology: if Jesus is the human face of God, then every human being carries a similar possibility to manifest the divine and every human being has immense value.

Many Models Historically

Over the centuries members of the church have been drawn to various models. The same will be true today. Many church leaders and the more traditionally oriented Christians will tend toward the model of Jesus as the second person of the Blessed Trinity. These believers know such a model persists, firmly rooted in church tradition and in their personal history. Those involved in the social mission will probably choose the model of ethical liberator or the man for others; the charismatic will choose the model of Lord and Savior; the skeptical believer will be more at ease with the mythological figure; the speculative theologian, especially one educated in existential phenomenology, might prefer the human face of God or follow the more traditional model of Jesus as the second person of the Blessed Trinity.

Often these various groups will react strongly against certain other models. Some will completely reject the mythological figure and feel insecure about the liberator or the man for others. The social mission group may dismiss the second person of the Blessed Trinity as being totally irrelevant, lacking any meaning today. The charismatic may avoid the theological models and may also react against the skepticism that might be associated with the mythological Christ. Can one conclude "*Chacun a son gout*," "To each his own"?

At the very least, the cross-fertilization of models should permeate the church. No one should think that one particular model has all of the answers or that no one can learn from other models. A good, healthy skepticism can help Christians, even when generated by those who see Jesus as mythological, and the enthusiastic acceptance of Jesus as personal Savior might do a world of good for the speculative theologian as well as for church bureaucrats.

Each model has its value and place. Such has been the working hypothesis throughout this study. Each has some insight into the meaning of Jesus as experienced and pondered through two millennia of Christianity. The model of Jesus as the second person of the Blessed Trinity has as its great contribution the stress on the divinity of Jesus; the mythological figure guards against falling into a false absolutism or a false supernaturalism; the liberator and the man for others center more upon the mission of Jesus and the church, especially with regard to suffering minorities; the human face of God emphasizes the humanity as the expression of the divinity; Lord and Savior concentrate on Jesus-for-me, offering salvation.

Limiting Qualifications

People, however, should not just accept the six models without qualification. They do not agree in every way, and often they emphasize one aspect to the detriment of another. More problematically, they suggest different priorities that will profoundly affect the movement of Christianity in the century to come. If some are taken as absolutes, they could have a disastrous effect on Christianity within a generation.

The model of Jesus as second person of the Blessed Trinity tends to develop an ecclesiastical approach with little relationship to people's lives. In the past some have used this model to be rigid and conformist. Often those who maintain such a model have authority in the church and have tended to be critical of other approaches. Thus used, the model may stifle free thought. Some who have been brought up on this model can also experience a sense of inferiority. Often, the very divine Jesus appears too strong a model for sinful human beings.

The liberator can and has involved the church in revolution and the support of violence in the name of Jesus. Some who follow this model also maintain the illusion that the gospel cannot be preached as long as the economically and socially deprived continue to exist.

The human face of God can so emphasize the humanity of Jesus that people lose all sense of the divine. It can also undermine the sense of structure in theology and in the church by assuming that all the church needs is a basic theology of serving others. Subjectivism may then follow.

The man for others, like the liberator, can be without much theological substance and can present Christians as a group of social workers. Jesus becomes just another good person who suffered and died.

Finally the Lord and Savior can lead to fanaticism in its search for the experience of Jesus as Savior. Followers can become very critical of all others who do not believe as they do, resulting in Christian elitism.

Search for a Paradigm

Aware of the major contribution of each model and the major drawbacks if the model becomes accepted exclusively, can anyone find a paradigm, one model that responds to more of the unanswered questions and problems than all of the others, without totally excluding them? Will such a pursuit lead to naught?

The models presented here are not the only possible models. Christian history knows others: Jesus the wise man, the teacher, the superstar, the king, the priest, the prophet, the servant. These six have been chosen because they seem to cover most of the territory. They are major models. No one model would be adequate for christology for all time. The models of Jesus also involve the mystery of human life as well as the mystery of God, and surely there can never be an adequate expression of those realities. Better to work with models that are, and will always remain, even if all models exist far removed from the reality they seek to express.

One possible method would be to harmonize the models in such a way that their differences become complementary. This demands criticizing each of the models in the light of the others. In this way some might come to an understanding of Jesus that transcends the limitations inherent in each of the models. The models can interact and allow each other to emphasize good points and counter weaknesses. Theologians and believers may want to base their christology on Jesus as the human face of God, but then include in that the model of Jesus as liberator to encompass the mission aspect of the faith as actually lived. In Latin America a theologian or believer may take the ethical liberator as the fundamental model, but join to this the model of Jesus as the human face of God, or second person of the Blessed Trinity. These same believers may pay attention to the mythological character in order to maintain a healthy skepticism about ideologies in the struggle to renew the face of the earth.

The model of Jesus as the human face of God offers many possibilities. It can include in it the sense of social mission as well as what-Jesus-means for-me; it maintains the divinity without the limitations often associated with the model of Jesus as the second person of the Blessed Trinity. More than any other model, it can help foster a good sense of personal worth, which every individual needs, whether socially, economically or politically oppressed or not.

Of the six models, that of the second person of the Blessed Trinity seems to have the least interest for many. For centuries it has been the predominant paradigm. In the light of developments that have taken place in recent years, however, many do not pay great attention to this strong traditional approach to Jesus. Somehow it seems less suited than other models to the demands that are being made upon Christianity today.

Readers should not try to harmonize all the models nor homogenize them. Each model must be seen against its own background. They still involve the age-old mystery of the relationship between God and people. That will always cause everyone to pause before trying to solve all the problems and answer all the questions. The helpful will be preserved; what is not helpful can be easily ignored. What is of God will last; what is not will fade (Acts 5:35-39).

The completion of this study encourages a little prophetic activity.[228] Certain aspects of Christology that have emerged in the recent past will in all probability continue:

1. Christology will be more and more related to the Trinity even if the model of Jesus as the second person of the Trinity may continue to fade. Jesus came not to reveal himself but to reveal the Father through the power of the Spirit. The understanding of Jesus as the one who is the human face of God, just as the word has been traditionally understood as the expression of God, will continue with a greater sense of the trinitarian understanding of faith. It will not, however, be Augustine's study of the Trinity nor that of the scholastics, but an attempt to relate the revelation of God in a human being, Jesus of Nazareth, to the experience of all people. This will include them in the mystery of God that is characterized by community. Christology will not encourage isolation, but solidarity with God understood and loved as Father.

2. The impact of the liberal and often radical economic and social movement will continue to influence christology. Since Jesus lived for others and had a special predilection for the downtrodden, all the oppressed peoples of the world, those socially or economically or politically or sexually oppressed, will have their special claim on Jesus. Their struggles for equality and freedom will profoundly influence the understanding of Jesus.

3. The need for believing that each person is good and can experience salvation in Jesus through an enthusiastic movement or in some other personal way will continue. The meaning for the individual that Jesus offers has great importance for the continuance of Christianity.

4. Pluralism in christology, with new approaches, will contribute to a continuing development in the understanding of Jesus of Nazareth. Theology will never reach the eschatological, never-to-be-changed paradigm. Pilgrim people in theology as well as in faith will remain.

These predictions seem to be warranted both by the current ferment in christology as well as by the current awareness of the social dimensions of Christianity. If the church functions in the world, it has to be aware of the movements that will affect the understanding of Jesus and must allow for the fulfillment of all of the potential that lies within the human spirit.

STUDY TOPICS AND QUESTIONS

1. Evaluate each model using your own criteria.

2. Do you have a personal paradigm? Why?

3. Do you also have a secondary model? How do the two relate.

4. Draw up a list of advantages to accepting many approaches to Jesus:

    a. for the church

    b. for theology

    c. for personal spiritual life

    d. for feeling part of the Christian community

    e. for yourself

CONCLUSION

Many models of Jesus have characterized Christianity from the experience of Jesus himself by his disciples. In the New Testament, each gospel has one predominant model and several secondary ones. The history of the Church also bears witness to many models. Some have predominated, and especially since Chalcedon the second person of the Blessed Trinity has been the paradigm. If so many models have been accepted within the church for centuries, the broad Roman Catholic tradition as well as other Christian traditions can accept new models in this century and for centuries to come.

In preaching and in religious education, the model which may well be in fact the paradigm, if not in theory, seems to be the human face of God. Preachers easily help listeners relate to this Jesus.

In a world in which too many people suffer needlessly, the social aspect of Jesus must also be considered. Whether Jesus as liberator or Jesus the man for others answers that need depends upon many factors, not least of which is history and the social economic order.

Jesus as Lord and Savior has always appealed to many for personal reasons. And so it will in the future. For theology the second person of the Blessed Trinity must remain significant but not necessarily the paradigm. Probably theologians, like most others believers, have a basic model which is paradigmatic and then have a secondary model which will help fill out the personal understanding of Jesus. For believers to know where they stand in this search for an approach to Jesus can be most helpful.

This work began as a journey that did not know its final point. Now that the last page is reached, all should be aware that the journey in understanding Jesus of Nazareth will never end. The history of Christianity has only attained way stations along the road in understanding Jesus of Nazareth. Those stopping places, however, are not without value, since they have been blessed by the labor of believers who nobly continued to seek a response to that haunting question of Jesus himself: "Who do you say that I am?"

NOTES

1. See *Rome and the Study of Scripture* (St. Meinrad: Grail, 1962).

2. See *The Pope Speaks*, vol. 10 (1964-65), 86-90. Also published in R. Brown, *Crisis Facing the Church* (New York: Paulist, 1975). For a review of American biblical study see Gerald Fogarty, "American Catholic Biblical Scholarship: A Review," *Theological Studies*, Vol. 50 (1989), 219-43.

3. Avery Dulles, *Models of the Church* (New York: Doubleday, 1974). Richard McBrien, *The Remaking of the Church* (New York: Harper & Row, 1973).

4. See *The Pope Speaks*, vol. 17 (1972-73), 64-68.

5. *Ibid.* 65.

6. *Ibid.* 69.

7. *Ibid.* 67.

8. *The Evangelist*, June 18, 1992, 8.

9. *Ibid.*

10. Cf. *The Virginal Conception and Bodily Resurrection of Jesus* (New York: Paulist, 1973), 66.

11. "The Brothers and Sisters of Jesus in Ecumenical Perspective," Vol. 54 (1992), 27.

12. *Ibid.* 27-28.

13. John Meier, *A Marginal Jew* (New York: Doubleday, 1991).

14. Dominic Crossan, *The Historical Jesus: The Life of a Mediterranean Jewish Pesant* (San Francisco: Harper, 1991).

15. Bernard Cooke, *God's Beloved: Jesus' Experience of the Transcendent* (Philadelphia: Trinity Press, 1992).

16. Jerome Neyrey, S.J., *Christ Is Community* (Collegeville: Liturgical Press, 1990).

17. Albert Nolan, O.P., *Jesus Before Christianity* (Maryknoll: Orbis, 1992).

18. Joseph Fitzmyer, S.J., *A Christological Catechism* (New York: Paulist, 1982).

19. *Acta Apostolicae Sedis,* 54 (1962), 792.

20. In Mk 13:32, Jesus remarks that not even the Son knows the day of judgment. Theologians have developed a host of responses in attempting to explain this lack of knowledge, instead of taking the words at their face value.

21. See John F. O'Grady, *Jesus, Lord and Christ* (New York: Paulist, 1972), Chapter 8.

22. See J. Sobrino, *Christology at the Crossroads* (Maryknoll: Orbis, 1978).

23. *Teachings of the Catholic Church,* ed. K. Rahner (Staten Island: Alba House, 1967), 154.

24. Karl Rahner, "Chalkedon—Ende oder Anfang," *Das Konzil von Chalkedon,* ed. A. Grillmeier and H. Bacht, vol. 3 (Wurzburg, 1954), 3-49.

25. See Karl Rahner, "The Concept of Mystery in Catholic Theology," *Theological Investigations,* vol. 4 (Baltimore: Helicon, 1966), 36-73. Raymond Brown, "The Semitic Background of the New Testament *Mysterion,*" *Biblica,* 39 (1958) 42-48; 40 (1959), 70-87.

26. K. Rahner and Herbert Vorgrimler, *Theological Dictionary* (New York: Herder and Herder, 1965, 300-301.

27. Rahner, "*The Concept. . .*" 41-43.

28. "Lumen Gentium," *Documents of Vatican II,* ed. Walter Abbott (New York: America Press, 1966).

29. See Karl Rahner, "The Theology of the Symbol," *Theological Investigations,* vol. IV (Baltimore: Helicon, 1966), 221-52.

30. *Ibid.*

31. Francis Thompson, "In No Strange Land," *The Oxford Book of English Verse* (New York: Oxford University Press, 1940).

32. J.A.T. Robinson, *The Human Face of God* (Philadelphia, Westminster, 1967).

33. Karl Barth, *The Humanity of God* (Richmond: John Knox, 1960).

34. D. Bonhoeffer, *Letters and Papers from Prison* (New York: Macmillan, 1967).

35. Edward Schillebeeckx, *Christ the Sacrament of Encounter With God* (New York: Herder and Herder, 1963). See also *Jesus: An Experiment in Christology* (New York: Seabury, 1979).

36. Karl Rahner, *Foundations of Christian Faith* (New York: Seabury, 1978), Chapter VI.

37. Cf. B. Cooke *God's Beloved: Jesus' Experience of the Transcendent* (Philadelphia: Trinity Press International, 1992).

38. Quoted in Dulles, *Models of the Church*, 20.

39. I.T. Ramsey, *Models and Mysteries* (New York: Oxford, 1964).

40. Ibid. 4. See also Max Black, *Models and Metaphors* (Ithaca: Cornell University Press, 1962).

41. E. Cousins, "Models and the Future of Ministry," *Continuum* 7 (1969), 78-91. John McIntyre, in *The Shape of Christology* (London: SCM Press, 1966), is the first theologian, as far as I can establish, to attempt to use the approach of models in christology. His particular theological stance differs considerably from mine, but I have profited by his attempts and acknowledge the debt.

42. *Ibid.*

43. Karl Rahner, *The Dynamic Element in the Church* (New York: Herder and Herder, 1964), 168.

44. John Powell, *The Mystery of the Church* (Milwaukee: Bruce, 1967), 8.

45. T. S. *Kuhn, The Structure of Scientific Revolutions* (Chicago: University Press, 1970), 175.

46. For a general review of the quest for the historical Jesus, see W. Thompson, *The Jesus Debate* (New York, Paulist, 1985). Thompson summarizes the debate up to the recent works by Crossan, Meier, etc.

47. Howard Clark Kee, *What Can We Know About Jesus?* (Cambridge: University Pess, 1990), gives an accurate, brief summary of the historical evidence for Jesus in chapter 1.

48. Cf. *The Historical Jesus,* xiii-xxvi. Crossan has summarized the results of his study and I in turn have summarized Crossan. The reader should refer to these pages of the author for a fuller explanation of what Crossan accepts coming from the historical Jesus.

49. Cf. J. Jeremias, *New Testament Theology,* Vol. 1 (London: SCM Press, 1971), 61-67.

50. *Jesus: An Experiment in Christology* (New York: Seabury, 1979), 256-69. For a feminiist critique which questions whether Jesus actually used this title and its meaning, see Mary Rose D'Angelo, "Abba and the 'Father': Imperial Theology and the Jesus Traditions," *Journal of Biblical Literature,* Vol. 111 (1992), 611-30.

51. Cf. *God's Beloved,* 1-24.

52. Cf. Carl Braaten, *Christ and Counter-Christ: Apocalyptic Themes in Theology and Culture* (Philadelphia: Fortress, 1972).

53. Any general biblical dictionary will offer overviews of the apocalyptic and the eschatological. See, for example, the entries on "Apocalypses and Apocolypticism" and "Eschatology" in *The Anchor Bible Dictionary* (New York: Doubleday, 1992). After each article the various authors offer extensive bibliographies.

54. This image of Jesus is also found in *The Catechism of the Catholic Church* (New York: Paulist, 1994).

55. Braatan, 107-18.

56. Cf. *Jesus the Magician* (San Francisco: Harper, 1978).

57. The concept of "mystery" as previously discussed finds expression here in the study of the New Testament.

58. Cf. W. Meeks, *The First Urban Christians* (New Haven: Yale University Press, 1983).

59. Cooke, *God's Beloved,* presents many of these particular aspects of the life of Jesus, in particular Jesus as a Jewish male and his experience as an Israelitic prophet. Meier, *A Marginal Jew* and Crossan, *The Historical Jesus* also offer exceptional insights into the Jewish background of Jesus.

60. Two such attempts immediately come to mind, written twenty years apart, both of which merit study for a fuller picture of the many christologies of the New Testament: John Reumann, *Jesus* (Philadelphia: Fortress, 1968) and Earl Richard, *Jesus: One and Many:*

The Christological Concept of New Testament Authors (Wilmington: Glazier, 1988).

61. See R. Fuller, *Foundations of New Testament Christology* (New York: Scribner's, 1965), 143-73; J.A.T. Robinson, "The Most Primitive Christology of All," *Journal of Theological Studies*, vol. 7 (1956), 177-89; D. Stanley, "The Primitive Preaching," *Concilium*, vol. 2 (1966), 47-52.

62. The gospel of John, and to a lesser extent the gospel of Luke, offer a realized eschatology. See John F. O'Grady, *The Jesus Tradition and the Four Gospels* (New York: Paulist, 1989), part III, chapter 5.

63. See R. Brown, *The Birth of the Messiah* (New York: Doubleday, 1977), 29-32.

64. Cf. Joseph Fitzmyer, *Paul and His Theology* (Englewood Cliffs: Prentice Hall, 1987). J. C. Beker, *Heirs of Paul* (Minneapolis: Fortress, 1991). A. Tambasco, *In the Days of Paul.* (New York: Paulist), 1991. J.F. O'Grady, *Pillars of Paul's Gospel* (New York: Paulist 1992).

65. W. Carroll, "The Jesus of Mark's Gospel," *The Bible Today*, #103 (1979), 2105-12; J. Donahue, "Jesus as the Parable of God in the Gospel of Mark," *Interpretation*, 32 (1978), pp. 369-86; T. Weeden, *Traditions in Conflict* (Philadelphia: Fortress, 1971); W. Harrington, "The Gospel of Mark: A Theologia Crucis," *Doctrine and Life*, vol. 26 (1976), 24-33; J. Lambrecht, "The Christology of Mark," *Biblical Theology Bulletin*, 3 (1973), 256-73. Richard, Jesus op. cit.; V.K. Robbins, *Jesus the Teacher* (Philadelphia: Fortress, 1984).

66. See E. Gaston, "The Messiah of Israel as Teacher of the Gentiles," *Interpretation*, vol. 29 (1975), 2410; M. Johnson, "Reflections on a Wisdom Approach to Matthew's Christology," *Catholic Biblical Quarterly*, vol. 36 (1974), 44-64; J. Kingsbury, *Matthew: Structure, Christology, Kingdom* (Philadelphia: Fortress, 1975); J. Meier, *The Vision of Matthew* (New York: Paulist, 1979); M. Suggs, *Wisdom, Christology and Law in Matthew's Gospel* (Cambridge: Harvard University Press, 1970). Richard, *Jesus, op cit.*; L. Morris, *The Gospel According to Matthew* (Grand Rapids: Eerdmans, 1992).

67. See O. Betz, "The Kerygma of Luke," *Interpretation*, vol. 22 (1968), 131-46; D. Jones, "The Title 'Christos' in Luke-Acts," *New Testament Studies*, vol. 18 (1971-72), 39-53; C. Talbert, "An Anti-Gnostic Tendency in Lukan Christology," *New Testament Studies,* vol. 14 (1967-68), 259-71; E. LaVerdiere, *Luke* (Wilmington: Glazier, 1980); D. Tiede, *Luke* (Minneapolis: Augsburg, 1988); Richard, *Jesus, op cit.*

68. See J. Giblet, "The Johannine Theology of the Logos," *The Word* (New York: Kenedy, 1964), 104-46; M. Boismard, "Jesus the Savior According to John," *Word and Mystery* (Westminster: Newman, 1968), 69-86; R Collins, "The Representative Figures of the Fourth Gospel," *Downdiside Review,* vol. 94 (1976), 26-45, 118-32; R. Fortna, "Christology in the Fourth Gospel: Redaction-Critical Perspectives," *New Testament Studies,* vol. 21 (1975), 489-504; P. Harner, *The "I am" of the Fourth Gospel* (Philadelphia: Fortress, 1970); D. Rensberger, *Johannine Faith and Liberating Community* (Philadelphia: Westminster, 1988); M. Thompson, *The Humanity of Jesus in the Fourth Gospel* (Philadelphia: Fortress, 1988). R. Karris, *Jesus and the Marginalized in John's Gospel* (Collegeville: Liturgical Press, 1990); R. Collins, *John and His Witness* (Collegeville: Liturgical Press, 1991).

69. *The Pope Speaks,* vol. 17 (1972-73), 64-68.

70. See K. Rahner, "Chalcedon, *art. cit.*

71. For a general overview of this council, any standard encyclopedia of theology is helpful. See *Sacramentum Mundi,* vol. 3 (New York: Herder and Herder, 1969), 201-03; also A. Greilmeier, *Christ in Christian Tradition* (London: Mowbray, 1965). G. Tavard, *Images of the Christ* (Washington: University of America Press, 1982), presents an excellent overview of the council including the background for the controversy, 36-44.

72. See *Teachings of the Catholic Church,* 151-53.

73. *Ibid.* This formulation by Leo became the foundation for the debate during the Council of Chalcedon, as well as the previous Council of Ephesus. Cf. Tavard, 29-36.

74. *Ibid.* 153-54. As a result of this formulation, most Christians are aware of the statement regarding two natures in one person, but are not aware of the controversy surrounding the formulation.

75. *Ibid.* 169-70. The debate at the Third Council of Constantinople preserved the human will of Jesus and human operations. If this had not been formulated, the humanity could easily have been absorbed into divinity in developing theology. Cf. Tavard, 44-47.

76. Tavard, 40.

77. Greilmeier, 492. This authoritative study on the history of christological controversy is invaluable, even though I cannot agree that the Jesus of the New Testament can be heard with undiminished strength

in the philosophical discussions. Rather, the unresolved questions of the New Testament concerning the precise relationship between humanity and divinity laid the foundation for the philosophical development as expressed in these conciliar declarations.

78. See *Dictionnaire de theologie catholique*, VII, 1466-1511. Also see K. Rahner, *Foundations of Christian Faith*, 214ff. Since the main concern was the theology of the Trinity and the three persons were seen as equal in all things, it would be a logical conclusion that, although any of the three persons could have become incarnate, it was fitting that it was the Word, since the Word proceeded directly from the Father.

79. Tavard summarizes well the medieval speculation on the motivation of the incarnation (58-63). His conclusion helps to situate the question: "The chief question was not the hypothetical problem of an incarnation 'had there been no fall of Adam.' It was that of the primacy, in the purpose of God, of elevating creation to glory, and one man, Jesus, to be the highest glory" (62-63).

80. *Summa Theologica*, III, q. 1, a. 3.

81. *Reportata Parisiensia*, 3, dist. 7, 1, 3 and 4.

82. K. Adams, *The Christ of Faith* (New York: Pantheon, 1957), 24. See also M. Scheeben, *The Mysteries of Christianity* (St. Louis: Herder, 1946), 331. "It [the humanity] participates in the nature of the divinity." Accordingly, then, the humanity will receive the adoration due to the divinity.

83. *Ibid.* 240. Also Scheeben, 329-30, 332. "For the anointing of Christ is nothing less than the fullness of the divinity of the Logos, which is substantially joined to the humanity and dwells in it incarnate."

84. *Ibid.* 246.

85. *Ibid.* 247.

86. *Ibid.* 247-54. The efforts to reinterpret the gospels to avoid any act by Jesus that would be considered less than perfect has a long tradition. The early fathers of the church were also quick to offer explanations for his cursing the fig tree, the harsh words to the Canaanite woman, etc.

87. Cf Brown, *The Virginal Conception and Bodily Resurrection of Jesus*, *op. cit.* Also J.F. O'Grady, "Jesus in History: His Birth and Resurrection," *Chicago Studies*, Vol. 26 (1987).

88. The model of Jesus as incarnate second person of the Blessed Trinity sometimes affected the understanding of sexuality in Christian tradition especially on the level of personal piety. The entrance of the Logos into history was based solely upon his relationship to God, thus avoiding any human paternity; this view frequently cast a shadow over the positive value of human generation. Spiritual writers could use the perpetual virginity of Mary as well as the extraordinary conception of Jesus to separate sexuality from spirituality. Easily, some concluded that to imitate both Jesus and Mary, a distance from all sexuality could prove meritorious. Such theology also had implications for the doctrine of the perpetual virginity of Mary and often presented unusual implications for the true humanity of Jesus.

89. Cf. J.N.D. Kelly, *Early Christian Creeds* (London: Longman, 1960), 144-45.

90. Brown, *The Virginal Conception. . .,* pp. 52-68. Also see Brown, "Gospel Infancy Narrative Research from 1976-1986, Part I (Matthew), *Catholic Biblical Quarterly,* Vol. 48 (1986), #3 and Part II (Luke), Vol. 48 (1986), #4. Recall the remarks of Pope John Paul II quoted earlier in chapter 1.

91. One possible source for this tradition is the accusation by Jews that Jesus was illegitimate. Cf. Brown, *The Birth of the Messiah* (New York: Doubleday, 1977), 28-29, 142-43, 150, 534-42.

92. F. Ferrier, *What Is the Incarnation?* (New York: Hawthorne, 1962), 158. This work is a popularization of the principal theological positions held by most christologists up until the very recent past. See M. Scheeben, 330: "In its own actions the humanity becomes the *instrumentum conjunctum* of this divine person and these actions themselves thereby receive an infinite dignity and efficacy—in a word, an infinite value." See also E. Mersch, *The Theology of the Mystical Body* (St. Louis: Herder, 1951), 229ff.

93. Ferrier, 159. See also Mersch, 228: "The incarnation established a new human species, or rather effected a renewal of the species: Divinized humanity." For a well-argued understanding of instrumental causality in Thomas Aquinas, see Paul Crowley, "*Instrumentum Divinitatis* in Thomas Aquinas: Recovering the Divinity of Jesus," *Theological Studies,* Vol. 52 (1991), 451-75. This essay does not apply directly to the examination of this model, but indirectly the author demonstrates the value of this model in preserving the divinity of Jesus.

94. Ferrier, 159.

95. Ferrier, 160. The traditional understanding of the "communication of idioms" allows us to say that God died on the cross but not that divinity died on the cross.

96. Rahner would disagree with this opinion. For him, Jesus had to die to achieve redemption. See *On The Theology of Death*. New York: Herder and Herder, 1961). Mersch would maintain a similar position for different reasons: "The God-man by being the God-man in the sinful humanity is intrinsically the redeemer consecrated to death; conversely by being the redeemer who died on the cross, He emerges most clearly as the God-man in sinful humanity" (285).

97. *Summa Theologica*, III, q. 19, a. 1. See also Crowley, "Instrumentum Divinitatis. . ." *art. cit.*

98. Cf. Engelbert Gutwenger, "The Problem of Christ's Knowledge," *Who Is Jesus of Nazareth?* (New York: Paulist, 1965), 91-105; William Thompson, *Christ and Consciousness* (New York: Paulist, 1977); Gerald O'Collins and Daniel Kendall, "The Faith of Jesus," *Theological Studies*, Vol. 53 (1992), 403-23 The recent christological documents from the International Theological Commission (1979, 1981, 1985) never claim that Jesus possessed the beatific vision but did claim that Jesus was aware of this pre-existence. See M. Sharkey, *International Theological Commission, Texts and Documents, 1969-1985* (San Francisco: Ignatius Press, 1989).

99. Pope Pius XII, *Mystici Corporis*, paragraph 48. See also the recent christological documents quoted above.

100. M. Vigue, *Le Christ* (Paris, 1947), 571.

101. Ferrier, 169. The popularization of these theories encouraged Christians to believe that Jesus knew everything that would happen to him as well as to everyone else. Even if there could be limitations on infused knowledge (most of the time there were not), Jesus, as the divine person, always had divine knowledge.

102. *Summa Theologica*, III, q. 12, a. 2.

103. In recent years many works have appeared on the exegetical and theological understanding of the resurrection. Gerald O'Collins in particular has written several works on the resurrection, including *Jesus Risen* (New York: Paulist, 1987), and *Interpreting the Resurrection* (New York: Paulist 1988). See also Jerome Neyrey, *The Resurrection Stories*

(Wilmington: Glazier, 1988) and a classical text, Reginald Fuller, *The Formation of the Resurrection Narratives* (New York: Macmillan, 1971).

104. Cf. *The Catechism of the Catholic Church* (New York: Paulist, 1994).

105. For a good summary of the weaknesses of liberal Protestantism of the nineteenth century, see Barth, *The Humanity of God,* 11-33. The author reacted strongly against this tendency; from this reaction came the rebirth of a transcendent theology in Protestantism.

106. J.A.T. Robinson, *Honest to God* (Philadelphia: Westminster, 1963), 24-48.

107. John Hick, ed., *The Myth of God Incarnate* (Philadelphia: Westminster, 1977).

108. C. Talbert, ed., *Reimarus: Fragments* (Philadelphia: Fortress, 1974).

109. Cf. Hugh Schonfield, *The Passover Plot* (New York: Geis Associates, 1965). Jesus is depicted as a schemer who fakes his own death by a drug-induced coma and then plans to stage a resurrection but unfortunately he is too weak after the fake crucifixion and dies. The disciples then claim to have seen the "risen Lord." For Schonfield, Christianity is based on a fraud.

110. See D.F. Strauss, *The Life of Jesus Critically Examined* (London, 1846); *A New Life of Jesus* (London, 1865).

111. See A. Schweitzer, *The Quest for the Historical Jesus* (New York: Macmillan, 1961), 137-68.

112. R. Bultmann, *Kerygma and Myth* (New York: Harper & Row, 1961); *Jesus Christ and Mythology* (New York: Scribner's, 1958).

113. See E. McKnight, *What Is Form Criticism?* (Philadelphia: Fortress, 1969), and R. Bultmann, *The History of the Synoptic Problem* (New York: Harper & Row, 1963).

114. See R. Bultmann, *Jesus Christ and Mythology,* 19-21; *Kerygma and Myth,* 10.

115. R. Bultmann, "The Historical Jesus and the Kerygmatic Christ," in C. Braaten and R Harrisville, eds., *The Historical Jesus and the Kerygmatic Christ* (Nashville: Abingdon, 1964), 15-42. N. Perrin, *The Promise of Bultmann* (Philadelphia: Lippincott, 1969).

116. See Perrin, 22-36.

117. See H. Jonas, *The Gnostic Religion* (Boston: Beacon Press, 1963).

118. M. Goulder, "Jesus, the Man of Universal Destiny," in *The Myth of God Incarnate,* 49.

119. F. Young, "Two Roots of a Tangled Mass," in *The Myth of God Incarnate,* 117-18.

120. Cf. Kee *What Can We Know About Jesus?* (Cambridge: University Press, 1990), 6-16.

121. Shortly after the publication of this work, several English theologians published their answer in *The Truth of God Incarnate,* ed. M. Green (London: Hodder and Stoughton, 1977).

122. Most of these scholars have already been mentioned: Crossan, Fitzmyer, Nolan, Meier, all of whom are Roman Catholic. Here I would add Howard Clark Kee, *What Can We Know About Jesus?* (Cambridge: University Press, 1990).

123. I add "at this time" since John Meier is preparing his second volume which will be followed by an additional volume.

124. *The Historical. . .,* 375.

125. *Ibid.* 394.

126. *Ibid.* 372.

127. I make reference to "many" early Christian documents since Crossan in his study includes the apocryphal writings, e.g. the Gospel of Peter, the Gospel of Thomas, as well as writings of the early fathers, Clement, Ignatius, the Didache, and the writings of pagans and other Jewish writings of the period.

128. Cf. *ibid.* xiii-xxvi. For a summary see in this volume Part II, 47.

129. No one need accept everything Crossan writes. I have serious reservations on his dating of documents and would be less hesitant in ascribing to all of the writings of the period the same level of authority.

130. For a good introduction to Bultmann the believer, see *Jesus and the Word* (New York: Scribner's, 1958).

131. Leonardo Boff, a Brazilian leader of this distinctive approach to theology and christology, and former Franciscan priest, explained simply of his decision to seek laicization: "Everything has a limit and I had arrived at my limit." "Boff Explains," *National Catholic Reporter,* July 17, 1992, 13. See also Dennis Doyle, "Communion, Ecclesiology and the Silencing of Boff," *America,* 12, September 1992, 139-43.

132. "Boff Explains," *National Catholic Reporter*, July 17, 1992, 13.

133. Sobrino discusses the differences between European and Latin American theology in *The True Church and the Poor* (Maryknoll: Orbis, 1984), chapter 1.

134. See E. Cardenal, *The Gospel in Solentiname*, vol II (Maryknoll: Orbis, 1978), 2.

135. *Ibid.* 4.

136. See H. Assmann, *Theology for a Nomad Church* (Maryknoll: Orbis, 1976); G. Gutierrez, *A Theology of Liberation* (Maryknoll: Orbis, 1973); R Alves, *A Theology of Human Hope* (Washington: Corpus, 1969); J. Miranda, *Being and the Messiah* (Maryknoll: Orbis, 1977); L. Boff, "Salvation in Christ and the Process of Liberation," *Concilium*, vol. 96 (New York: Paulist, 1974); J. Segundo, *Liberation Theology* (Maryknoll: Orbis, 1975); G. Gutierrez and R Shaull, *Liberation and Change* (Atlanta: John Knox, 1977).

137. See J. Sobrino, *Christology at the Crossroads* (Maryknoll: Orbis, 1978); *Jesus in Latin America* (Maryknoll: Orbis, 1987) See also Paul Ritt, "The Lordship of Jesus Christ: Balthasar and Sobrino", *Theological Studies*, Vol. 49 (1988) 709-29. Ritt attempts to combine the mystical theology of Balthasar with the more liberation or political christolgy of Sobrino. L Boff, *Jesus Christ Liberator* (Maryknoll: Orbis, 1978). C. Bussman, *Who do you say? Jesus Christ in Latin American Theology* (Maryknoll: Orbis, 1985).

138. Sobrino, 12.

139. *Ibid.* 13.

140. Cf. Albert Nolan, *Jesus, op. cit.* Nolan examines various episodes in the gospels and makes application based upon his personal experience as a missionary working in the third world.

141. J. Ernst, "Der Nonkonformisus Jesus," in *Anfang der Christologie* (Stuttgart, 1972), 145-58. The nonconformist attitude is evident in a reading of the gospels. See also E. Kasemann, *Jesus Means Freedom* (Philadelphia: Fortress, 1970).

142. Kasemann, Chapter 1.

143. See M. Hengel, *Was Jesus a Revolutionary?* (Philadelphia: Fortress, 1971). This work contains an extensive bibliography on works prior to

1970. See also O. Cullmann, *Jesus and the Revolutionaries* (New York: Harper & Row, 1975).

144. See C. Duquoc, "Liberation and Salvation in Jesus Christ," in *Liberation Theology and the Message of Salvation* (Pittsburgh: Pickwick, 1978), 53. This collection of essays, mainly by European theologians, contains many valuable insights into the meaning of liberation theology.

145. Cf. John F. O'Grady, *Jesus Lord and Christ* (New York: Paulist, 1972), chapter 5.

146. Cardenal, 4.

147. See *Concilium*, vol. 2, #10 and vol. 6, #10. Both issues are devoted to the question of liberation theology. The contributors are Latin Americans as well as European.

148. See G. Montague, "Hermeneutics and the Teaching of Scripture," *Catholic Biblical Quarterly*, vol. 41 (1979), 1-17.

149. Boff, "Salvation in Christ and the Process of Liberation," in *Concilium*, 80. The Latin of the first means: "The very intention of Jesus"; the second, "the very words of Jesus."

150. G. Casalis, "Jesus de Nazareth, 'Che' Guevara et les Conquistadores" A shorter version is "Jesus, ni vaincu ni monarque celeste." *Temoignage Chretien*, #1503, April 1973, 17-18. Quoted in G. Casalis, "Liberation and Conscientization in Latin America," *Liberation Theology and the Message of Salvation*, 114.

151. Paul VI, *Progressio Populorum* (New York: Paulist, 1967). John Paul, II, *Laborem Exercens* (New York: McGrath Publishing, 1981), *Solicitudo Rei Socialis* (Washington: USCC, 1988); *Centesimus Annus, The Pope Speaks*, vol. 36 (1990-1991), 273-310.

152. Leonardo Boff's writings on the church and the need for the liberalization of its structure seems to have contributed significantly to his problems with Rome. He personally could not preach a liberation theology without calling for a liberation in church structures. Cf. *National Catholic Reporter*, July 17, 1992, 12-13.

153. This chapter has avoided separating the various oppressed groups and has tried to deal with general themes that might be applied to all of the oppressed. For the treatment of the black liberation movement in the United States, see the works of James Cone, especially *God of the Oppressed* (New York: Seabury, 1975) and *A Black Theology of Liberation* (Philadelphia: Lippincott, 1970). See also Raymond Moloney, "African

Christology," *Theological Studies,* Vol. 48 (1987), 505-15. With regard to feminist theology, much of the contemporary literature, in the opinions of the authors themselves, has gone beyond Christianity. For the Christian perspective see L. Russell, *Human Liberation in a Feminist Perspective–A Theology* (Philadelphia: Westminster, 1974); R. Ruether, *Religion and Sexism* (New York: Simon & Schuster, 1974); Elisabeth Schussler Fiorenza, *In Memory of Her* (New York: Crossroad, 1985). The early Mary Daly writings, e.g. *The Church and the Second Sex* (New York: Harper & Row, 1968) are Christian. Her later works are professedly post-Christian. Almost nothing from the gay liberation movement can be termed Christian other than rebuttals of church pronouncements condemning homosexuality and attempts at calling attention to the question. The basic principles presented in this chapter should apply to all minority groups and to any oppressed person or peoples.

154. While I may emphasize this as a limitation I also am aware of the simplicity of my critique. Liberation christology, as noted in its advantages, tends to energize people who then need to work out the details. Certain guidelines rise to the surface such as inclusiveness, community, and social justice. But how can these be expressed in the complex societies of this and the coming century? Also, all will admit of the need for such programs as part of society but then who will actually pay for them? Disagreements on this last item on the agenda of liberation christology continues without any sign of resolution.

155. (Philadelphia: Westminster, 1963). See also Routley, *The Man for Others* (New York: Oxford University Press, 1964).

156. J.A.T. Robinson, *Can We Trust the New Testament?* (Grand Rapids: Eerdmans, 1977). This work has not met with the same enthusiasm as the previous work.

157. P. Tillich, *Systematic Theology* (Chicago: University of Chicago Press, 1953-66).

158. D. Bonhoeffer, *Letters and Papers from Prison,* rev. ed. (New York: Macmillan, 1967).

159. *Ibid.* 209-10

160. I noted in the first chapter my inclination to exclude this model in this revised edition. Upon more careful thought, I concluded that this approach to Jesus not only remains timely, but should include in its purview those followers of Jesus who live a life based on Jesus precisely as the "man for others" without any further attempt at theology.

161. Robinson, *Honest to God*, 65.

162. Cf. Bonhoeffer, *Christ the Center* (New York: Harper & Row, 1960); *The Cost of Discipleship* (New York: Macmillan, 1967); *Creation and Fall* (New York: Macmillan, 1966); *Ethics* (New York: Macmillan, 1964); *The Communion of Saints* (New York: Harper & Row, 1963). See also John Phillips, *Christ for Us in the Theology of Dietrich Bonhoeffer* (New York: Harper & Row, 1967) and B. Reise, *The Promise of Bonhoeffer* (Philadelphia: Lippincott, 1969).

163. See Bonhoeffer, *Letters and Papers from Prison*, 151-57.

164. Robinson, *Honest to God*, 75.

165. Bonhoeffer, *Christ the Center*.

166. *Ibid.* 49-60.

167. *Ibid.* 61-68.

168. See J. Pelikan, "The Early Answer to the Questions Concerning Jesus Christ: Bonhoeffer's Christology of 1933," in M. Marty, *The Place of Bonhoeffer* (New York: Association Press, 1962), 147-66.

169. Bonhoeffer, *Christ the Center*, 47.

170. *Ibid.* 49-53.

171. *Ibid.* 53-59.

172. *Ibid.* 59-61.

173. *Ibid.* 62-67.

174. *Ibid.* 63-66.

175. *Ibid.* 66-67.

176. *Ibid.* 106-10.

177. *Ibid.* 110-18.

178. In the earlier edition of this book this chapter was titled: "Jesus, Personal Savior." I have changed the title of this model since Lord and Savior follows the more general understanding of this approach to Jesus rather than personal Savior. Personal Savior is more the result of the individual's attitude flowing from the acceptance of Jesus as Lord and Savior.

179. Cf. Julia Duin "Charismatics, After 25 Years, Seek New Spark," *National Catholic Reporter*, June 19, 1992, 5.

180. Kilian McDonald and George Montague, *Fanning the Flame* (Collegeville: Liturgical Press, 1990).

181. R. Knox, *Enthusiasm* (New York: Oxford University Press, 1949). See Larry Christenson, *A Message to the Charismatic Movement* (Minneapolis: Division, 1972). This author compares the Catholic apostolic church of the late nineteenth century to the present movement and sees the former as a forerunner of the latter.

182. *Ibid.* 1.

183. *Ibid.* 2.

184. *Ibid.* 4.

185. *Ibid.* 591.

186. *Ibid.*

187. See "Redemption," *Dictionary of the Bible,* John L. McKenzie (Milwaukee: Bruce, 1965).

188. O'Grady, *Jesus, Lord and Christ,* 71-75.

189. See S. Clark, *Baptized in the Spirit* (Pecos, 1970); S. Tugwell, *Did You Receive the Spirit?* (New York: Paulist, 1972); G. Montague, *The Spirit and His Gifts* (New York, 1974); J. Dunn, *Baptism in the Holy Spirit* (London: SCM Press, 1970); E. Jorstad, ed., *The Holy Spirit in Today's Church* (New York: Abingdon, 1973). Jorstad gives a summary in Chapter 6, 58-76.

190. See Rene Laurentin, *Catholic Pentecostals* (New York: Doubleday, 1977), 100-31. Also cf. Jorstad, Chapter 8, 100-18, as well as his section on demonology.

191. See E. O'Connor, *The Pentecostal Movement in the Catholic Church* (South Bend: Notre Dame Press, 1971), and Laurentin, 115-16. See also J. Gunstone, *Greater Things Than These* (New York: Faith Press, 1974), 64-65.

192. Knox, *Enthusiasm,* 2.

193. The leaders in the Roman Catholic charismatic renewal frequently warn against the pitfalls of this fundamentalism. See especially Gelpi and Montague.

194. Many of the Roman Catholics in the charismatic movement remain integrated into their parishes and dioceses. These comments are not meant to indict anyone or any particular group within the

movement. The model itself can encourage this separation from the organized church and often has in the past.

195. Cf. H. Nouwen, *In Memoriam* (Notre Dame: Ave Maria, 1979).

196. Knox, 591.

197. See K. Rahner, "Christianity Within an Evolutionary View of the World," *Theological Investigations*, vol. 5 (Baltimore: Helicon, 1965), 173ff; also *Theological Foundations*, 208 ff.

198. See the comments by R. North concerning A. Hulsbosch in "Recent Christology and Theological Method," *Continuum*, vol. 7 (1969), 63-77. See also Mark Schoof, "Dutch Catholic Theology: A New Approach to Christology," *Cross Currents*, vol. 22 (1973), 415-27.

199. Karl Barth, *The Humanity of God;* also H. Kung, *On Being a Christian* (New York: Doubleday, 1976).

200. See P. Schoonenberg, *The Christ* (New York: Herder and Herder, 1971); "God's Presence in Jesus: An Exchange of Viewpoints," *Theology Digest*, vol. 19 (1971), 29-38; "Is Jesus 'Man plus God'?" *Theology Digest*, vol. 23 (1975), 59-70, plus a letter from Schoonenberg, 22-25. See also S. Pujdak, "Schoonenberg's Christology in Context," *Louvain Studies*, vol. 6 (1976), 338-53; Herwi Rikhof, "God's Changeability and Unchangeability: The Vision of Piet Schoonenberg," *Louvain Studies*, Vol. 18 (1993), 21-37; Piet Schoonenberg, "The Doctrine of the Trinity: empty dogma or fruitful theologoumenon?" *Theology Digest*, Vol. 39 (1992), 23-31.

201. Cf. Cooke, *God's Beloved, op. cit.*

202. J.A.T. Robinson, *The Human Face of God* (Philadelphia: Westminster, 1973).

203. See J. O'Grady, *Christian Anthropology* (New York: Paulist, 1976), Chapter 1.

204. E. Schillebeeckx, *Jesus: An Experiment in Christology* (New York: Seabury, 1979), 601.

205. It is true that in the gospel of Matthew Jesus speaks of "our" Father (Mt 6:9). This, however, is recognized by scripture scholars as a liturgical formula, with the parallel place in Luke considered to be the original (Lk 11:2).

206. See Mt 11:27; Lk 10:22; Mk 13:32; Jn 8:42; 10:25ff, 12:49; 13:5.10.23, etc.

207. See William James. *The Variety of Religious Experience* (New York: Longman, Green, 1929) and R. Otto, *The Idea of the Holy* (New York: Oxford University Press, 1958).

208. Cooke, *God's Beloved, op. cit.*, 11. For a feminisit critique see Mary Rose D'Angelo, "*Abba* and 'Father': Imperial Theology and the Jesus Traditions," *Journal of Biblical Literature*, Vol. 111 (1992), 611-30.

209. The Christian understanding of original sin gives the theological foundation for this aspect of human life. See O'Grady, *Christian Anthropology*, Chapter 4.

210. Schillebeeckx, *Jesus, op. cit.*, 603.

211. The careful reading of the gospel of John and how this gospel has expressed the meaning of Jesus, will give the reader the source for my emphasis on Jesus as the human face of God. Each of the gospels portrays Jesus as revealing God the Father but the fourth gospel seems to emphasize this facet of Jesus more than the others.

212. Cf. Crossan, chapters 5-10; Meier, chapters 8-10, Cooke, chapters 2-4.

213. See O'Grady, *Jesus, Lord and Christ*, 10-16.

214. See Schillebeeckx, 644-50; Rahner, Theological Dictionary, op. cit., 264-84; Rahner, *On the Theology...*

215. K. Rahner, *On the Theology of Death*, 69-70.

216. Only recently in Roman Catholic theology has the resurrection been seen in its pivotal position. Previously it was viewed chiefly as the greatest of miracles and thus used in an apologetic sense. The renewal in resurrection theology can be traced to the influence of the following: F. X Durwell, The *Resurrection* (New York: Sheed and Ward, 1960); David Stanley, *Christ's Resurrection in Pauline Soteriology* (Rome: Biblical Institute Press, 1961); John Galvin, "The Origin of Faith in the Resurrection of Jesus: Two Recent Perspectives," *Theological Studies*, Vol. 49 (1988), 25-44. With these works as a foundation, further study has been made especially by G. O'Collins as previously cited.

217. Thompson, *The Jesus. . .*, 223-24.

218. See the various critiques of some contemporary approaches: A. Dulles, "Contemporary Approaches to Christology: Analysis and Reflection," *Living Light*, vol. 13 (1976), 119-25; Thomas Clarke, "Current Christologies," *Worship*, vol 53 (1979), 438-49; Gerald

O'Collins, "Jesus in Current Theology," *The Way,* vol 16 (1976), 291-308; Donald Gray, "The Divine and the Human in Jesus Christ," *CTSAP,* vol. 31 (1976), 21-39; Peter Chirico, "Kung's Christology: An Evaluation of Its Presuppositions," *Theological Studies,* vol. 40 (1979), 256-72.

219. It is this point that Schillebeeckx makes so well; see *Jesus, op. cit.,* 657-61.

220. In addition to the works already cited, see "Current Problems in Christology," *Theological Investigations,* vol. 1 (Baltimore: Helicon, 1961), 149-200, and "The Theology of tho Incarnation," *Theological Investigations,* vol. 4 (Baltimore: Helicon, 1966).

221. The chief weakness of Schoonenberg is his apparent lack of a philosophical foundation. See the works cited above for a critique and his reaction.

222. Hulsbosch's work is known mainly through secondary sources. In addition to the works cited above, see R. North, "Soul-Body Unity and God-Man Unit," *Theological Studies,* vol. 30 (1969), 63-77.

223. Schillebeeckx does not deal in any systematic way with his philosophical foundations. However, the existential phenomenology associated with many Dutch theologians in the past thirty years seems to form the foundation for his thought in the opinion of this writer.

224. Cf. the critiques of Kung as mentioned above.

225. Gerard Manley Hopkins, "As Kingfishers Catch Fire," in *A Hopkins Reader* (New York: Doubleday, 1966), 67.

226. In the earlier edition I proposed seven criteria. I have added the eighth one. The concern for further understanding of Jesus whether through preaching or through religious education should be part of the analysis of models of Jesus.

227. This has not always been the case in history as previously noted. The French school of spirituality still has many followers.

228. The following limited predictions remain in this *Models of Jesus Revisited.* The interest in Spirit christology supports the first prediction. The continued interest in the social mission of the church from pope to laity supports the second. The impact of personal commitment and enthusiasm seems to have lessened in the charismatic movement. With others in the church, however, the return to a more mystical communion with God through Jesus supports the need for an awareness of the saving presence of God in life. Pluralism continues.

INDEX

Abba, God as, 33, 43, 67, 76, 115, 179-80, 181, 182, 184
Alexandria, school of, 175
Antioch, school of, 175
Apocryphal gospels, 98
Aquinas, Thomas, 93, 98, 100, 147
Art, images of Jesus in, 15
Augustine, 206

Baptism in the Spirit, 166
Barth, Karl, 19, 101
Bauer, Bruno, 109-10, 120
Bible, 5-6, 35-36, 108-13; *see also* New Testament; Old Testament
Boethius, 90
Boff, Leonardo, 122, 123
Bonhoeffer, Dietrich, 19, 142-53, 155, 156, 157
Born-again Christians, 161, 165
Brown, Raymond, 8
Brulle, Pierre de, 103
Bultmann, Rudolf, 110-15, 117, 118, 119, 120

Can We Trust the New Testament? (Robinson), 142
Cardenal, Ernesto, 122, 123

Catholic Biblical Quarterly, The, 8
Chalcedon, Council of. *See* Council of Chalcedon (451)
Charismatic movement, 159-63, 167, 172-73; baptism in the Spirit, 166
Christ. *See* Jesus
Christ is Community (Neyrey), 9
Christological Catechism, A (Fitzmyer), 9
Christology, 5-28; Biblical concerns, 5-6; church concerns, 7-8; exaltation christology, 38-39; images of the church, 6; scholarly activity, 8-10; *see also* Jesus; and specific headings
Church Dogmatics (Barth), 101
Church: and community, 144, 168-69, 176; crisis of images, 18-19; and human needs, 145-46; images of, 6; models of, 11-12; "religionless Christianity," 144-45, 157
Colson, Charles, 166
Community: church and, 144, 168-69, 176; and meaning of life, 168-69
Compassion, 154

229

163; in gospel of Matthew, 8, 39-40, 56-63, 68, 80; as ground of being, 22; as healer, 61-62, 166-68; historical Jesus, 31-40, 107-08, 113, 114-15, 117, 118, 119-20, 125, 126, 151-52; as human face of God, 19, 22, 175-96, 202-03, 204, 205,206; humanity of, 77-81, 93-94, 175-96; humiliation, 152-53; hypostatic union, 88, 89, 91, 94; images of, 10-11, 20-21; Incarnation, 91, 92-93, 95, 151-52; as Jewish charismatic, 35; kindness, 154; knowledge of, 98-100; as liberator, 10, 24, 124-41, 201, 203, 204, 205, 208; as Lord, 57, 67-68; as Lord and Savior, 159-74, 202, 203, 204, 208; as magician, 35; as man for others, 19, 22, 142-58, 202, 203, 204, 208; as man of prayer, 64-65; as Messiah, 47-48, 49, 57, 68-69, 81, 110; as miracle worker, 55-56; mystery of, 13-15, 45; mythological Christ, 109-21, 201, 203-04, 205; and nature, 150-51; non-conformity of, 129-30; as perfect Greek gentleman, 64, 157; as perfected human person, 19; personal awareness of goodness, 180-81; and personal existence, 149-50; as political revolutionary, 34; as prophet, 62; resurrection, 44, 45, 48, 100-01, 114, 125, 131, 152; as ruler, 25; as sacrament of encounter, 19; as sacrament of God, 22; as Savior, 42, 45, 61, 165-66; as second person of Blessed Trinity, 22, 26, 34, 87-106, 200, 203, 204, 205-06, 208; signs and symbols of, 17-18; sin, 94, 180-81; as Son, 48, 71, 74-75; as Son of God, 53, 59-60, 62, 69-70, 74, 117; as son of Joseph, 78; as Son of Man, 50, 52-53, 60, 70-71, 73, 78, 80, 156-57, 163; as Son of Mary, 78; as suffering servant, 57, 58; as sacrament, 149; as teacher, 53, 54-55, 56, 60-61, 62; theandric acts, 96-98, 102; universalism, 65-66, 130, 153, 175, 182; value and purpose, 181-83; as Word of God, 40, 71-73, 77-78, 95, 96-98, 125, 148-49; worship of humanity of, 93-94; in writings of Paul, 37, 41-49, 83

Jesus Before Christianity (Nolan), 9
John, gospel of, 71-83, 110, 157, 193; *ego eimi*, 75-77; humanity of Jesus, 77-82; Jesus as Son of God, 52, 74-75; Jesus as Son of Man, 52-53, 73, 80-81; Jesus as Word of God, 40, 72-73
John Paul II, Pope, 8, 23, 142
John Paul XXIII, Pope, 9
Joseph, Jesus as son of, 78

Kerygma, 39, 112-13, 113-14, 115
Kindness, 154
Knox, Ronald, 161-63, 172, 173
Kung, H., 191
Kyrios, 62-63

Leo the Great, Pope, 88
Leontius, 90
Lessing, G.E., 108
Letters and Papers from Prison (Bonhoeffer), 142
Liberation theology, 122-41
Liberator, Jesus as, 10, 24, 124-41, 201, 203, 204, 205, 208
Logos, 40, 72-73, 79-80, 91, 94, 95, 96, 190, 193
Luke, gospel of, 8, 63-71, 110, 111; history in, 66; Jesus as